Between Image and Identity

Between Image and Identity

Transnational Fantasy, Symbolic Violence, and Feminist Misrecognition

Karina Eileraas

LEXINGTON BOOKS

A division of
ROWMAN & LITTLEFIELD PUBLISHERS, INC.
Lanham • Boulder • New York • Toronto • Plymouth, UK

LEXINGTON BOOKS

A division of Rowman & Littlefield Publishers, Inc.
A wholly owned subsidiary of The Rowman & Littlefield Publishing Group, Inc.
4501 Forbes Boulevard, Suite 200
Lanham, MD 20706

Estover Road
Plymouth PL6 7PY
United Kingdom

British Library Cataloguing in Publication Information Available

Library of Congress Cataloging-in-Publication Data

Eileraas, Karina, 1971-
Between image and identity : transnational fantasy, symbolic violence, and feminist misrecognition / Karina Eileraas.
p. cm.
Includes bibliographical references and index.
ISBN-13: 978-0-7391-1811-5 (cloth : alk. paper)
ISBN-10: 0-7391-1811-0 (cloth : alk. paper)
ISBN-13: 978-0-7391-1812-2 (pbk. : alk. paper)
ISBN-10: 0-7391-1812-9 (pbk. : alk. paper)
1. Feminist theory—Political aspects. 2. Sex role—Political aspects. 3. Women—Violence against. 4. Postcolonialism. 5. Symbolism. 6. Identity (Psychology) 7. Women authors. 8. Women artists. I. Title.
HQ1190.E36 2007
305.48'9692—dc22 009276

Printed in the United States of America

∞™ The paper used in this publication meets the minimum requirements of American National Standard for Information Sciences—Permanence of Paper for Printed Library Materials, ANSI/NISO Z39.48-1992.

To my sister and brother, examples of how to inhabit the world with insatiable curiosity, depth, drive, and an outrageous sense of humor. Also to my father, for reminding me how much can be achieved with ambition, vision, loyalty, and a profound sense of honor.

To Lawrence and Annelise, for your creativity, support, chocolate chip cookies, and sense of wonder. Thank you for always reminding—and enabling—me to embrace the pleasures of our intricate lives.

And to my mother, for her indomitable spirit, unwavering faith, and commitment to profound beauty. Thank you for a million examples of how to live with passion, optimism, and style; for your belief in dreams and poetry . . . and for insisting that anything is possible.

Contents

Acknowledgments

How to sufficiently acknowledge the many sources of inspiration that enable one to conceive, write, and eventually publish a book? Not an easy task, but I will attempt it here nonetheless.

The seeds of this work were planted during my undergraduate studies at Wesleyan University, unbeknownst to me at the time. Wesleyan provided me with a lively, intense, and passionate community within which to pursue political and academic debates, one to which I am forever indebted. Although the people who inspired me while at Wesleyan are too numerous to cite here, I especially wish to thank Khachig Tololyan, Christina Crosby, Jeff Rider, Richard Stamelman, Aashraf Rushdy, Ann Cvetkovich, Audrey Prins Patt, and Carol Grosman, all of whom ensured that my days at Wesleyan were endlessly rich, stimulating, and profound.

I completed much of the work for this book during my graduate studies at Northwestern University and UCLA, where I was surrounded by a supportive, creative, and dynamic circle of faculty members in the departments of French, Women's Studies, Comparative Literature, History, and Art History. I especially want to thank Françoise Lionnet, whose intellectual and creative accomplishments I so admired that I decided to follow her from Northwestern to UCLA! Thank you, Françoise, for your warm friendship and guidance in academics and in life, and for sharing such rich examples of scholarly innovation and interdisciplinary cross-pollination in your courses, research, and publications. Profound thanks also to Lynn Hunt, Saloni Mathur, and Anne Mellor at UCLA, who so generously agreed to be a part of my dissertation committee. Your brilliant insights and in-depth critique contributed more than you know to the shape, direction, and final execution of this work; and your stellar examples of scholarly achievement and intellectual curiosity continue to inspire my own path in academe.

I also wish to express my gratitude to Scott Durham, Jane Winston, Mireille Rosello, Hélène Cixous, and Margaret Thompson-Drewal, all of whom inspired and nurtured my work in various capacities during my studies at Northwestern University. The Performance Studies Department at Northwestern proved to be a particularly rich source of intellectual and creative inspiration for my own work and evolution as a scholar. Similarly, I cannot say enough about the vitality, intellectual rigor, and dynamism of the emerging Women's Studies Program and Center for the Study of Women at UCLA, where I was delighted to find an extraordinarily rich community that provided ongoing inspiration, friendship, and lively exchange. My profound thanks also to the UC Multi-Campus Research Group on Transnational and Transcolonial Studies, which supported my research and writing, surrounded me with a dynamic network of scholars, and provided me with invaluable opportunities to pursue transnational work while at UCLA. Thanks especially to Chris Littleton, Sandra Harding, Sondra Hale, Susan McClary, Shu-Mei Shih, Sonia Saldivar-Hull, Dominic Thomas, Rachel Lee, Victor Wolfenstein, Aamir Mufti, and Kirstie McClure, all of whom either directly or indirectly enriched my own efforts of critical analysis, research, teaching, and writing.

I would surely not have been able to complete this book without the generous award of a Mellon Postdoctoral Fellowship from Carleton College. While at Carleton, I completed my final manuscript, taught courses in the Women's and Gender Studies Program, and participated in several lively academic conferences. Thanks to the Carleton faculty members who stimulated my thinking, including Annette Igra and Dana Strand, and to the many students who, perhaps unwittingly, helped to challenge and refine my ideas.

Several other individuals have made lasting impressions on me at various stages of my academic career, whether or not they are aware of their influence on my life and work. I especially wish to acknowledge Bernard Aresu and Anna Caflisch of Rice University, as well as Sunaina Maira from U-Mass Amherst. Thanks also to Philippe Barbé, Margaret Werry, Alison Rice, Sharmila Lodhia, and Louis Fishman, fellow graduate students and teachers at Northwestern University, UCLA, and Carleton College, for days filled with stimulating conversation and commiseration. I also wish to thank Marc Garanger for gracious permission to reprint his photographs; Suzanne Roos at *MLN*; and the editorial staff at *TDR* for being among the first to "officially" recognize and encourage my work. Finally, I want to thank my students at Northwestern, UCLA, and Carleton College—all of whom, as it turns out, have challenged, inspired, and taught me more than I could possibly have taught them.

Introduction

Women Between Nations

Violence and the (Im)possibilities of Representation

> The act of representing others almost always involves violence to the subject of representation.
>
> —Edward Said, "In the Shadow of the West"

> Feminist figures of humanity must somehow both resist representation and still erupt in powerful new tropes, new turns of historical possibility . . . History can have another shape, articulated through differences that matter.
>
> —Donna Haraway, "Ecce Homo, Ain't (Ar'n't) I a Woman, and Inappropriate/d Others: The Human in a Post-Humanist Landscape"

In a surprising chain of events last spring, a series of cartoon images sparked a worldwide controversy that eventually erupted in violent protest. Cartoons of the prophet Mohammed were first published by the Danish newspaper *Jyllands-Posten*, and subsequently reprinted by several European presses. Thousands of people around the world took offense to these images, regardless of their religious affiliation. Many responded by organizing street protests throughout Europe and the Middle East, some of which culminated in acts of violence toward foreign embassies and their employees. As the crisis unfolded, cultural critics, scholars, and foreign policy analysts scrambled to understand how and why cartoons had the capacity to ignite such controversy.

What most clearly emerged from this international political debacle was an appreciation for the startling power of images—especially their capacity to distort, wound, transgress, and incite violence.[1] In a global economy that is in many ways dependent upon the circulation of images, the choice of what, whether, and how to represent often begets cultural, religious, and political scandal. Within this context, it is vital to understand the force of images; their relation to formulations and practices of identity; their potential to spark violence; and the complex web of cultural meanings in which they are inextricably embedded.

My work is vitally concerned with this constitutive power of images, especially with the ways in which postcolonial women forge relationships between image and identity. My manuscript addresses the autobiographical art and literature of postcolonial Francophone women from the Maghreb and Southeast Asia including Leila Sebbar, Assia Djebar, Marguerite Duras, Theresa Cha, and Hélène Cixous. Adopting a comparative approach, I consider how these artists choose to represent—and often reinvent—experiences of transnational trauma such as colonization, revolution, sexual violence, and exile. I conclude that the subjects of my study variously seek to challenge or "misrecognize" nationalist, colonialist, and Orientalist imagery, especially by confronting the racial and sexual fantasies embedded in colonial photography, film, and Orientalist painting. By exploring the creative powers of fantasy, alienation, and misrecognition in their autobiographical work, they vitally rewrite postcolonial history, and reimagine the relationships between image, identity, and national memory.

At issue in my project are the silence and marginalization that often define postcolonial women's status *vis-à-vis* the nation. This silence is hauntingly evoked by Dai Sil Kim-Gibson's film *Silence Broken* which tells the stories of several Korean comfort women who were sexually enslaved by the Japanese military during WWII.[2] Interweaving personal testimony with dramatic reenactment, *Silence Broken* explores the traumatic psychological, medical, and political effects of state-sanctioned sexual violence against women. Most compellingly, *Silence Broken* exposes the plight of women struggling to forge an autonomous sense of identity and to trace accountability in the interstices between two nations. To this end, the film evokes the haunting *silence* surrounding women's experiences of transnational trauma—especially sex trafficking, forced prostitution, and rape—during wartime and registers a repeated unwillingness on the part of nation-states to take responsibility for these crimes. It especially condemns government censorship that has dictated whose voices will be heard in public, which histories will be included in academic curricula in Japan, and whose stories will be officially recognized and validated by the state.[3] Ultimately, silence lingers as a potent symbol of women's uneasy integration into national and transnational political projects.

The deliberate censure of state-sponsored violence against women has disturbing legal and political implications. In March 2003, for example, the Japanese Supreme Court denied the claims of a group of Korean comfort women seeking compensation for their experiences of sexual servitude.[4] Because the statute of limitations had expired, the Court ruled that the Japanese government owed comfort women neither financial remedy nor formal apology. What echoes in this ruling is a political will to silence: or rather, an unwillingness to grant formal recognition and legal redress to female victims of transnational, sexual trauma. Most disturbingly, this will to silence underscores the virtual impossibility of representing sexual violence within the national imaginary. Yet this inability or unwillingness to represent sexual violence is certainly not unique to Japan; instead, we find it replicated on a global scale in the wake of nationalism, colonization, war, revolution, and other periods of political turmoil.

At the same time, state censorship of women's experiences of abuse often masks popular racial, sexual, and national fantasies about women that continually inform collective memory. In this book, I will consider such collective fantasies to exert a form of symbolic violence with material effects. In turn, I will explore feminist aesthetic efforts to transmute these forms of violence into aesthetic and political strategies of resistance. At the heart of my inquiry are female artists and writers who occupy the borderlands in between nations due to experiences of war, revolution, colonization, and exile.

Yet it is impossible to consider how "resistant" transnational subjectivities might be forged without first reflecting on the psychological dimensions of trauma and identification, as well as the ethical imperatives of representation. In a groundbreaking essay entitled "Under Western Eyes: Feminist Scholarship and Colonial Discourses," Chandra Talpade Mohanty demonstrates how Western feminist representations of "third world women" often engage in a form of ethnocentric reductionism that has traumatizing effects for postcolonial women. Because of its tendency to evoke "third world women" as the static, monolithic objects of discourse, Western feminist analysis effectively "colonizes" third world women by appropriating their subjectivity for its own scholarly purposes.[5] Mohanty especially critiques the perception of third world women as eternal victims, frozen in time and space and lacking political and historical agency.

To challenge reductive portrayals of third world women, Mohanty advocates a postcolonial feminist approach to theorizing identity and difference that would proceed from the following premises:

1. the idea of the simultaneity of oppressions as fundamental to the experience of social and political marginality;
2. the crucial role of a hegemonic state in circumscribing women's daily lives and survival struggles;
3. the significance of memory and writing in the creation of oppositional agency; and
4. the differences, conflicts, and contradictions internal to third world women's organizations and communities.[6]

To encourage complex re-visionings of history grounded in the specific locations and struggles of postcolonial women, Mohanty also urges feminist scholars to explore the dynamic relationships between feminist, antiracist, and nationalist liberation movements.

Reflecting on the 1989 Tiananmen Square massacre in Beijing, Rey Chow similarly explores the politics of representing "third world women."[7] She concludes that one cannot simply "read" a political crisis through the lens of gender without simultaneously addressing issues of race, class, and nationality. Like Mohanty, Chow advocates an intersectional approach to understanding oppression and resistance. In particular, she calls upon feminists to engage in more rigorous analysis of the role of the gaze in political projects of colonization. Because she conceives of the other's gaze as constitutive of identity, Chow critiques Western portrayals of "third world women" that presume passive resemblance and depict "natives" as lifeless objects of the Western feminist gaze. Emphasizing the traumatizing powers of this gaze, Chow tries to imagine an alternative space of negotiation between image and identity:

> How do we construct the native's "identity"? What processes of identification are involved? We cannot approach this politics without being critical of a particular relation to *images* that is in question . . . Whether positive or negative, the construction of the native remains at the level of image-identification, a process in which "our" own identity is measured in terms of the degrees to which we resemble her and to which she resembles us. Is there a way of conceiving of the native beyond imagistic resemblance?[8]

As Chow suggests, only by dispensing with binary notions of the autonomous Western "subject" and native "object" of the gaze can we hope to appreciate the complex dynamics of identification, desire, and resistance that circumscribe diasporic subjectivity. She urges us to rethink the relationship between colonial imagery and postcolonial identity, especially by contesting the ideals of likeness and recognition as aesthetic and political objectives. Although Chow's perspective is grounded in the ethical imperative to assume responsibility for image creation and consumption, it also acknowledges potentially empowering aspects of fantasy and disidentification for postcolonial women.

Western feminist theory has yet to fully engage with the experiences of third world women, especially women who inhabit the murky space in between nations. To promote a paradigmatic shift within feminist theory, contemporary postcolonial feminist critics like Mohanty and Chow have repeatedly called for more self-conscious and sophisticated formulations of difference, agency, and representation. At stake is the potential to make visible a broad range of postcolonial feminist tactics of political intervention and disidentification relative to the image. As Chow concludes:

> It is only when we acknowledge the fact that the subaltern cannot speak that we can begin to plot a different kind of process of identification for the native . . . The agency of the native cannot simply be imagined in terms of a resistance against the image—that is, *after* the image has been formed—nor in terms of a subjectivity that existed *before*, beneath, inside, or outside of the image. It needs to be re-thought as that which bears witness to its own demolition—in a form which is at once image and gaze, but a gaze that exceeds the moment of colonization.[9]

It is this gaze to which I hope to bear witness in my work, which asks how women located in the margins between nations engage with popular ethnic, racial, and sexual fantasies to create novel visions of transnational trauma and feminist resistance. Throughout this book, I will consider the intersectional aspects of identity coupled with the constitutive effects of violence in order to ask how oppositional forms of agency are both conceived and enacted in transnational feminist art and literature. Most importantly, I will ask how feminist restagings of the relationship between image and identity might promote new ways of imagining the creative, political, and ethical dimensions of difference, or the "encounter between self and other."[10]

As a child of Norwegian immigrants to the United States, I have always been invested in efforts to theorize and represent transnational existence. During childhood, I was fascinated by tales of daring relatives who operated ham radios or otherwise aided the underground Resistance movement following the Nazi invasion of Norway in 1940. So it was with great interest that I learned recently of an entirely different, arguably "un-heroic" group of Norwegians: women who entered into relationships with German Wehrmacht officers during WWII. In many ways, these women embody the problematic status of transnational subjectivity. Their tenuous sociopolitical position recalls the perilous intersections between personal identity, national memory, sexual politics, and abjection that often circumscribe women's lives.

The German military regarded these primarily blonde, fair-skinned Norwegian women as the perfect specimens with which to enact Hitler's dream of an Aryan race. If women conceived during their affairs with German soldiers, they became beneficiaries of the SS's Lebensborn program, which provided child support and shelter for expectant mothers in one of ten homes scattered throughout Norway. The Lebensborn network of financial assistance and refuge proved critical to such women, who were publicly scorned and disowned by their families once word of their pregnancies began to spread throughout the community.

Considered Nazi collaborators and traitors to the Norwegian nation, most Lebensborn beneficiaries were either deported or confined to internment camps by the war's end. Abandoned, their children were left to fend for themselves in a sociopolitical climate of intense resentment and hostility. Regarded as symbols of their mothers' shame and transgression, Lebensborn children were ostracized by their fellow Norwegians. Historian Kare Olsen recently documented the plight of these children, many of whom were needlessly confined to long-term hospitalization in mental asylums. In December 2002, the Norwegian Parliament voted to provide financial compensation to these children as partial remedy for their experiences of social ostracism and alienation.[11]

One of the most compelling aspects of this little-known history is the fate of Lebensborn women, who remain outsiders *vis-à-vis* Norway and Germany. Represented as Nazi conspirators within both national communities, these women constitute a caste of untouchables that has been virtually ignored by scholars and government officials alike. Yet Lebensborn women's status as transnational scapegoats demands more complex feminist analysis. In particular, their relationships with German soldiers can only be understood within the context of the Lebensborn program, which provided powerful incentives for Nazi soldiers to pursue Norwegian women in order to achieve Hitler's racial, ethnic, and international political objectives. Although Norwegian women may have willingly entered into such relationships, German political objectives most often provided the impetus for their initial meetings and eventual involvement. Within this framework, German-Norwegian wartime couplings cannot be viewed as purely voluntary or love-based; nor can we unambiguously evoke Lebensborn women as enemies of the state.

National belonging is always haunted by the specters of race, ethnicity, and religious affiliation. Yet, as *Silence Broken* and the fate of Lebensborn women demonstrate, nationalism is an especially tenuous proposition for women, who typically inhabit the national imaginary as symbols of tradition and cultural purity, markers of sexual difference, and vehicles for strategic propagation of the "race" or species. Although sexuality and motherhood constitute the most intimate of human experiences, they nonetheless generate intense public scrutiny and state regulatory practices that profoundly impact women's daily lives. Disproportionately, it is women who must negotiate the treacherous interface between national, international, and sexual politics, and who most often suffer shame, social stigma, and ostracism from the national community as they attempt such negotiations.

Women's ambivalent experiences relative to the nation repeatedly test the ethical limits of community, nation, and representation. For postcolonial women, national belonging and the very concept of "home" are profoundly complicated and unstable propositions. Postcolonial feminist artwork, in particular, transforms traditional feminist analytical paradigms by emphasizing the need to reimagine home and community from transnational perspectives—especially since the majority of the world's refugee population consists of women and children, many of whom are victims of gender-based human rights violations such as rape and sex trafficking.[12]

How to represent sexual difference, and especially sexual violence, within the national imaginary presents an intractable political problem for the modern nation-state. If, as Ernest Renan has claimed, nationalism depends upon forgetting, then this form of collective amnesia exacts a particularly heavy toll on women. Indeed, women remain perhaps the most "forgotten" or repressed constituents of the body politic, even though their own bodies are so often made to signify national identity and cultural belonging.[13]

When I first began to sketch the outlines of this book in Los Angeles in June 2002, a *loya jirga* (grand assembly) was meeting across the globe in Kabul to lay the foundations for the future government of Afghanistan. This assembly marked a significant crossroads in Afghanistan's political history, coming on the heels of Taliban rule and on the eve of democratic elections projected for 2004. During this transitional period, the *loya jirga* wrestled with key political issues: Who should lead Afghanistan? Which form of government would most benefit the Afghan people? As these questions echoed in the minds of *loya jirga* delegates and foreign policy analysts, a general consensus seemed to emerge: women should play a role in Afghanistan's restructured administration. After years of human rights abuses by the Taliban, Afghan women *must* be represented in the new government.

Perhaps this desire to involve women in the future governance of Afghanistan revealed a collective longing to redress the sex inequalities engineered by the Taliban regime. While in power, the Taliban denied access to healthcare, education, legal representation, and the professions to girls and women. More disturbingly, it routinely subjected women to kidnapping, rape, assault and battery, forced marriage, sex trafficking, and public execution.

Yet Afghan women's sudden emergence into the political limelight came at a price. Dr. Sima Samar, the first interim minister for women's affairs in Afghanistan, later assumed the less visible position of human rights commissioner after receiving thousands of death threats. Her plight epitomizes the problematic status of "woman," more broadly, *vis-à-vis* the nation. At stake is not only the future of the Afghan polity, but also the potential to represent or integrate past injustices against women within the national imaginary, and to empower women to assume leadership roles in domestic and global politics. If the abuse of women figures in the Afghan psyche is an open wound, then the contemporary rush to recognize women's rights aims to stop this wound from bleeding and indelibly staining national memory.

But the stain is already there. Because a transitional government inherits the past, old grievances inevitably haunt new administrations. Trauma leaves a residual trace on the national imaginary, one that persists as a reminder of the human limits of community, law, and democracy. In light of this stain, new leaders are obliged to reconcile past suffering with contemporary desires for retribution. In this sense, the status of women in the Afghan polity is not exceptional, but representative of broader trends within international politics.

In English, the word "representation" evokes both political agency and visual culture. Although particular to the English language, this double entendre dramatically captures the synergy of political and artistic visions. Often, works of art are called upon to resolve lingering tensions between political trauma, collective memory, and the desire for redemption. Since injustice would be "repeated into oblivion"[14] without efforts to represent the past, artists—as mediators between past and present—"carry the burden of remembering and working through the trauma of the past"[15] in order to facilitate national mourning. I mean to evoke the act of remembering here not as a quiet effort of introspection, but as a "painful re-membering, a putting together of the dismembered past to make sense of the trauma of the present."[16]

German artist Anselm Kiefer's paintings epitomize this capacity to assume the ethical burdens of representation and commemoration.[17] By mixing materials such as lead, tar, sand, and straw on his canvases, Kiefer evokes the Holocaust as a haunting presence within the German imaginary in order to work through the unspeakability of traumatic memory.[18] His unconventional materials dramatically contrast the fragility of life with the heaviness of remembrance. Similarly, Assia Djebar's autobiographical work *L'amour, la fantasia* evokes the bloody, mutilated hand of an Algerian woman killed on a battlefield to symbolize at once the urgency, yet the impossibility, of representing women's experiences of transnational trauma—and, more broadly, ethnic, cultural, and sexual difference—within the national imaginary.

Insisting on the dual aesthetic and political dimensions of representation, this book will address the following questions with respect to women's experiences of transnational trauma. First, what does it mean not only to inhabit the schismatic space in between nations, but also to try to transmute this space of exile into a feminist politics and aesthetics? Although the notion of split subjectivity or schizophrenia is repeatedly invoked to describe a generic condition of postmodern malaise, what are its specific manifestations and implications in the context of postcolonial or diasporic existence? And how might it help to articulate feminist strategies of resistance?

Next, what does it mean to insist on the visual as a form of violence? How might Lebensborn women, for example, experience and respond to their image as "traitors" to two nations? How does symbolism exert violence that exceeds the seemingly benign realm of the imaginary in order to impact the material conditions of women's lives? Why does Assia Djebar, an Algerian-French writer, constantly couple her descriptions of the French military conquest of Algeria in 1840 with scathing commentary about the violence of the artistic impulse to *represent* "difference," exotically conceived? Finally, how do postcolonial feminist artists participate in the violence of representation to promote sexual as well as national decolonization? How might women's participation in this violence contribute to what Gayatri Spivak refers to as "alternate storying,"[19] or transnational feminist re-visionings of history, genealogy, national memory, and the colonizing gaze?

Since the late 1980s, feminist analyses of nationalism, colonization, and war have gained increasing momentum. Yet as a whole, this body of scholarship has failed to connect the aesthetic and political dimensions of colonization as envisioned by postcolonial feminist critics like Mohanty and Chow. In particular, few scholars have asked how women's creation and consumption of images might foster subversive political tactics of intervention and disidentification with the nation. Still fewer critics have considered how feminist representations of transnational trauma often enlist innovative aesthetic and ethical strategies for representing "difference." To address this scholarly lacuna, I will explore the intersecting psychological, political, and aesthetic components of representation and identification in order to reflect in greater detail on women's problematic symbolic status *vis-à-vis* the nation.[20]

This book will explore how women existing "in between" nations, or on the margins of national communities, portray their experiences of transnational trauma in semiautobiographical art and literature.[21] Specifically, I will ask how transnational feminist artists navigate the overlapping fantasies embedded in popular Orientalist, colonialist, and nationalist imagery. I am most interested in how women artists and writers choose to represent personal experiences of revolution, colonization, and exile. My work contends that feminist writers and artists who have experienced transnational trauma often invent bold aesthetic strategies for resisting—or misrecognizing—dominant sexual, racial, ethnic, and national fantasies, as well as hegemonic bids for identification.

My manuscript hopes to engage with several of the most pressing debates in contemporary feminist scholarship regarding nationalism and transnational studies, sexuality, colonization, autobiography, and visual culture. These debates can be summarized as follows. First, what might it mean to integrate women's traumatic experience within the national imaginary? How do women represent themselves *vis-à-vis* the nation—especially when national solidarity is so often founded on a certain tolerance for, if not incitement to, violence against women? How do feminist artists variously negotiate the "wounding" images that they have inherited—especially the simultaneous erasure, sexualization, and overdetermination of the feminine within nationalist symbolism?[22] How do they reformulate relationships between sexual, national, colonial, and visual politics in their work?

Yet I also want to provoke a new series of questions regarding misrecognition as a transnational feminist strategy for engaging with the violence and ambivalence of colonizing images. In particular, what are the political potentials of misrecognizing, rather than simply accepting or rejecting, stereotypical representations of women relative to the nation? How might feminist strategies of misrecognition allow for creative reformulations of identity and national memory? How do postcolonial feminist artists challenge binary conceptions of the "subject" and "object" of the gaze? How do they deploy fantasy as an integral element of identity and political expression? Finally, how might a closer reading of women's experiences "in between" nations help us to understand the complexity of women's polyvalent subject positions—and of their negotiations *vis-à-vis* the nation, transnational migration, and dominant modes of representing ethnic, racial, or sexual "difference"?

To answer these questions, I will explore literary and artistic works by Leila Sebbar, Theresa Cha, Hélène Cixous, and Assia Djebar. Although these artists hail from diverse geopolitical, ethnic, and socioeconomic backgrounds, their works similarly approach the nation as an object of critical inquiry, and leverage an intersectional model of "identity-in-difference"[23] as the basis for transnational feminist visions of community, genealogy, and history. Their shared emphasis on the subversive potentials of cultural consumption or spectatorship is especially radical when viewed alongside canonical texts on colonization, Orientalism, and visual culture by Roland Barthes, Frantz Fanon, Malek Alloula, David Henry Hwang, and Edward Said, among others. Feminist writers and artists constantly recall the blind spots of those canonical texts, such as Frantz Fanon's relative indifference to the complexities of female subjectivity as lived in the crossfire between colonialism and masculinist nationalism.

The writers and artists at the heart of my inquiry consistently trouble the presumed "subject" of Western feminist thought. As Chicana feminist theorist Norma Alarcón points out, "the most popular subject of Anglo-American feminism is an autonomous, self-making, self-determining subject who first proceeds according to a logic of identification."[24] This logic presumes that women must identify with the male subject position in order to achieve social parity. Inherent to this approach is an understanding of gender as the "primary" component of women's oppression, and on literal equality or sameness as the goal of feminist liberation. By contrast, transnational feminist analysis demands radical interrogation of Western concepts of consciousness and sovereignty, highlighting a need to address the intersecting variables that circumscribe women's experiences of oppression, including gender, race, class, ethnicity, and sexuality. For feminist artists who explore how identity is produced in relation to the transnational flows, images, and affiliations spurred by colonization, the logic of identification fails to capture the complex interface between trauma, agency, and representation.

In response to these insights, I will adopt a comparative approach to argue that transnational feminist artists often devise creative tactics for "misrecognizing" hegemonic imagery, and for complicating the presumed opposition between "subject" and "object" of the Orientalist, colonial, and masculinist nationalist gaze. Rather than emphasizing a need for mutual recognition, these artists often mobilize the gap between image and identity as a space within which to navigate transnational fantasy and trauma, and to promote a transformational politics and aesthetics of misrecognition.

This book will problematize the humanist ideal of recognition, especially as evoked in masculinist nationalist and colonialist discourse. Instead, I will explore feminist attempts to conceive of misrecognition in creative and politically empowering ways—especially to affirm difference and disjunction as sites of mutual permeability, and as the starting points for potentially liberating modes of exchange between self and other.

My usage of the term "misrecognition" both draws upon and departs from Jacques Lacan's psychoanalytical concept of *méconnaissance.* Like Lacan, I will use this term to allude to the primary role that fantasy plays in any encounter between the self and other (or the self *as* other). But I will also use it to describe self-conscious personal, political, and creative strategies for responding to "wounding" representations. Whereas Lacan construes misrecognition as an unconscious error of perception or cognition on the part of a generic, "apprehending" (viewing or speaking) subject, I will reframe it as a self-conscious strategy of aesthetic and political resistance adopted from specific locations of identity and difference. In this sense, I mean to propose it as a destructively creative tactic of disidentification, one that emerges in response to the wounding effects of colonizing or "controlling" images within postcolonial feminist art and autobiographical fiction.[25]

The subjects of my study address sexual and ethnic difference, violation, and collective memory as the foundations on which national ethical dilemmas are both articulated and resolved. Especially, they ask what is at stake in efforts to represent "difference" *vis-à-vis* the national community. Their works yield fresh perspectives on the relationship between trauma, image, and identity by strategically mining the aesthetic and political possibilities of misrecognition. Recalling the violence at the heart of any representational project, they encourage us to imagine its provocative and destabilizing, rather than crippling, possibilities for diasporic subjectivity.

Interestingly, none of these artists seeks to mitigate symbolic violence, or to reverse the hierarchical subject and object of the colonizing gaze. Instead, they ask how the violence of imagery constitutes postcolonial identity in terms of difference, internal division, and alienation. Moreover, they actively engage in symbolic violence in order to creatively rework hierarchical relations between self and other. They explore not only the aesthetic potentials of such reconfigurations, but also the ethical implications of differently imagining intersubjective relations within the nation. By so doing, they approach the violence of representation as a means of asserting aesthetic agency, and as a catalyst for conceiving of community in terms not of sameness or identification, but of difference and misrecognition.

One of the primary inspirations for my work, Frantz Fanon's *Black Skin, White Masks*,[26] powerfully attests to the wounding potentials of fantasy for minority and postcolonial identity. Like Edward Said's critique of Orientalism, Fanon's analysis of racist representation highlights its splitting effects for black subjectivity and consciousness. Although Fanon was one of the first theorists to link the political project of colonization with psychological effects, he had little to say on the subject of postcolonial women.

Contemporary feminist scholars including Ranjana Khanna and Ann Laura Stoler[27] have had much more to say about how fantasies about sexuality and gender identity inform colonial projects. My project departs from theirs in scope and geographic area of specialization. Focusing on the Maghreb and Southeast Asia, my work unites a feminist investigation into the psychological effects of colonization with an emphasis on visual culture, trauma studies, and feminist critiques of nationalism. Drawing on a range of critical perspectives,[28] I ask how transnational feminist artists variously deploy a critique of the nation in their artistic practices.

Another impetus for my work, Malek Alloula's *The Colonial Harem*[29] asks how images—especially colonial photographs—supported French colonization by reinforcing Orientalist fantasies about Algerian women. Yet Alloula's innovative study does not ask how Algerian women might have responded to their role in image-making—indeed, how they might have participated in photo-shoots as creative agents and manipulators of the colonial gaze. Drawing on Roland Barthes' insights about the potentials for creative manipulation and interpretation of photography in *Camera Lucida*,[30] my manuscript explores how postcolonial women artists from the Maghreb and Southeast Asia evoke nationalist, colonialist, and Orientalist imagery throughout their work in order to participate in the violence of image-creation, and to subversively reframe the relation between image and identity. Although Fanon, like David Henry Hwang in *M. Butterfly*,[31] believed that the only antidote to stereotypical representation lies in a recognition of the humanity and identity of the "other," the artists whose work I explore adopt creative tactics of misrecognition in order to complicate the notion of national belonging and to sculpt creative passages between fantasy and identity.

My first chapter lays out the theoretical framework that will inform subsequent analysis. I begin by considering Frantz Fanon's assessment of the link between the colonial gaze and minority identity, which inspires some of the primary questions behind my own work. What does it mean to look at, and identify with, colonial imagery? How might one look differently? How do differences in socioeconomic status, political affiliation, and historical context impact experiences of alienation or identification *vis-à-vis* the image? And how do postcolonial feminist artists confound resemblance and recognition as aesthetic and ethical objectives? This chapter will engage with the fantasies of sexual, racial, ethnic, and national otherness that so often collide in cross-cultural representation. By exploring Fanon's portrayal of women during the Algerian revolution alongside select literary, cinematic, and theoretical narratives by Marguerite Duras, Roland Barthes, Jacques Lacan, David Henry Hwang, and Rey Chow, I hope to develop a critical and creative lens through which to view postcolonial women's accounts of transnational trauma and colonial iconography.

Chapter 2 discusses the contemporary French-Algerian writer Leila Sebbar, whose work is vitally concerned with the relationship between colonial representation and postcolonial identity. Sebbar has written a trilogy of nomadic novels featuring Sherazade, a Beur or second-generation Algerian immigrant living in Paris. Sherazade constantly seeks out opportunities to participate in the violence of representation. In the first volume of the trilogy, for example, she shoots a .45 at a poster of Che Guevara, one of many nationalist leaders who was famously reluctant to involve women in the struggle for national liberation. Sherazade also tricks a French pornographic photographer as he attempts to arrange a studio shoot of her and her friends. Creatively mobilizing the Orientalist racial and sexual fantasies at play in his photo-shoot, Sherazade aims a fake gun at the photographer, simultaneously breaking his camera and demanding immediate payment for her services. In this and many other scenes of subversive reframing, she interrupts the process of image-making in order to upset the binary distinction between the presumed "subject" and "object" of representation. As a result, Sebbar's protagonist provocatively stages alternative means of identifying with and against the colonizing gaze.

Chapter 3 addresses the works of Hélène Cixous and Theresa Hak Kyung Cha. In *First Days of the Year*, the French-Algerian feminist writer Hélène Cixous provocatively imagines autobiography as the "self-portrait of a blind woman."[32] What does this mean? How might a blind woman accomplish her self-portrait? For Cixous, autobiography is above all an artistic pursuit: a bricolage of fantasy, imperfect memory, and the limits of self-knowledge. By approaching autobiography as a blind person's art, Cixous evokes self-representation as necessarily mediated by a limited access to the self. Unless another individual paints the self-portrait, the blind woman can best imagine herself from the inside out. Thus, Cixous anticipates the "I" as recognizable only through another's eyes, in passages between intimacy and alterity.

Theresa Hak Kyung Cha, a Korean-American conceptual artist and writer, challenges traditional forms of representation throughout her literary and visual oeuvre. In a photographic installation entitled "Chronology," Cha displays photographs that seem to constitute a family album. Yet she refuses to identify her photographic subjects, choosing instead to pair anonymous images with haunting text. Cha also repeats certain photographs throughout the exhibit rather than displaying the linear progression of images over time implied by her title. By resisting the imperatives of naming and classification that typically accompany autobiographical and genealogical projects, Cha marks a traumatic rupture in her own family history. At the same time, she troubles the fantasy of the harmonious "national family" by creating space for subversive performances of difference, incongruity, and alienation within the boundaries of the nation.

My fourth and final chapter will discuss Assia Djebar, a contemporary Algerian-French writer who centers representation as a problem throughout her work. Although she chooses to write in French, she constantly comments on the painful yet subversive potentials of speaking in the enemy's tongue. As she describes the French colonization of Algeria in her autobiographical novel *Fantasia*, Djebar highlights the ubiquity of painters and writers employed by the French government to record battle scenes. She constantly catches these artists in the act of representing war and, especially, the "exotic otherness" of Algerians. Demonstrating how the violence of representation vitally supports colonial politics and hegemonic visions of "difference," Djebar suggests that feminist visions of postcolonial identity, community, and history can only be articulated by formulating alternative symbolic economies or transnational feminist imaginaries. *Fantasia*'s conclusion evokes a woman's severed hand, left lying on the battlefield, to signify the impossibility of integrating sexual difference within an Orientalist or masculinist nationalist imaginary. Djebar's version of a postcolonial feminist imaginary enlists the details of the female body, desire, and cry in order to posit sexual liberation as tantamount to national decolonization.

Although these artists all foreground women's experiences of national and colonial trauma, they reach slightly different conclusions regarding the possibilities for women's integration, recognition, and identification within the national imaginary. Most notably, they adopt varied tactics for engaging with the colonizing gaze. For example, although Leila Sebbar's protagonist violently subverts the Orientalist gaze, she does not suggest that this participation in violence might lay the foundations for a feminist identity politics. The author resists facile efforts to categorize her own identity as either French or Algerian in order to honor the complexity of her mixed ethnic origins (French and Algerian). Assia Djebar, on the other hand, posits sexual decolonization as a vital goal for feminist activism and identity politics. She regards it as tantamount to national liberation, and claims that both depend upon the creation of new imaginaries and new modes of trafficking between image and identity that might enable alternative ethical approaches to political and aesthetic representation. Finally, although Theresa Hak Kyung Cha is careful to specify her subject position as a Korean-American artist, her work ultimately moves beyond identity politics to explore the problems of recognition and assimilation in the broader context of immigration and diaspora. In a sense, Cha constantly challenges and reworks the violence and alienation that lie just beneath images. By simultaneously engaging in and resisting the act of representation in her work, she asks what it means to represent the traumatized self to others, and how such representation depends upon fantasy, rupture, irresolution, and misrecognition. For Cha, identification and national solidarity remain elusive, if not impossible, goals.

The originality of my work lies in my adaptation of the Lacanian concept of misrecognition as an analytical tool with which to understand diverse postcolonial feminist aesthetic projects. The postcolonial feminist artists at the heart of my inquiry understand identity only in relation to experiences of transnational trauma including war, colonization, and exile. Consequently, I ask how their work navigates existing representations in order to trace a more complex space of trauma within national memory—one that acknowledges the ambivalence of women's roles and contributions.

My conceptual model of "creative misrecognition" draws upon critical perspectives in Francophone literary theory, psychoanalysis, postcolonial feminist and queer theory, ethnic and diaspora studies, philosophy, and aesthetics. Especially since 1999 or so, transnational feminist and queer theorists have struggled to understand how traumatic experiences impact gender, ethnic, and sexual identification. In the context of transnational queer performance art, Jose Muñoz (1999) has perhaps most provocatively conceptualized "disidentification" as an aesthetic response to sexual and ethnic marginalization. Postcolonial Francophone and ethnic studies scholars including Homi Bhabha, Ranjana Khanna, Lisa Lowe, Marianne Hirsch, Inderpal Grewal, Ella Shohat, and Anne Anlin Cheng have increasingly contributed to trauma studies as well, many returning to the work of Frantz Fanon in order to think anew about the relationship between racial and sexual stereotypes, colonization, identity, and possibilities for resistance.

Most recently, in the wake of September 11, 2001, ethnic studies scholars have asked pressing questions about how state-sanctioned forms of stereotyping and marginalization, such as Orientalist imagery and racial profiling, have inspired an increasingly volatile mix of disidentification with the "nation" coupled with a retreat to fundamentalist or conservative forms of religious expression and identification. In light of recent controversy regarding the international news media's publication of cartoon representations of the prophet Mohammed, scholars have thought especially hard about the unique power of images to inspire political turmoil and disidentification.

In response to, and in dialogue with, these evolving lines of inquiry, I develop an analytical lens of "creative misrecognition" with which to think about how trauma—especially nationalism, colonization, and sexual violence—impacts women's experiences of the space between image and identity—or identification and visual culture—in Francophone autobiographical literature and artwork. My work is primarily concerned with representation and resistance, but I imagine possibilities for resistance only in relation to the psychological impact of trauma, the work of identifying with or against images, and the various impossibilities of expressing traumatic experience.

My work hopes to unite diverse, interdisciplinary perspectives in order to promote new lines of vision, questioning, and analysis. Throughout this book, I bring feminist aesthetic and psychoanalytic theories of representation, identification, and misrecognition to bear on postcolonial women's literature and artwork. I analyze visual materials throughout my work, blending postcolonial feminist and aesthetic theory with trauma studies in a fashion that I have not encountered elsewhere.

For example, I analyze Theresa Cha's visual and performance art in conjunction with *Dictée* as a personal and national "family album" of sorts. This perspective is unique for its commitment to understanding the synergy between Cha's literary and artistic work. Similarly, I discuss Leila Sebbar's work as an active engagement with the violence of representation by reading her literary efforts alongside critical theories of the gaze and look. To my knowledge, few scholars have interpreted her work through the intersecting lenses of postcolonial politics and feminist aesthetics. Finally, I theorize Assia Djebar's *Fantasia* relative to the Nietzschean genealogical and epistemological project of "going under," and in relation to a feminist political commitment to exploring the female body, sexuality, and sexual violence as integral components of national identity and international politics.

My primary motivations for pursuing interdisciplinary scholarship include the desire to promote connections between disparate bodies of knowledge and to address multiple audiences. In particular, I hope that this work will speak to a wide range of students and scholars in the fields of Francophone literature and theory, literary criticism, autobiography, cultural and ethnic studies, feminist and queer theory, aesthetics, nationalism, sexuality, revolution, colonization, postcolonial theory, and trauma studies. Throughout this book, my discussions of heterogeneous artists and writers are united by a commitment to exploring how the psychological work of identifying with and against images might yield feminist strategies of resistance.

NOTES

1. See for example Michael Kimmelman, "A Startling New Lesson in the Power of Imagery," *The New York Times*, Feb. 8, 2006.

2. Dai Sil Kim-Gibson, *Silence Broken: Korean Comfort Women* (1999).

3. Japan has recently experienced a flurry of public debate regarding the omission of discussions of comfort women from history textbooks in Japanese primary schools.

4. "Korean Woman Loses WWII Sex Slave Case," *Los Angeles Times*, A20, Mar. 29, 2003.

5. Chandra Talpade Mohanty, "Under Western Eyes: Feminist Scholarship and Colonial Discourses," in Mohanty, Russo, and Torres, eds., *Third World Women and the Politics of Feminism* (Bloomington: Indiana University Press, 1991), 51.

6. Mohanty 1991: 10.

7. Rey Chow, "Violence in the Other Country: China as Crisis, Spectacle, and Woman," in Mohanty, ed. 1991: 81–100.

8. Rey Chow, *Writing Diaspora: Tactics of Intervention in Contemporary Cultural Studies* (Bloomington: Indiana University Press, 1993), 28–34.

9. Chow 1993: 51.

10. Peggy Phelan, "Broken Symmetries: Memory, Sight, Love," in Amelia Jones, ed., *The Feminism and Visual Culture Reader* (New York: Routledge, 2003), 112.

11. Kare Olsen, *Krigensbarn: De norske krigsbarna og deres modre* (Oslo: Forlaget Forum, 1998). For contemporary developments regarding Norway's compensation of Lebensborn children, see Gregory Crouch, "Norway Tries to Resolve a Lasting Nazi Legacy," *The New York Times*, December 16, 2002 and Gregory Crouch, "Norway: Payments for 'German Children,'" *The New York Times*, Dec. 17, 2002.

12. According to International Organization for Migration estimates, as many as two million women and children were trafficked across borders in 2001. See *UNIFEM Currents* (March 2003).

13. Ernest Renan, *Qu'est-ce qu'une nation?* (Pocket: Paris, 1992), 41. Renan first delivered this address at a conference of the same name held at La Sorbonne in Paris on March 11, 1882.

14. Theresa Hak Kyung Cha, *Dictée* (Berkeley: Third Woman Press, 1995; reprint, New York: Tanam Press, 1982), 33 (page references are to reprint edition).

15. Linda Belau, "Introduction: Remembering, Repeating, and Working-Through: Trauma and the Limit of Knowledge," in Belau and Ramadanovic, eds., *Topologies of Trauma: Essays on the Limit of Knowledge and Memory* (New York: Other Press, 2002), xxvi.

16. Homi Bhabha, "Foreword: Remembering Fanon," in Frantz Fanon, *Black Skin, White Masks*, trans. Charles Lam Markmann (London: Pluto Press, 1986), xxiii.

17. See John Tagg, *The Burden of Representation: Essays on Photographies and Histories* (Minneapolis: University of Minnesota Press, 1988).

18. Herman Rapaport, "Representation, History, and Trauma: Abstract Art after 1945," in Belau, ed. 2002: 246.

19. Gayatri Spivak, "Bonding in Difference," in Alfred Arteaga, ed., *An Other Tongue* (Durham, NC: Duke University Press, 1994), 283–84.

20. My usage of the terms "colonialist representation" or the "colonizing gaze" intends to evoke a broad range of hegemonic or "colonizing" ideologies, including masculinist nationalist, in addition to colonialist, discourse.

21. I use the term "semiautobiographical" here to address works that self-consciously interweave autobiographical detail with fantasy and fiction.

22. Roland Barthes approaches representation, specifically photography, as a wound in *Camera Lucida*. See Roland Barthes, *Camera Lucida*, trans. Richard Howard (New York: Farrar, Straus & Giroux, 1981), 21.

23. This expression refers to a popular feminist deconstructivist understanding of identity as constituted in and through difference.

24. Norma Alarcón, "The Theoretical Subject(s) of *This Bridge Called My Back* and Anglo-American Feminism," in Gloria Anzaldúa, ed., *Making Face, Making Soul: Creative and Critical Perspectives by Feminists of Color* (San Francisco: Aunt Lute Books, 1990), 357.

25. For a discussion of "controlling images"—or stereotypical imagery that supports a political economy of domination—see Patricia Hill Collins, *Black Feminist Thought: Knowledge, Consciousness, and the Politics of Empowerment* (New York: Routledge, 1990), 67–90.

26. Frantz Fanon, *Black Skin, White Masks*, trans. Charles Lam Markmann (New York: Grove Press, 1967).

27. Ranjana Khanna, *Dark Continents: Psychoanalysis and Colonialism* (Durham, NC: Duke University Press, 2003); Ann Laura Stoler, *Race and the Education of Desire: Foucault's* History of Sexuality *and the Colonial Order of Things* (Durham, NC: Duke University Press, 1995).

28. My work is especially influenced by the following: Ernest Renan (*Qu'est-ce qu'une nation?* Paris: Poche, 1992), Benedict Anderson (*Imagined Communities: Reflections on the Origin and Spread of Nationalism*, London: Verso, 1991), Homi Bhabha (*The Location of Culture*, New York: Routledge, 1994), Lauren Berlant (*The Queen of America Goes to Washington City: Essays on Sex and Citizenship*, Durham, NC: Duke University Press, 1997), Anne McClintock (*Imperial Leather: Race, Gender and Sexuality in the Colonial Context*, New York: Routledge, 1995), Marnia Lazreg (*The Eloquence of Silence: Algerian Women in Question*, New York: Rout-

ledge, 1994), Jarrod Hayes (*Queer Nations: Marginal Sexualities in the Maghreb*, Chicago: University of Chicago Press, 2000), and Marie-Aimee Helie-Lucas ("Women, Nationalism, and Religion in the Algerian Liberation Struggle," in M. Badran and M. Cooke, eds., *Opening the Gates: A Century of Arab Feminist Writing*, Bloomington: Indiana University Press, 1990).

29. Malek Alloula, *The Colonial Harem*, trans. W. Godzich (Minneapolis: University of Minnesota Press, 1986).

30. Roland Barthes, *Camera Lucida*, trans. Richard Howard (New York: Hill and Wang, 1981).

31. David Henry Hwang, *M. Butterfly* (New York: Penguin, 1989).

32. Hélène Cixous, *First Days of the Year*, trans. Catherine MacGillivray (Minneapolis: University of Minnesota Press, 1998), originally published as *Jours de l'an* (Paris: Les editions des femmes, 1990), 101.

Chapter One

Fantasizing the Self

Identifying With and Against Images

People seek to have their photographs taken because they believe that they are "made real by photographs." The clicking of the actual or metaphoric camera signifies that social acknowledgment or "recognition" upon which all subjectivity depends.

—Kaja Silverman, *The Threshold of the Visible*

The questions of identification, recognition, self-definition, or the very possibility of envisaging oneself as a subject are fundamental questions for feminism. If identification is the operation whereby the human subject is constituted . . . then it must be all the more important, theoretically and politically, for women who have never before represented ourselves as subjects, and whose images and subjectivities—until very recently, if at all—have not been ours to shape, portray, or create.

—Teresa de Lauretis, "Aesthetic and Feminist Theory: Rethinking Women's Cinema"

What are the possibilities of politicizing the experience of disidentification or misrecognition, this uneasy sense of standing under a sign to which one does and does not belong? . . . It may be that the affirmation of that slippage, that the failure of identification, is itself the point of departure for a more democratizing affirmation of difference.

—Judith Butler, *Bodies That Matter*

I. LOOKING AT PICTURES

Scenes from a film viewed in the fourth grade swirl around in my memory. More than its title or content, I recall my restless sense of alienation while watching the film. As I looked up at the screen, I focused on the mouths until they no longer signified anything but movement. And from the vague sea of parting lips I distinctly felt that I would learn more from this film, that I would be more engaged by it, if it included female characters in addition to boys and men.

Fifth grade heralded a very different, yet equally formative, cinematic moment. As I sat enthralled by a British production of Robert Louis Stevenson's *Treasure Island*, I heard snickers and complaints rise from the surrounding audience of my classmates—mimicry and cries of "I don't understand this!" and "what are they saying?" The more jeering that I overheard, the more closely I identified with the foreign accents of the British "others," and recognized myself as a grateful outsider to the crowd. Growing up as part of an immigrant family in a conservative Midwestern town, I had already developed an acute understanding of language as either an obstacle or an enabler, a badge of belonging or a stigma that positioned one as the outcast and scapegoat of a "native" community.

These childhood memories foreground the issues of representation and identification that I hope to explore in this chapter, which lays out the theoretical framework for my subsequent analysis. I will begin by considering Frantz Fanon's evaluation of the compelling relationship between minority identity and the colonial gaze, which is one of the primary motivations for my own work. What does it mean to look at, and identify with, colonial imagery? How might one look differently? How do differences in socioeconomic status impact possibilities for identification? How do these possibilities vary according to political and historical circumstance? And finally, do postcolonial feminist art and literature present any alternatives to recognition as an aesthetic and ethical objective?

This chapter will explore Fanon's portrayal of women in the Algerian revolution together with select literary, cinematic, and theoretical narratives by Marguerite Duras, Roland Barthes, Jacques Lacan, David Henry Hwang, David Cronenberg, and Rey Chow. By juxtaposing these seemingly disparate voices, I hope to develop a critical and creative lens through which to view postcolonial women's portrayals of national trauma and colonial representation. This is vital since, as Anne Anlin Cheng notes, liberal discourse has "studiously avoided confronting either the subjective implications of domination or its accompanying network of fantasy."[1] To counter this silence, I will discuss feminist engagements with a broad spectrum of fantasies (sexual, racial, ethnic, national, cultural, colonial) that collide in intercultural representation. My analytical perspective emphasizes feminist tactics of misrecognition and disidentification, which I will elucidate in the following discussion. In particular, I hope to illuminate fantasy's role in mediating acts of representation and identification.

II. FIXING THE IMAGE: FANON, COLONIZATION, AND REPRESENTATION

> To exist is to be called into being in relation to an Otherness, its look or locus. The very place of identification is a space of splitting.
>
> —Homi Bhabha, "Foreword," *Black Skin, White Masks*

> Since the other hesitated to recognize me, there remained only one solution: to make myself known.
>
> —Frantz Fanon, *Black Skin, White Masks*

In *Black Skin, White Masks*, Frantz Fanon powerfully evokes the profoundly damaging effects of racist imagery for minority identity. While relaying a particularly offensive encounter aboard a train in France, Fanon confesses that the racist language and images seemed to tear into the very surface of his skin, and to shatter his sense of self beyond all possible reconstitution:

> I was battered down by tom-toms, cannibalism, intellectual deficiency, fetishism, and racial defects. On that day, completely dislocated, I took myself far off from my own presence, far indeed, and made myself an object. *What else could it be for me* but an amputation, an excision, a hemorrhage that spattered my whole body with black blood? My body was given back to me sprawled out, distorted, recolored, clad in mourning on that white winter day.[2]

Fanon's anguished meditation on the wounding potentials of racist representation never ceases to haunt me. Bombarded by dehumanizing images of blackness within French society, Fanon calls attention to the daily state of emergency in which he feels compelled to exist.[3] Most compellingly, he describes his body and psyche as called into being—or interpellated in the Althusserian sense[4]—on the basis of their perceived alterity, pathology, and inhumanity. Whereas racist discourse both hails and refuses to address Fanon as a black male subject, it simultaneously "fixes" or binds him to an identification that can never exceed what he calls the racial "epidermal schema," or the hypervisibility of his skin as social signifier.[5]

Fanon describes the "fixing" potentials of racist representation in aesthetic, personal, and political terms. In his words, "the glances of the other fixed me there, in the sense in which a chemical solution is fixed by a dye. I burst apart."[6] Fanon's evocation of the fixative power of the colonial gaze is enriched by a psychoanalytic understanding of the self as constituted in and through the gaze of the other. As Slavoj Žižek explains,

> The subject is always fastened, pinned, to a signifier which represents him for the other, and through this pinning he is loaded with a symbolic mandate [a particular positioning within symbolic relations]. Loaded with this mandate, the subject is automatically confronted with a question of the Other: "*why am I what you are saying that I am?*"[7]

Fanon's highly original analysis of the constitutive effects of racist representation for identity foreshadows similar concerns that have been voiced by women of color in the United States, especially since the mid-1980s. Fanon's theoretical paradigm, symbolized by the opposing constructs of black skin and white mask at play in the title of his work, construes minority identity as the site of split subjectivity or plural positioning. Chicana feminist theorist Alma Garcia has similarly evoked this metaphor of split subjectivity to describe the experiences of Chicana women *vis-à-vis* the Chicano nationalist movement and Anglo-American feminist scholarship. Because the lives of women of color are impacted not only by gender or ethnicity, but also by race, class, and sexuality, Garcia insists that feminist theory and practice must address the interwoven strands of women's oppression in order to grasp the diversity and complexity of their experiences.[8]

To encourage feminist theorists and legal practitioners alike to account for split subjectivity as experienced by women of color in the United States, feminist legal theorist Kimberlé Williams Crenshaw pioneered the concept of "intersectionality" in the early 1990s.[9] A founding principle within the legal field of critical race theory (CRT), intersectionality refers to the multiple and simultaneous factors—including race, class, gender, religion, and sexuality—that coalesce in women's experiences of oppression, and, in Crenshaw's words, often reduce women of color to a "location that resists telling."[10] Today, intersectionality or "multiple consciousness" has gained popular currency in U.S. third world feminist scholarship to express the ways in which plural aspects of identity compound women's experiences of societal oppression.[11]

The convergence of minority and feminist discourse on the issue of split subjectivity points to the inadequacy of gender (or race, or class) as an isolated category with which to understand experiences of violence and subjugation. Feminist activists, especially advocates for the rights of battered women, emphasize the need to address the multifaceted variables of oppression that differentially impact women's experiences of, and abilities to respond to, domestic violence, sexual harassment, rape, reproductive health, and poverty. As Clarence Thomas' Senate confirmation hearings in 1991 powerfully demonstrated, these differential variables often lead to competing claims for community allegiance and loyalty among women of color.[12] The personal and political stakes of these conflicting bids for identification should not be underestimated. Several feminist legal theorists have adopted an intersectional approach in their advocacy work in order to revise legal principles such as the "reasonable person standard" and "battered woman's syndrome."[13] As litmus tests that measure the appropriateness or "authenticity" of personal responses to violence, these principles often work to marginalize or pathologize the nonconformist behaviors of women who are subject to multiple forms of oppression.

Although articulated within a very different social and historical context, Fanon's critique of split subjectivity similarly seeks to challenge hierarchical constructions of identity and difference. Fanon parallels his existence within the African diaspora in France to the Algerian experience of French colonization, both of which he perceives to exercise shattering effects on minority identity. For Fanon, colonial power plays out most forcefully "through image and fantasy."[14] He embraces a Lacanian view of fantasy as the space of negotiation between individual desire or self-image and the demands of the other.

In terms that recall Gloria Anzaldúa's evocation of the colonized United States–Mexico border as a bleeding wound (*una herida abierta*),[15] Fanon articulates the fracturing effects—or "gaping wound"—of colonial fantasy for both body and psyche. Although Fanon adopts the Lacanian premise that ego-formation always involves self-schism, he highlights the unusually painful effects of this process for colonized people. Fanon understands colonial oppression to etch dehumanizing images, myths, and fantasies onto the bodies and minds of the colonized. Drawing upon case studies of patients treated during his career as a clinical psychiatrist in revolutionary Algeria, Fanon identifies the shattering effects of colonial representation as foundational to the self-image of colonized people. As his clinical and theoretical work affirms, identification is forever haunted by colonial politics.

Fanon insightfully foregrounds the constitutive effects of colonial representation for subjectivity. As Diana Fuss has noted, his work "asks us to remember the violence" of representation, as well as the symbolic and material practices of domination and exclusion that "transform 'other' subjects into subjected others."[16] Colonization initiates not only a rupture in the political life and history of a colonized land; it also occasions a profound break in representation. In particular, colonialism informs the collective imaginary of what it means to be human. For the colonized subject, humanity is virtually off-limits: "every ontology is made unattainable."[17]

Yet part of the project to recall the violence at the origins of national identity entails a critique of nationalism itself, which—as Ernest Renan contends—depends on the forgetfulness of citizens.[18] The blind spot of Fanon's analysis lies partly in his failure to acknowledge the ways in which individuals are differently situated relative to the incipient nation. Although he anticipates the impact of racial stereotypes on the minority subject's ability to identify with the colonial other and, by extension, the nation, he discounts other factors that coincide with race to compound experiences of oppression, such as class, gender, and sexuality. For example, Fanon discounts and even pathologizes homosexuality throughout his text. Also, despite his lengthy and essentialist reflections on white female psychosexuality, he claims to "have nothing to say" and to "know nothing" about women of color.[19] Yet for those who are constructed as marginal to a national community on the basis of intersecting elements of identity, including queers and women of color, the need to remember the violence at the origins of nationalism is especially acute. Fanon's erasure of black female subjectivity in *Black Skin, White Masks* not only repeats the founding exclusions of nationalist discourse; it also reduces violence against women of color, including rape, to a "location that resists telling."[20]

During the Algerian revolution, violent clashes between colonialists and nationalists specifically impacted Algerian women. Targeted by campaigns of rape, strategic impregnation, and forced veiling or unveiling by French and Algerian militants, women inhabited the crossfire between nationalist and colonialist ideologies. Many women expressed their situation as one of double colonization, first by French colonizers and subsequently by patriarchal nationalists. Algerian sociologist Djamila Amrane, who conducted an extensive survey of war veterans after the revolution, found that most Algerian women nationalists were restricted to domestic roles during the revolution, where they served as cooks, laundresses, and nurses.[21] Although about 2 percent of female nationalists did engage in suicide bombings or other militant activities, the vast majority was granted peripheral and stereotypically "feminine" tasks *vis-à-vis* the nascent nation.

Fanon's analysis of the splitting effects of colonization for male subjectivity draws its impetus from the Hegelian master/slave dialectic. Like Hegel, Fanon believes that mutual recognition is the only basis for egalitarian relations and political empowerment. He concludes that "in order to win the certainty of oneself, the incorporation of the concept of recognition is essential" to colonized people.[22] Images are especially powerful throughout Fanon's analysis because they confer upon individuals precisely this form of "recognition" or acknowledgment upon which subjectivity depends.

I appreciate Fanon's strategic call for recognition in projects to oppose what Gayatri Spivak has called the "epistemic violence" of colonial representation, or its injurious effects on identity. However, I believe that misrecognition is a more promising political strategy for postcolonial artists and writers. My work will consider tactics of misrecognition that abound in postcolonial feminist art and literature, precisely because they call into question the very possibility of the founding "I" and its ability to identify with images of self and nation in times of trauma. To counter Fanon's emphasis on recognition as an ethical imperative, I will explore feminist strategies of misrecognition that test the limits of national identity, memory, and representation by promoting violent collisions between fantasy, identity, and politics.

Fanon's question—"what else could [stereotypical imagery] be for me?"—clearly haunts the work of contemporary postcolonial feminist artists and writers. Yet how do postcolonial women artists differently respond to this question? That is, what else might representation offer them, beyond recognition? I am especially interested in women's experiences of identification with, or against, the nation and national iconography.

My analysis highlights feminist attempts to negotiate transnational trauma, visual culture, and collective memory in order to forge resistant histories, identities, and imaginaries. In particular, I will suggest that creative feminist engagements with representation invite us to re-vision the relationship between image and identity. Rather than conceiving of the image solely as a weapon that wounds or an envelope that contains its subject, we might re-frame the image as a double, mask, or "thrown-off-skin" that the subject can reject, parody, or refuse to wear.[23] To provide a richer framework within which to understand women's engagements with the violence of colonial imagery, let us now turn to another of Fanon's essays entitled "Algeria Unveiled," which specifically addresses women's experiences during anticolonial revolution.

III. FANON UNVEILED: ALGERIAN WOMEN, REVOLUTION, AND IDENTIFICATION

> Because the women of Algeria have been fashioned as living symbols of the nation, feminist analysis must come to terms with and dismantle this aspect of national identity.
>
> —Winifred Woodhull, *Transfigurations of the Maghreb*

How are women evoked in historical accounts of the Algerian revolution, and how did nationalist symbolism help to establish parameters of belonging to the budding nation throughout wartime? Perhaps the most familiar stories of women's involvement in the Algerian revolution come from the work of Frantz Fanon, a French-Martinican psychiatrist who served on medical duty in revolutionary Algeria. During his clinical work, Fanon found striking parallels between the psychological effects of racist objectification in France and French colonization in Algeria.

Along with the film *The Battle of Algiers* (1966), Fanon's essay "Algeria Unveiled," written during the fifth year of war, remains among the most influential informants of the Western imagination regarding Algerian women's participation in revolution.[24] The popularity of Fanon's work bespeaks its analytical power relative to the ideological construction of colonized subjects and the strategic role of anticolonial violence. Written primarily during the revolution, Fanon's essays undoubtedly influenced the leadership of the Algerian nationalist liberation movement (FLN). Their frequent publication in *El Moudjahid*, the official newspaper of the FLN—where Fanon served for some time as an editor and active member of the FLN—suggests that revolutionary leaders embraced his ideas.

In "Algeria Unveiled," Fanon discusses the veil as a fetishistic marker of national identity and anticolonial resistance. In particular, he analyzes Algerian women's shifting deployment of the veil throughout the revolution. As Fanon points out, some women concealed bombs beneath their veils in order to transport them to popular French cafés and milk bars in Algiers.

Fanon predicted that by participating in anticolonial violence, women would help to bring about gender equality in postrevolutionary Algerian society.[25] He also believed that the revolutionary activities of the male-female (conjugal) couple would lay the foundations for national and social emancipation. In his view, "the united militant couple, participating in the birth of the nation, becomes the basic cell of the commonwealth, the fertile nucleus of the nation. There is a simultaneous and effervescent emergence of the citizen, the patriot, and the modern spouse."[26] Fanon assumed that the image of courageous women wielding bombs under their veils would become foundational to national consciousness. In particular, he believed that this powerful symbolism would linger in the national imaginary long enough to spark social change, especially sexual decolonization, in postcolonial Algeria.

Algerian writer Assia Djebar painted a strikingly different picture of women's fate in postcolonial Algeria. In *L'amour, la fantasia* (*Fantasia*), she spoke of a "black sun" that would dawn for Algerian women in the postwar period. Of course, since it was written decades after the revolution, *Fantasia* might be said to benefit from the infallibility of hindsight. Yet even Djebar's earlier work, *Les alouettes naïves*—written only five years after the intoxicating eve of liberation[27]—pessimistically imagined women's roles within postrevolutionary Algerian society. Countering Fanon's perspective on the wartime heterosexual couple as the harbinger of postcolonial sex equality, *Les alouettes naïves* predicted instead that the war between France and Algeria would "live on" in postrevolutionary Algeria as a civil war within the conjugal couple.[28]

What accounts for these divergent predictions for women's status in postcolonial Algeria? Their difference stems from varying levels of complexity in both writers' analyses of the founding images of the Algerian national imaginary—especially those related to sexuality, identification, and nationalist representation. Like Simone de Beauvoir, Fanon assumes that women will achieve equality, or accede to the "universal" subject position, by adopting traditionally masculine roles. Fanon's vision is grounded in a Marxist analysis of class oppression coupled with an unwavering faith in the transcendental subject. Ultimately, Fanon believes that the ideal of women's liberation will be "made real" by popular imagery. In particular, the radical image of women acting in masculine roles during the revolution will become so foundational to Algerian national memory that it will authorize a radical rewriting of sexual politics postindependence.

In "Algeria Unveiled," Fanon offers a nationalist perspective on revolutionary practices of veiling and unveiling, or what came to be known as the battle of the veil. From this perspective, the French policy of unveiling Algerian women constitutes an effort to Westernize Algerian society. In response, Algerian nationalist leaders urged women to retain their veils as symbols of defiance against French "modernization." As Fanon points out, many women strategically utilized the veil to express their allegiance to the Algerian community. They donned the veil to affirm Muslim religious and cultural beliefs, and also to conceal messages, guns, and bombs during wartime. Given its pivotal role in symbolic politics, Fanon evokes the veil as an integral component of anticolonial resistance.

Although some Algerian women did appropriate the veil as a strategy of political resistance and empowerment during the revolution, Fanon's analysis of the veil's liberating potentials rests on a disturbing oversimplification. By reading women's veiling practices solely in terms of anticolonial defiance, Fanon minimizes the complexity of women's social and symbolic status in revolutionary Algeria. In particular, he ignores how women's strategic assumption of the veil might have problematically aligned them with patriarchal interpretations of the Qur'an and, more broadly, Algerian culture. The revolutionary nationalist movement evoked women as symbols of the nascent Algerian nation; as guardians of pure or authentic Algerian culture; and as repositories of tradition, to be protected at all costs from colonial infiltration. In this sense, women came to represent "pure" indigenous culture and tradition as opposed to Western corruption, modernity, and sociopolitical reform. In a painfully literal enactment of this symbolism, both Algerian and French men raped Algerian women throughout the revolution. As an effort to assert cultural and political dominance, sexual violation transfigured female bodies into disputed possessions at the heart of international political struggle.

During the revolution, the Algerian nationalist movement encouraged women to support the war effort by categorically rejecting French "modernizing" proposals such as the call to unveil. Women found themselves embroiled in an intense debate regarding the political meaning of veiling. Could the veil be considered a symbol of patriarchal oppression, as French colonialists intimated? Or was it an integral component of indigenous culture jeopardized by colonial infiltration? Competing constructions of the strategic import of the veil testified, above all, to the precariousness of women's position—both symbolic and physical—*vis-à-vis* colonial and nationalist communities.

Nationalist leaders consistently rejected feminist critiques of veiling as a form of collusion with imperialist ideology. By positing an irreconcilable tension between the goals of nationalism and feminism, the FLN leadership delegitimized feminist aspirations. At the same time, it downplayed the Western origins of nationalist ideology. Nationalist rhetoric and symbolism—which problematized women's loyalty and rendered them objects of contestation between French and Algerian men—was reinforced by a careful regulation of space and sexuality within the *maquis*, or revolutionary nationalist underground. In covert operations throughout the revolution, nationalist directives ordered women to deploy their veils in ways that overwhelmingly upheld women's symbolic alignment with "traditional" Algerian culture. The antirevolutionary and antifeminist implications of this nationalist association between feminism and colonialism became clear only in independent Algeria, where feminist calls for social and legal reform, including a repeal of the conservative Family Code, were repeatedly denounced as incompatible with indigenous cultural practice and national political objectives.

Fanon's analysis of the liberating potential of women's revolutionary activities would benefit from a closer look at these dynamics of institutionalized resistance to changing the social and symbolic status of women. Although women's participation in national liberation movements does threaten to perturb gender norms, this threat may, as in Algeria, be effectively contained within an economy of masculinist national symbolism and regulation, only to reinforce patriarchal conceptions of sexual difference, family, and the nation following revolution. In fact, this is a central paradigm for the enduring legacies of third world feminists.

In "Algeria Unveiled," Fanon uncritically adopts nationalist symbolism aligning women with Algerian tradition. This equation plays out most noticeably in Fanon's essentialist characterizations of women. Despite his eloquent portrayal of the splitting effects of colonization for Algerian men, Fanon makes no attempt to theorize its particularly traumatic effects for female subjectivity. For example, although he discusses mimicry as a symptom of the alienation experienced by colonized men, he presumes that Algerian women's mimetic usage of the veil during revolution is straightforward and instinctive. Fanon does not imagine that women might experience their position—at the discursive intersection of French and Algerian calls to veil or unveil—as the site of an impossibly divided allegiance. Instead, he maintains that women effectively mobilize their traditional dress and domestic inclinations in order to nurse, clothe, feed, and shelter male rebels during the revolution. Furthermore, he suggests that women's dutiful domestic and religious performances will promote feminist liberation.[29]

As an anticolonialist, Fanon condemns French campaigns of forced unveiling. He understands these campaigns as attempts to incite Algerian women's identification with "liberated" French women and civilization, and as efforts to procure French sexual access to the bodies of Algerian women. Because Fanon does not allow that Algerian women might experience certain traditional cultural practices as oppressive, however, he presumes that Algerian women will unanimously oppose French calls to unveil.

Yet in his effort to contrast the psychological effects of forced versus strategic unveiling, Fanon obscures a broader spectrum of female subjectivity and agency. In his view, Algerian women unveiled for solely strategic purposes throughout the revolution; their mimicry of Western dress and behavior on those occasions in no way prompted them to identify with French women. Nor did women's behavior awaken in them a desire to challenge the Islamic practice of veiling. Because Fanon identifies the veil as a defensible marker of "traditional" sexual and cultural identity, he presumes women's strategic unveiling during revolution to be an act of mimesis without identification.

Although Fanon interviews several women who experience unveiling as a dramatic liberation of the female body and mobility, he ignores the possibility that these women might henceforth reassess the cultural and religious practice of veiling as the product of an unnecessarily restrictive or patriarchal interpretation of the Qur'an.[30] Instead, Fanon cites women's experiences as testament to the liberating potentials of their participation in anticolonial violence. For Fanon, Algerian women's reassumption of the veil after brief periods of strategic unveiling proved, above all, that "it was not true that woman liberated herself at the invitation of France and of General de Gaulle."[31] Although Fanon's analysis purports to address the shifting connotations of the veil, it ultimately records a male contest to impose nationalist and sexualized meanings on women's bodies. Ordered by French and Algerian men to alternately veil and unveil, Algerian women emerge from Fanon's text as partially effaced historical subjects, and as the perpetual objects of exchange among men.

Fanon's analysis of the veil as a barometer of nationalist allegiance overlooks the intersecting elements of women's oppression, as well as their complicated positioning *vis-à-vis* the nation. His interpretive lens is especially distorting because, as feminist political theorist Cynthia Enloe points out:

> Women haven't had an easy relationship with nationalism. Even when they have suffered abuse at the hands of colonialists and racists, they have often been treated more as symbols than as active participants by nationalist movements organized to end colonialism and racism.[32]

Whereas Fanon rightly attributes anticolonial significance to the veil as a symbol of national, cultural, and religious identity, he fails to imagine that this symbolism might have ambivalent—rather than purely liberating—implications for Algerian women. Although many contemporary Islamic feminists affirm the empowering or emancipatory potentials of wearing the *hijab*, especially within Western societies, most acknowledge that the veiled woman as national symbol has a complicated history of meanings and material implications for women's lives.[33] Fanon's privileging of the socially revolutionary aspects of unveiling precludes a similarly nuanced analysis of the epistemological struggle between feminist and nationalist objectives.[34] His account especially ignores the potentially negative implications of Algerian women's mandate to identify with masculinist conceptions of patriotic duty throughout the revolution. Ultimately, Fanon's position bespeaks an unwillingness to imagine the complex relationships between female mimicry and identification that later erupted in feminist challenges to patriarchal interpretations of "tradition" in independent Algeria.[35]

Because Fanon fails to imagine the compounding effects of nationalism and colonialism as intersecting forces in Algerian women's social subordination, he ignores the competing claims of these discourses on women's efforts to identify with various communities. Especially, he fails to recognize that nationalist symbolism might authorize brutal acts of violence against women, including military campaigns of rape. In this sense, Fanon's assessment of colonial mimicry:

> runs aground on the question of sexual difference. Fanon's otherwise powerful critique of the scene of colonial representation does not fundamentally question the many sexualized determinations of that scene.[36]

Fanon's essentialist portrait of Algerian women has moot consequences for his project of decolonization. Significantly, his failure to give voice to the complexity and diversity of women's experiences of nationalism, colonization, and identification undermines his broader claims about revolution as a catalyst for sexual and social change. Perhaps most disturbingly, Fanon's critical lacuna exemplifies the masculinist undertones of the nationalist movement, which ultimately prevented women from achieving equality in postcolonial Algeria.

From the blind spot of "Algeria Unveiled," I will next consider a missing photograph at issue in Marguerite Duras' semiautobiographical novel, *The Lover*. By making this leap, I hope to highlight women's efforts to create from the spaces of silence and erasure that haunt masculinist texts. My discussion of *The Lover* will zoom in on aesthetic and psychoanalytic debates about representation, fantasy, and identification. On the basis of this discussion, I will develop a feminist analytical framework responsive to the complexity of women's experiences of intersectional identity, nationalism, and colonial representation, especially in the context of transnational trauma and immigration.

IV. MISSING PHOTOGRAPHS: IDENTITY À LA DURAS

> As a representation of the real the image is always, partially, phantasmatic. In doubting the authenticity of the image, one questions as well the veracity of she who makes and describes it. To doubt the subject seized by the eye is to doubt the subjectivity of the seeing "I."
>
> —Peggy Phelan, *Broken Symmetries*

> I often think of the image only I can see now, and of which I've never spoken. It's always there, in the same silence, amazing. It's the only image of myself I like, the only one in which I recognize myself, in which I delight. It might have existed; a photograph might have been taken. But it wasn't. And it's to this failure, this failure to have been created, that the image owes its virtue.
>
> —Marguerite Duras, *The Lover*

Imagine leafing through your favorite photo album. How and when do you most recognize yourself in its photographs? Do you identify with a wry smile, a funky outfit, a favorite hairstyle, or a knowing glance? In *The Lover*, Marguerite Duras describes the picture that best captures her identity as a fictitious image: a photograph never taken.[37] Forgotten or omitted, this image is most striking for its absence and failure to represent. Yet for Duras, it spurs delight, recognition, and a journey through years of private memory in a relentless attempt to present and re-present, or retouch, the self.

Duras explores the relationship between image and identity as a source of overflow, creativity, loss, and impossibility. For Duras, only one real photograph approximates the power of her fictional image: a picture of her twenty-year-old son. In this picture, her son poses as a drifter in the California wilderness, smiling arrogantly at the camera and imbuing his image with an aura of mystery and material poverty. As his mother wryly notes, "He's so thin, you'd think he was a white Ugandan. That's how he likes to see himself, poor, with that poor boy's look" (*The Lover*: 13). Like the portrait of Duras that was never actually taken, her son's photograph captures the relationship between image and identity as elusive and phantasmic. These two photographs—one real, the other imagined—spark the enigmatic art of self-fashioning that animates Duras' narrative.

As for Duras' imaginary self-portrait, it is *not* taken on a momentous occasion of polyphonic crossing in her life.[38] In one solitary journey, she simultaneously crosses a river, bridges two cultures, and traverses the precarious threshold between youth and adulthood. Her trip foretells a myriad of transgressions and vocations that Duras will pursue later in life, including interracial, interclass, and intergenerational sex; alcohol; and writing. Ironically, what best allows her to identify herself—or to make repeated and contradictory attempts to tell the story behind her "ravaged" face—is the missing photograph: blueprint of a receding past, cherished persona, and fading memory.

Whereas an actual photograph would inventory the precise details of Duras' journey, the missing image instead confirms, through its absence, that the story of her life "does not exist. There's never any center to it. There are great spaces where you pretend there used to be someone, but it's not true. There was no one" (*The Lover*: 8). This uncreated photograph cannot be framed, just as Duras' identity seems to elude containment within the insular "I."

Narrating her life story, Duras claims that by age fifteen, she already had a face that prefigured the one she would acquire in middle age. Ravaged by time, her face was—even in youth—marked by untimely knowledge. Her look preceded experience, and exuded an insatiable appetite for pleasure. Despite the recognizable attributes and contours of her face, however—which she identifies as the origin and, in some ways, the author of her journey—Duras constructs her identity and life story as radically unstable, decentered, and fluid.

Duras' unphotographed crossing of the Mekong River constitutes a highly significant and complex passage in her life. She admits that the missing photograph "could *only* have been taken if someone could have known in advance how important it was to be in my life, that event, that crossing of the river" (*The Lover*: 10). At the time of this crossing, she is a fifteen-and-a-half year-old, lower-middle-class *colon*,[39] traversing the Mekong River from Sadec to Vinh Long, Vietnam, en route to a state boarding school in Saigon. At her mother's wishes, she also attends a French colonial lycée in Vietnam. On her routine bus ride to and from school, she sits near the driver, "in the front section reserved for white passengers" (*The Lover*: 9). By explicitly marking the intersecting strands of her identity, the narrator insinuates herself in the interstices between privileged whiteness and disadvantaged class status. At the same time, she specifically maps her experience of crossing within the geopolitical framework of colonization.

On this pivotal day of crossing, Duras wears a low-cut, sepia-colored silk dress borrowed from her mother. After generations of use, the dress is so threadbare as to appear virtually transparent. To complement her risqué dress, Duras sports cherry red lipstick, a "man's hat," and the "famous" shoes: a pair of gold lamé stilettos bought on clearance (*The Lover*: 11). Duras' ensemble stakes out her identity as a space of ambiguity, fantasy, appropriation, and playful contradiction. Her clothing signals the various (incipient or manifest) "crossings" at play within her identity: class (everything is either a hand-me-down or bargain item); sexuality (the precocious gold heels, threadbare dress, and dark makeup on a schoolgirl); and gender-bending (the masculine hat coupled with ultra-feminine shoes, the "crucial ambiguity" of the image). Her ensemble also signals a desire to defy neat categorization. In fact, Duras suggests that such defiance is the hallmark of her identity. She notes, for example, that because her shoes and hat are contradictory, "they're right for me" (*The Lover*: 13).

Duras vaguely recalls how she discovered her hat: she must have seen it in a shop window and tried it on for fun. In the process, she began to conceive of gender identity as an opportunity for play and experimentation. By placing a man's hat on her female body, Duras awakened to the thrill of gender-bending. She delighted in the seeming contradictions between her material body and the conventional props of sexual difference. By situating herself at the boundaries of gender identity, Duras makes herself "available to all eyes, in circulation for cities, journeys, desire" (*The Lover*: 13). Delighting in the possibilities of gender ambiguity, Duras asks her mother to buy the man's hat as a birthday gift. She wears it religiously from that day forward, exulting in its mixed messages.

The bus, the Mekong River, her outfit: all evoke Duras as an embodiment of transgression. She dwells in the borderlands between cultures (i.e., colony and metropole), genders, generations, races, and classes. Although Duras relishes the hybridity and fluidity of her identity, her crossing of the Mekong

River portends ominous journeys yet to come. Its prelude—especially her last moments waiting on dock, where she is "always afraid"—ripples with fear and desire. As Duras eyes the forceful current, it seems likely to sweep everything away, and to forecast "a storm blowing inside the water. A wind raging" (*The Lover*: 11).

Precarious indeed: this day of crossing finds Duras on the brink of adulthood. Aching to shed childhood innocence, she hovers nervously on the edges of adolescence. On this journey, Duras will meet a lover who allows her to simultaneously transcend the boundaries of sex, race, age, class, and nation.

Aboard the ferry, the scene quickly turns silent and unsettled. Duras senses the soundlessness of the water beneath her flowing imperceptibly, "like the blood in the body"(*The Lover*: 21). On one hand, this silence is perilous: Duras imagines the Mekong River as both a conduit for contamination and a provocateur of unseemly encounters. Within her narrative, the river stealthily gathers refuse from each brush with the shore. Debris from rice paddies and dead birds from Cambodia are "all stuck together. Everything flows toward the Pacific" (*The Lover*: 22). On the other hand, Duras evokes this silent tide as a means of sustenance (ingestion, expulsion) and transmission on her journey. More than just a significant moment in her life, this passage along the Mekong River is as vital to her as the blood in her veins—her identity, circulation, and self-creation depend on it.

This monumental scene of crossing—formative, yet never captured or photographed—imaginatively evokes what is, for Duras, radically unrepresentable: the self. Because the various threads of her identity (class, race, sexuality, ethnicity) resist all efforts to represent, they are necessarily constituted in and through fantasy. In this sense, a representational lacuna spurs Duras' autobiographical impulse. The missing photograph in which she most recognizes herself allows her to embark on voyages of creative misrecognition within her text. Ultimately, the nonexistent image invites endless attempts at self-representation, through which Duras continuously composes and retouches her self-image and life story. From this space of absence, Duras inaugurates a million attempts to tell the story behind her ravaged face. She expresses herself as she would most like to be seen (or not seen), while inventing a personal history that fuses memory and longing. The creative process of writing and its endless potentials for revision satiate Duras' desire to both map and unmap the "I" as an infinite ray of perilous, pleasurable, and provocative crossings.

The art of self-fashioning and re-visioning that transforms the practice of autobiography in *The Lover* parallels the creative efforts that I will discuss within postcolonial feminist art and literature. I am specifically interested in Teresa de Lauretis' conception of "re-visioning" as an effort to enact another vision, and to construct new objects and subjects of representation:

> The project of women's cinema is no longer that of destroying or disrupting man-centered vision by representing its blind spots, its gaps or its repressed. The effort and challenge now are how to effect another vision . . . and to formulate the conditions of representability of another social subject.[40]

As Adrienne Rich notes, to re-vision or see with fresh eyes is, for women, an act of survival. It involves a project of reclaiming vision, or "seeing difference differently," in order to shift critical emphasis from specific images of women to the visual economy that works to produce certain visions.[41]

To analyze postcolonial feminist acts of re-visioning, I begin with a Fanonian understanding of identification and representation as primary sources of trauma for colonized people. These feminist re-visions are further illuminated by the Durassien vision of identity as a fleshy collision of sexual, racial, ethnic, national, and cultural fantasies; and by U.S. third world feminist reflections on the intersecting components of women's oppression. This book will explore postcolonial feminist articulations of "hyphenated identities" which have taken shape especially in the interstices between France and Algeria, Korea and the United States.[42] The writers whose work I will examine invent diverse tactics of misrecognition that challenge traditional psychoanalytic models of identification and ego-formation. They also reject the Hegelian (and Fanonian) emphasis on recognition as crucial to self-expression and validation. Instead, their work incorporates fantasy and parallax to interact with inherited images on the basis not of recognition, but of disidentification and misrecognition.

Contemporary transnational feminist artists and writers repeatedly attest to the complicated and often painful intersections between nationalism, sexuality, colonization, and Orientalist representation in their work. Yet they also approach the relationship between image and identity as a form of dissemblance that can promote creative decompositions and re-visionings of sexuality and subjectivity. Their work strategically severs "the umbilical cord of [national] memory"[43] in order to formulate alternative symbolic economies that account for intersectional feminist identities.[44] These writers construct identities that are lived in varying proximity to, and self-conscious complicity with, traditional implements of representation and dissection, such as the camera lens, painterly canvas, mirror, and surgical scalpel. Because they derail traditional processes of reflection and identification, the writers that I will study displace the conventional opposition between the subject and object (or surveyor/surveyed) of an image.

My work takes seriously the insight of cultural theorist Rey Chow, who remarks that

> the agency of the native cannot simply be imagined in terms of a resistance against a [preexisting] image, nor in terms of a subjectivity that existed before

> or outside the image. It needs to be rethought as *that which bears witness to its own demolition*—in a form which is at once image and gaze, but a gaze that exceeds the moment of colonization.[45]

I am most interested in transnational feminist engagements with the image, where "thought seeks itself, puts itself in question, and finds new paths for itself."[46] By understanding representation as a domain of creative negotiation, I hope to elicit more nuanced portraits of female subjectivity than typically emerge from nationalist and anticolonial scholarship. This book will highlight alternative modes of seeing that complicate the positions of "looker" and "looked at" at the heart of contemporary debates about culture, power, and representation. To better understand the power of images and image-making in transnational feminist art and literature, I will begin with Roland Barthes' philosophical meditations on photography, especially his effort to develop an art of "reading" or unpacking the image.

V. BARTHES ON PHOTOGRAPHY AND MISRECOGNITION

> Are there not equal amounts of fantasy and dreaming in what we claim to see as there are of objective apprehending?
>
> —Gilles Deleuze and Felix Guattari, *Cinema 2*

> You don't put into a photograph what's going to come out. Or, vice versa, what comes out is not what you put in.
>
> —Diane Arbus

In *Camera Lucida*, Roland Barthes—a self-described aesthetic realist, despite his work on the semiotics of imagery—approaches the photograph as a ghostly trace; incontrovertible evidence of something or someone "that-has-been." For Barthes, "every photograph is a certificate of presence,"[47] or an exercise in pure denotation that is inevitably grounded in the Real. His reading downplays photographic style, manipulation, and creative license. Instead, he confronts the photograph as an "image without code," a transparent frame for the truth of its referent or subject.[48] Despite his objectivist framework, Barthes struggles to understand why the act of viewing photography, especially pictures of ourselves and those we know, is so often an exercise in misrecognition and defamiliarization. He observes that ultimately, "a photograph looks like anyone *except* the person it represents."[49]

In a related essay, Barthes acknowledges that photographers use several techniques to overlay a photograph, or analogon, with connotative or cultural meanings.[50] These "connotation procedures" include lighting, exposure, composition, perspective, framing, pose, and darkroom manipulation. Barthes pays special attention to the act of posing, through which the photographed subject becomes an active participant in the creation of his or her image(s). With regard to his own experiences of posing for a photograph, Barthes notes that

> "Myself" never coincides with my image. Once I feel myself observed by the lens, everything changes: I constitute myself in the process of "posing," I make another body for myself, I transform myself in advance into an image.[51]

Reflecting on these techniques for blending photographic and cultural meaning, Barthes lays out what he calls the "photographic paradox." At the heart of any photographic image are two contradictory messages: one with and one without a code. Barthes understands the image not as a union of connotative and denotative messages; rather, he asserts that the connoted meaning develops *on the basis of* the image without a code. In light of this paradox, Barthes regards photography as both language and social institution. His theoretical work tries to imagine strategies for "reading" images as simultaneously transparent and socially coded.

Using Barthes' ambivalent approach to photography as a starting point, I would like to pursue this question: why, so often, do we not recognize ourselves in photographs? Within the context of postcolonial literature, how have the political and aesthetic strategies of colonization and representation—especially Orientalism—impacted individual opportunities for recognition and identification? For example, how did some Algerian women challenge the Orientalist visions that they were enlisted to disseminate during the French colonial era? And how do postcolonial feminist writers, more broadly, creatively negotiate the Orientalist and nationalist "look"? This book will consider these questions as integrally tied to issues of fantasy, memory, and cross-cultural representation.

How to explain the power of an image—or rather, how can we understand the ways in which images wield power over us? Social meanings and desires are inevitably projected onto the body and identity. Within a photographic image, they are transmitted through the camera onto paper representations that constitute a "collective assemblage" of the photographed subject, the photographer's eye, and their shared or divergent cultural and political histories.[52] Because of the parallax that typically accompanies this process of inscription, I conceive of misrecognition as a site of productively creative tension for forging and undoing identities. Keeping in mind the need, as French feminist Luce Irigaray sees it, to "change the stock of the female imaginary,"[53] I will approach misrecognition as a complex response to the nationalist and colonialist politics of representation. This subversive tactic resembles Michel de Certeau's notion of *la perruque*, or everyday trickery and resistance.[54] By creatively engaging with fantasy, erasure, misperception, and parallax, postcolonial feminist writers act on the space outside the frame or beyond the limits of representation—they force silences and fissures to speak.

Barthes' reflection on photography provides an apt point of departure for my own work because of its highly original approach to the image as at once a language to be decoded and a sociopolitical frame of reference. I especially find useful Barthes' emphasis on the photograph's capacity to shock and disturb its audience. Interestingly, Barthes regards the consumption of images not as an experience of seamless perception and immediate categorization, as suggested by Piaget's theory of cognitive development. Instead, Barthes focuses on nonlinear or jarring responses to an image, including delays in verbalization; suspensions of language; blockages of meaning; and parallax or other perceptual errors. Barthes finds these uncustomary responses to visual cues highly interesting because they interrupt the usual mechanics of perception. As a result, they prompt questioning, anguish, discomfort, and trauma within the viewing subject or audience.[55]

Barthes' emphasis on the disruptive and wounding potentials of photography provides an extremely useful starting point from which to think about colonialist, nationalist, and Orientalist representation. By placing Barthes in dialogue with Fanon, Duras, Lacan, Hwang, and Chow in this chapter, I hope to fashion a critical interpretive lens through which to read feminist strategies of resistance to nationalist masculinist and imperialist imagery. I will evoke photography as a metonym for representation more broadly in order to think about the image's capacity to pierce; to pin down or "fix";[56] and to wound, especially within a cross-cultural context.

Despite Barthes' assertions to the contrary in *Camera Lucida*, photography involves more than a mere surrender to the visible. It is important to recall the plural artists of a photographic image; I will regard the photographer, viewer, and photographed subject as joint authors of photographic meaning. Together, they variously exploit the technological capacities of the camera and the aesthetic qualities of the subject at hand in order to ensure that a photograph will "keep haunting" its audience.[57]

My aim in this chapter is to elucidate a theoretical framework with which to read transnational feminist stagings of the relationship between fantasy, image, and identity. Subsequent chapters will address specific literary and artistic efforts to disorient and disown potentially wounding images including photographs, paintings, and stereotypes. I do not mean to suggest that creative engagements with traumatic images can somehow foreclose their wounding potential. Yet wounds may be deflected, scar tissue leveraged to promote constructive breaks with dominant ideology and representation. It is in this sense that I mean to recall the French verb *blesser*, "to injure," together with its English homonym *bless* or *blessing*. Can we be blessed by that which wounds us? In particular, can symbolic violence (of the sort effected by stereotypical images) give rise to empowering strategies of self-representation and self-invention for transnational women artists? I want to think about this in the realm of colonial representation: can misrepresentation—or, for Fanon, "amputation"—serve as both a wound and a potential blessing? To reflect on this question, I will first consider some of the operations and effects of photography, as a unique confluence of chemical, aesthetic, and subjective possibilities.

What exactly is a picture? In Barthes' opinion, "a photograph is always invisible: it is not *it* that we see."[58] The image functions as a screen for social meanings, and as a simulacrum that mechanically repeats moments that could not otherwise recur. Photography began as "an art of the person, of identity"; by tracing possible lines of identification, it provides the ambivalent record of "a time that is always elsewhere."[59] Consequently, every image raises questions about the captured moment: was it candid or posed? If posed, what does it reveal about the photographer's intent? Or, if candid, does a portrait reveal latent "truths" of identity? And does a posed photograph subtly alter its subject, or prevent any truth from spilling out onto the image?

In *Camera Lucida*, Barthes reflects on the art of photography by recalling personal encounters with the camera lens. He pays particular attention to the act of posing, an experience in which "I make another body for myself, I transform myself in advance into an image."[60] Because posing suggests actual or potential transformation, it often elicits anxiety on the part of the photographed subject who wonders how she will look, or how others will read her image. Photography inaugurates complicated circuits of looking that powerfully exceed mirror reflection. As a result, the attempt to identify with images of oneself is often an exercise in alienation.

By studying the mechanical operations and subjective effects of photography, Barthes constructs a partial "history of looking" (Barthes 1981:12). In his view, the invention of photography radically altered the experiences of representation and identity. Although a photograph is, for Barthes, anchored in the Real, it permits new relations to both the self and the outside world. As Barthes concludes, "the photograph is the advent of myself as other: a cunning dissociation of consciousness from identity."[61] The image's ability to construct self as "other" irritates Barthes, who regards the camera lens as a tool of objectification. In his words, "photography transforms subject into museum object" (Barthes 1981: 13) by effacing life, breath, and variability.

It is precisely as a *non*mirror image—or fusion of self and other—that the photograph disturbs. For in the time between photographic composition and exposure, the photographed subject cannot perceive the eye that is seeing her, or framing her as an aesthetic object. She can only hope that what she tries to hide will elude the camera's eye, or, conversely, that what she hopes to exude comes through in her portrait. She might also hope to favorably translate into a two-dimensional surface. Yet, as I have noted, often she will not—at least not without some experience of alienation. As Barthes explains,

> I want my image . . . altering with situation and age, to always coincide with my profound "self"; but it is the contrary that must be said: "myself" never coincides with my image; for it is the image which is heavy, motionless, and "myself" which is light, divided, dispersed . . . *myself doesn't hold still*.[62]

Photography violently decenters the "look" as a site of exclusive mastery and ownership. However one wishes for a photograph that will capture the profoundest truths of being, the photograph is always a becoming-other of the self: a lacuna between past and present, life and death. By a simple trick of light,[63] the camera transforms its subject into an object of aesthetic consumption. Because a photograph unites multiple viewpoints, it also raises questions of authorship and authenticity. The picture is always a likeness—but of whom? Who authors a photograph? Since its inception, photography has sparked heated debates regarding the proper attribution of authorship and creation.

Partly because of their inconclusive pedigree, photographic images may disrupt the perceived correspondence between representation and identity. Among postcolonial women writers, this gap between image and identity often promotes a deconstructive stance toward historical representation, and a dispossession of Cartesian models of identity as contingent upon faithful reflection and recognition.

Barthes highlights the traumatic potentials of representation by exploring photography not as an aesthetic question, but, rather, as a "wound."[64] For instance, he discusses "shock photos" (depictions of catastrophic events such as fire, war, and death) as images that are impossible to integrate with one's sense of self and history. Barthes understands these traumatic images as "photographs about which there is nothing to say"[65]; they radically destabilize cognition and connotation. In fact, Barthes avows that "the connotative effect of a photograph is inversely proportional to its traumatic effect."[66]

Although Barthes did not extend his analysis to imperial relations, I find in his work an extremely useful framework with which to make sense of colonial imagery. Unlike Barthes, I believe that images can be experienced as traumatic even when one acknowledges their roots in fantasy.[67] At the same time, I will highlight feminist attempts to sublimate or minimize the wounding effects of traumatic imagery. Whereas Barthes examines how representation "fixes" identity in various postures of melancholy and objectification, I want to think about the creative powers of authorship that might be discovered in and through one's consumption of potentially wounding images and fantasies.

Like other representational genres, photographs permit multiple and often contradictory readings. Although the photograph establishes a certain balance of power between its subject and object, it also offers its audience a particular framing of subjectivity that might spark desire, disgust, or identification. A picture may awaken dreams of being someone or somewhere else—it delivers us to the possibility of being-otherwise. In this sense, the act of engaging with images can be experienced as a profoundly creative endeavor.

To account for the photograph's capacity to transport us beyond its frame, Barthes discusses what he calls the photographic *punctum*. This is an accidental detail that somehow slips into a photograph against the photographer's will. The *punctum* is a surprising, accidental, and unconscious element—a heterogeneous detail that insinuates itself into the image. Like a punctuation mark, the *punctum* disrupts the intended composition and effect of an image. It resembles a pinprick, sting, wound, shock, or lightning bolt—an unnamable element that eludes the photographer's eye, yet bruises and often haunts the audience. As opposed to the predictable or intentional element of the photographic *studium*, the *punctum* establishes a "blind field" or counterforce to lure the viewer outside the photographic frame (Barthes 1981:57). In effect, the *punctum* makes possible a whole series of imaginative relationships to the outside of an image.

I evoke Barthes' notion of the *punctum* in order to think about feminist negotiations, or strategic "occupations," of wounding imagery. These interventions provoke dissonant formulations of the "self" as at once subject and object, mediator and agent, virgin papyrus and centuries-old palimpsest. The postcolonial works that I will study are primarily concerned with representation not as a producer of inauthentic versions of the self, but as a vehicle with which to challenge the ontological foundations and political effects of identity, authenticity, and recognition. To counter Barthes' claim that in photography nothing can be refused or transformed, I will argue that it is precisely by engaging with the founding fantasies of an image that one can envision creative lines of flight from, and effective forms of resistance to, its wounding potential.

The Fanonian ideal of recognition remains a legal and political imperative for minority subjects. Yet this ideal fails to acknowledge how minorities are differentially situated *vis-à-vis* the colonizing gaze. What I find most compelling within postcolonial feminist art and literature is an understanding of identity as the effect of competing fantasies about race, gender, sexuality, nation, and ethnicity. This approach encourages creative interventions into the relationship between image and identity rather than blind acceptance of the ideals of resemblance and recognition.

If the incompatibility of nationalist and colonialist discourse begets mourning among postcolonial women writers, it also invites radical experimentation with nonmirror imagery. In the discussion that follows, I will revisit the Lacanian psychoanalytic constructs of the "mirror phase" and *méconnaissance.* By so doing, I hope to reformulate women's experiences of identification and misrecognition in response to transnational trauma, especially sexual violence and colonization.

VI. LACAN, THE MIRROR PHASE, AND *MÉCONNAISSANCE*

> Imaginary identification is always identification *on behalf of a certain gaze in the Other*. The question to ask is: *for whom* is the subject enacting this role? Which gaze is considered when the subject identifies with a certain image?
>
> —Slavoj Žižek, *The Sublime Object of Ideology*

> The question of identification is never the affirmation of a pre-given identity—it is always the production of an "image" of identity and the transformation of the subject in assuming that image.
>
> —Homi Bhabha, "Remembering Fanon"

Psychoanalytic theory suggests that we achieve selfhood only through a series of wounding inscriptions. From a Lacanian perspective, the road to subjectivity begins with the mirror stage—a moment of primary narcissism that culminates in the birth of the self as other.[68] In early infancy, a child exists wholly in the realm of the Imaginary. She imagines herself as part of a fictional whole incorporating the child, mother, and immediate surroundings. The infant does not perceive her body as a separate entity capable of acting on the world. During the mirror stage, however, a child suddenly catches sight of her movements reflected in a mirror, and regards this mirror image as an integral component of her "self." As she progresses through this developmental stage, the child begins to perceive her body as distinct from others, yet crucially linked to her mirror image.

Through repeated play, gesture, and mimicry, the child delights in the perceived correspondence between image and identity, which she identifies as a relation of equivalence. The mirror stage thus launches a process of identification wherein the subject assumes a fictional unity of self. Because of the apparent primacy of the mirror stage to ego-formation, Lacan concludes that the self is founded on a fiction—one that only loses currency by way of one's progression from the Imaginary to the Symbolic realm of signification.

Feminist psychoanalytical critic Jacqueline Rose distinguishes two moments of the mirror phase: (1) that of the corporeal image, or primary narcissism, which is prior and resistant to symbolization; and (2) that of the relation to the other, or secondary narcissism, which *depends on* such symbolization.[69] Conceived in this way, these two moments shed light on the human tendency to forge relationships between image and identity, or the subject and object of the gaze.[70] Yet such relationships are possible only through a process of self-objectification, by conflating the gazes of self and other.

Humans have no direct access to the self; instead, the mirror image and the gaze of the other necessarily mediate our self-perceptions. Because we perceive ourselves solely on the basis of transmission and transmutation, misrecognition plays a primary role in ego-formation and the illusion of autonomy: I misrecognize myself as an image. It is in this sense that Lacan evokes "*un méconnaître essentiel à me connaître*," or misrecognition as vital to self-knowledge.[71] He characterizes misrecognition or *méconnaissance* not as a failure to recognize, but as a misperception that vitally constitutes the "I." Because it triggers misrecognition, the mirror stage inaugurates the fiction of the unified subject. From a Lacanian perspective, a child's subsequent entry into the Symbolic (and accession to language and the phallus, or Law of the Father) promotes a radical break with the fictive unity achieved during the mirror stage. Misrecognition—the self's enabling fiction—is dispelled upon the subject's entry into the Symbolic.

Yet I will part ways with Lacan here, for my sense is that different forms of misrecognition persist within the Symbolic depending on one's sociopolitical status. This is especially true when a subject's accession to the Symbolic is achieved within the political context of colonization, and in conjunction with the fracturing imperatives of colonized subjectivity. As Fanon powerfully elucidates, minority subjects are constantly confronted with racial, sexual, and national fantasies that attempt to "fix" their identities, or to coerce identifications with hegemonic imagery. I hope to show that these colonial fantasies and fixations also trigger tactics of symbolic disidentification and misrecognition, as is especially apparent in the work of transnational feminist artists.

My work will emphasize the decolonizing and deconstructive possibilities, rather than the tragic limits, of self-knowledge and representation. To this end, I will consider the plural meanings of misrecognition. It may help to recall that *méconnaissance* is not tantamount to ignorance; in fact, it is unthinkable without correlative *connaissance*—or "a kind of knowledge of what there is to misrecognize."[72] In this sense, I would argue that the Lacanian model of subjectification ignores the intersections between ego-formation and knowledge production that continuously impact one's experiences of identification. Colonization, in particular, promotes misrecognition of the native "other"—by way of the stereotype, gaze, and limited political representation—as an ongoing strategy for domination and dehumanization. In response, the postcolonial subject actively negotiates hegemonic images of herself. She often misrecognizes these images in order to interrupt imperialist understandings of self and other that assume, on one hand, faithful resemblance yet, on the other hand, radical—even inassimilable—difference.[73]

Postcolonial feminist narratives of identity often rework the Lacanian concept of misrecognition. Most significantly, they understand subaltern identity to develop alongside, and in relation to, colonial fantasy and representation. In light of the self-splitting imperatives of colonization, they mark a useful distinction between imaginary [constituted] and symbolic [constitutive] identification:

> To put it simply, imaginary identification is identification with the image in which we appear likeable to ourselves; and symbolic identification involves identification with the very place *from where* we are being observed, *from where* we look at ourselves.[74]

It is precisely in the gap between these two forms of identification—how I see myself, and the point of view from which I am observed—that transnational feminists stage fascinating and subversive interventions. Like Barthes' *punctum*, their works shock and disrupt traditional narratives of identity and psychoanalytic conceptions of identification. By investigating colonial, racist, ethnic, and sexual fantasies, they attempt to translate the desire of the other into a different sort of interpellation—one stripped of its ability to "fix" identifications. The protagonists of postcolonial feminist literature often identify with the other "precisely at a point at which he is inimitable, at the point which eludes resemblance."[75] By so doing, they accentuate the subversive potentials of symbolic identification and disidentification.

The Lacanian mirror phase ignores the ways in which subjects are differentially constituted along axes of gender, race, class, sexuality, age, and nationality. Yet the politics of difference is precisely what renders problematic a visual economy premised on specularity and reflection. Diasporic discourse highlights the experiences of misrecognition, asymmetry, dissonance, and dislocation that challenge psychoanalytic assumptions about universal patterns of identification and ego-formation.

My work will consider the disparate potentialities of the concept of "misrecognition" as it emerges in the autobiographical fiction of transnational women writers including Leila Sebbar, Theresa Hak Kyung Cha, Hélène Cixous, and Assia Djebar. Based on my readings of their texts, and especially the relationships that they establish between text, image, and identity, I will advocate a multifaceted understanding of misrecognition. I will regard it first, in a Deleuzian sense, as a relation to an excessive or unthought element within the real whereby "I" discover myself only insofar as I am passing into another world or identity. I will also conceive of misrecognition as an Imaginary relation to an image that constitutes an effect of illusory self-identity (Lacan's mirror stage, but also Fanon's notion of the colonialist image that fixes and fractures the "native"). Finally, I will explore misrecognition as a refusal of recognition, which might be read as a negation of an unconscious identification, or as a perverse disavowal of a preexisting and socially sanctioned identity. I am especially interested in the latter aspect of misrecognition, and want to ask what can happen when someone confronts an unrecognizable image with the disclaimer, "that's not me!" Significantly, this moment of misrecognition might constitute not a distancing from the "false," but rather a strategic attempt to provocatively employ fantasy, as an inevitable element of history, memory, and identity, in one's own becoming.

Insurgent literary tactics of misrecognition resemble surrealist collages by simultaneously juxtaposing diverse viewpoints. Like the photomontages of Hannah Höch, they birth the previously unthinkable by polluting and dismembering seemingly coherent narratives of identity. I will focus on misrecognition as a subversive manipulation of one's image that performs, in Homi Bhabha's terms, a "strategic return of that difference that informs and deforms the image of identity."[76] Like Bhabha, I regard tactics of misrecognition as hopeful rejoinders to Frantz Fanon's lament on the wounding potentials of identification *vis-à-vis* colonialist imagery.

In light of the works that I will discuss, I see a salient need to reframe debates about fantasy and cultural identity in terms of misrecognition rather than objectification, misrepresentation, or antiessentialism.[77] To this end, I will posit misrecognition—or a noted parallax between the image and the real, engendered by representation especially in a colonial context—as a tool for potentially creative decompositions and reworkings of identity.

My usage of misrecognition is closely allied with the Deleuzian notion of "minor literature."[78] The "minor" in a Deleuzian or musical sense is ambiguous: at once aligned to a major key, yet also capable of tracing lines of flight from it. Thus the minor can be imagined as fugitive, or as a continual variation—"as though music set out on a journey."[79] For Deleuze, the minor forces a "stammer" in the dominant by revealing its internal heterogeneity or noise within. Moroccan writer Abdelkebir Khatibi imagines this stammer as a form of ecstatic and embodied "bilingualism" (*bi-langue*) that, when employed by postcolonial Maghrebian writers, effects ironic distance in order to render the "true French" strangers in their own tongue.[80] With respect to postcolonial women's art and literature, I will understand this "stammer" of misrecognition as an act of creative and political intervention into inherited images of female subjectivity and sexuality.

As James Baldwin has observed, colonized "others" are typically construed as loathsome yet alluring mirrors of the colonizer, to be apprehended with both recognition and disavowal. Especially within the context of colonization, then, I find it imperative to reformulate the mirror stage—and, in particular, the "mirrored body"[81]—as a continuous literal and metaphorical *passage* between the self-splitting imperatives of representation and the fugitive possibilities of authorship, consumption, and self-fashioning. Whereas Lacan conceives of misrecognition as the ground zero of ego-formation, I will explore it as an effort to jam the psychic machinery of identification and recognition. To this end, I will study transnational feminist works of art and literature that frame the self as both the subject and object of knowledge, and that record the Cartesian "I" as an impossible achievement in the wake of war and colonization.

Fanon characterizes subjectivity as an endless battle with representation. For the postcolonial writers whose work I will discuss, this war necessitates battle with overlapping narratives of embodied subjectivity. These include the social meanings of the physical body and skin (the most immediately classifiable signifiers of identity); the self as objectified in popular discourse and representation (especially on the basis of its categorization within specific social groups); and the self as internally experienced. It is within the context of this struggle—as exemplified by Fanon's meditation on the fracturing effects of racist imagery for identity—that I will consider misrecognition as a subversive ethical and aesthetic strategy of "disidentification."[82] As a creative effort to insert schismatic selves into competing historical narratives, misrecognition can be construed as "the art of imagining what has not imagined you."[83] This effort of imagination is crucial for postcolonial feminists, whose intersectional experiences are so often effaced in the name of identity politics and national solidarity.

I hope to explore two interlocking practices: the ways in which colonization disrupts or defers the resolution of psychic processes of ego-formation and identification; and critical and creative attempts to establish alternative resolutions. I will address the work of several postcolonial writers who deploy misrecognition in response to the shattering experiences of colonial representation. I want to emphasize here that representation spurs both traumatic forms of identification and resistant acts of misrecognition among subaltern subjects. My claim is that misrecognition might authorize new visions of subjectivity, rather than merely symptomatic attempts to suture or evade the constitutive limits of a culturally or institutionally sanctioned self. Misrecognition makes it possible to live the wounding effects of colonial imagery as an opening onto the edges, borders, and limits of identity and representation.

By deconstructing the autonomous "I" and confronting the limits of its representation, postcolonial feminist artists "ruin the representative narrative of Western identity."[84] Their work gives birth to alternative representative economies wherein identification breaks down, and the colonizing gaze might be resisted. As Gayatri Spivak points out with regard to Isma, one of the primary narrative voices in Djebar's *Fantasia*, she is "not quite not Narcissus—she has some doubt about claiming the historico-philosophical 'I.'"[85] My work will explore the ways in which transnational feminist artists and writers distance themselves from the authoritative knowledge claims of the "I"—even when engaging in autobiographical practices—in order to imagine alternative transactions between self and other. These artists seize upon the decentering potentials of minor literature, enlisting fantasy to deconstruct the enabling conditions of both the Cartesian "I" and the colonial eye. To establish the mutual dependence of fantasy and identity, I will begin my analysis with a discussion of David Henry Hwang's fascinating play, *M. Butterfly*.

VII. VISIONS OF BUTTERFLIES: FANTASY AS THE POINT OF DEPARTURE FOR IDENTITY

> The Look is always potentially crazy: it is at once the effect of truth and the effect of madness.
>
> —Roland Barthes, *Camera Lucida*

> The corrective stance adopted to rehabilitate the image of the other through a critique mainly focused on stereotyping . . . is too predictable to continue to offer a productive place for analysis.
>
> —Trinh T. Minh-ha, *When the Moon Waxes Red*

When it made its stage debut in the late 1980s, David Henry Hwang's *M. Butterfly* provoked scandal and sensation worldwide.[86] Hwang's play ingeniously fuses the details of a contemporary espionage trial in France with Puccini's classical opera, *Madame Butterfly*. Puccini's opera tells the story of an American sailor (Benjamin Franklin Pinkerton) who marries, and soon abandons, a stereotypically "Oriental" woman (Butterfly) while serving on a tour of duty in Japan. Devastated by her husband's abandonment, Butterfly nonetheless fantasizes that he will return. Upon learning that Pinkerton has married an American woman instead, Butterfly commits suicide. Through its interwoven narratives of political and sexual conquest, *Madame Butterfly* presents an imperialist fantasy of female and Oriental submission.

Hwang's play reverses the fates of *Madame Butterfly*'s characters by overlaying Puccini's narrative with a true story of French espionage. A dramatic blend of sexual, national, and cultural fantasy and intrigue, the case of Bernard Boursicot and Shi Pei Pu gained international notoriety during its trial in 1986. Boursicot, a French accountant, was sent to China during the 1960s and 1970s to work for the French Embassy. While stationed in Peking, Boursicot met a Chinese opera diva, Shi Pei Pu, at a diplomatic soiree. Immediately beguiled by the singer's "Oriental" qualities, Boursicot soon fell in love with Pei Pu, whom he believed to be a woman.[87]

Thus began an affair that lasted for about two decades and appeared to produce a son.[88] In the final years of their affair, Pei Pu moved to Paris to share an apartment with Boursicot, whose job had been transferred back to France. Soon after Pei Pu's relocation to France, French intelligence officers launched an investigation into the relationship. In 1986, the French government officially accused Boursicot of passing national secrets to the Chinese government via his lover, Pei Pu.

Throughout a scandalous and titillating trial that attracted international attention, Boursicot reiterated to the incredulous jury and news media his undying belief that his lover was a woman. He admitted that he had construed Pei Pu's modesty as an authentically "feminine" expression of "Chinese custom."[89] He also professed a difficulty in differentiating between Chinese men and women. At the trial's closing, a Parisian judge sentenced Boursicot and Pei Pu to six-year prison terms for espionage.[90]

M. Butterfly probes the complex dynamics of deception at issue in the Boursicot case—and ultimately reverses the fate of Puccini's operatic personas—by staging "René Gallimard," the duped Orientalist (rather than Pei Pu or Butterfly, a.k.a. "Song Liling") as its tragic hero. To fully appreciate Hwang's efforts of cross-cultural fusion or palimpsest, it is important to trace the lineage of *M. Butterfly*'s operatic influences. Puccini's opera is an adaptation of American writer John Luther Long's short story of the same name (1898), which, in turn, draws upon Pierre Loti's *Madame Chrysanthemum* (1887). In this novel, Loti, a prolific French Orientalist writer, depicts an intercultural romance between a French man and Asian woman. Seizing on the multilayered cultural narratives at play in *Madame Butterfly*, Hwang's play scripts an explosive critique of sexual and national fantasies, especially their fusion in Orientalist representation and politics. Although *M. Butterfly* does not explicitly cite the Orientalist aesthetic, Hwang's play—especially the afterword—suggests familiarity with Edward Said's pioneering scholarship on the subject.[91]

By way of parody or ironic mimicry, *M. Butterfly* deliberately exploits Orientalist stereotypes in an attempt to deconstruct imperialist fantasy and desire. At issue throughout the play are Orientalizing tropes of sexual identity, including the "effeminate" Asian man and the "lotus blossom" or "butterfly" (modest, shy, and submissive yet hypersexualized) Asian woman. *M. Butterfly* also interrogates Western constructions of Chinese national identity as docile, undeveloped, and obsessed with the past. Insofar as the play highlights the socially constructed and performative aspects of sexual and national identities, it seems to deconstruct foundational categories of identity.[92] Gallimard's transvestite lover, Song Liling, is especially hailed in critical reviews of the play as an icon of national and sexual hybridity, border crossing, and indeterminacy.[93]

Despite its deconstructive aims, however, *M. Butterfly* often reinscribes the very categories of identity that it seeks to undermine by advancing didactic visions of cultural and sexual truth, authenticity, and difference. By foregrounding the injurious potential of emasculating stereotypes, for example, the play often indulges reductive portrayals of queer and female subjectivity. This has led at least one literary critic to describe *M. Butterfly* as "intermittently antifeminist and homophobic."[94] Whereas Gallimard and his friend Marc repeatedly voice misogynist and homophobic asides to the audience, the female lead Song Liling is rarely afforded the theatrical tool of the aside. This asymmetrical deployment of theatrical voice not only provides the audience with differential access to male and female subjectivity, but also seems, at several moments in the play, to legitimize misogynist and heteronormative discourse. By repeatedly denying Liling the tool of the aside, the play relegates Liling's (ostensibly "female") subjectivity to the shadows or margins of the production. This theatrical marginalization contributes to a potential reading of Liling as an inscrutable object to be viewed, desired, and translated by Gallimard and his intermittently sympathetic audience.[95]

At the same time, by repeatedly renouncing the Orientalist myth of Asian male effeminacy, *M. Butterfly* approaches colonial representation not as a shifting and ambivalent discourse that permits negotiation, but as a wounding falsification that demands reversal and recuperation.[96] In this sense, what seems most at stake throughout *M. Butterfly* is the preservation of a specifically masculinist fantasy of identity and sexual potency, despite Hwang's stated desire to challenge Orientalist perceptions of gender and cultural identity. Although the play explicitly addresses the confounding potentials and pitfalls of national, sexual, racial, and ethnic fantasies, it appears to be disproportionately concerned with the injury of emasculation.

Despite its deconstructive goals and interest in the productive possibilities of our investments in sexual and cultural fantasy, *M. Butterfly* ultimately presents a cautionary tale that leaves intact metaphysical presumptions about truth and authenticity, and associates fantasy with exclusively unethical exchange.

Hwang adopts a particularly antiessentialist tone in the play's afterword, which makes an appeal for relations based on truth rather than stereotype. He urges readers to "cut through layers of cultural and sexual misperception" (Hwang: 100) in order to promote truthful cross-cultural and sexual exchange. By directing his play's interpretation toward antiessentialist and didactic ends, Hwang abandons what is arguably *M. Butterfly*'s most radical potential: namely, the desire to explore fantasy and misrecognition as sites of deconstruction, transformation, and the "democratizing affirmation of internal difference"[97] for minority subjects.

Several years after the publication and initial stage production of *M. Butterfly*, filmmaker David Cronenberg adapted Hwang's screenplay for the cinema.[98] In an essay entitled "The Dream of a Butterfly," Rey Chow compares the stage and screen versions of *M. Butterfly* in order to tease out their implications for cross-cultural exchange, particularly between former imperial and colonized cultures.[99] Her work highlights several key differences between the play and film adaptation of *M. Butterfly*, and raises questions about fantasy and representation that are worth summarizing here in light of my foregoing argument.

From Chow's perspective, the play offers a cautionary tale of stereotyping that remains trapped within the framework of Edward Said's original critique of the intellectual and artistic tradition of Orientalism (1978).[100] She finds Cronenberg's film, on the other hand, to formulate a more compelling vision of the role that fantasy might play to mediate difference. Chow's distinction between film and play rests on a poststructuralist understanding of individual and collective identity not as fixed truths to be ascertained, but as illusory accomplishments apprehensible only through the psychic structures of fantasy, desire, language, and cognition.

For Chow, the film adaptation of *M. Butterfly* imagines what might happen when we explore, rather than dismiss, the possibilities of fantasy and stereotype. Chow regards fantasy not as necessarily dehumanizing, but instead as an integral facet of human relations. She suggests that mutual fascination and asymmetric sociopolitical status are constitutive elements of cross-cultural exchange which preclude the "truthful" cultural meetings romanticized by Hwang. By emphasizing the primacy of fantasy to interpersonal relations, Chow questions Hwang's faith in mutual recognition as the only viable antidote to racist, sexist, or ethnocentric representation, or as the only possible basis for ethical exchange.

Chow's analysis raises several key questions about fantasy and identification. First, how is fantasy implicated in our most basic, daily perceptions?[101] What might it mean to truthfully "identify" with another across cultural, racial, and sexual differences, given the psychological inseparability of fantasy and identity—that is, if we are always unconsciously invested in fantasies of the "other"? How useful is a corrective emphasis on cultural authenticity in light of the specific histories of colonization and immigration that have given rise to shifting affiliations and cross-pollination across national borders? And finally, what role—if any—should antiessentialism play in political efforts to promote mutual respect for differences?

Adopting a deconstructive stance, Chow destabilizes the "I" as a foundation of epistemological truth and certainty. By highlighting the strategic potentials for mobilizing fantasy and stereotype, Chow provocatively reframes transnational exchange as an opportunity to boldly engage with, and misrecognize, the disparate fantasies at play in identity. Her theoretical position is supported by a rich tradition of Asian art and literature that playfully leverages stereotypical imagery in order to destabilize ethnic identity.[102] In my own work, I wish to parlay Chow's insight into a creative and critical lens through which to view the intersecting strands of subjectivity (race, class, gender, sexuality, nationality, etc.) that complicate any claim to a singular "truth" of identity. By so doing, I hope to formulate new ways of reading transnational feminist reframings of the relationship between image and identity.

In light of Chow's insights, what I find most problematic about the play *M. Butterfly* is its political appeal to "truthful" recognition as a remedy for misperception, and its evocation of the sexed body in particular as a privileged site of such recognition. Although it troubles the notion of cultural authenticity, Hwang's play evokes the material body as a ground from which it is possible—indeed, imperative—to ascertain sexual truth and authenticity. Hwang's appeal to the "truth" of the body discounts the myriad ways in which our bodies assume meaning in and through a complex network of sociopolitical and cultural institutions, regulations, and contestations. This is an insight not only of poststructuralist and deconstructionist thought, but also of queer and feminist engagements with the "hard sciences" including biology, anatomy, and physiology.[103]

Overlooking this insight, Hwang's *M. Butterfly* ultimately posits the body as the site par excellence of ontological and epistemological certainty. The play's denouement features Song slowly and deliberately derobing onstage, which culminates in the revelation of his "true" sexual identity. Yet because the audience is presumably already privy to Song's biological sex, the physical evidence of Song's body "offers no key to this drama, just as it offers no key to Gallimard's psychical drama."[104] In this sense, Hwang abandons the most intriguing element of this story—namely, the constitutive and persuasive force of fantasy—in favor of the "real." Ultimately, *M. Butterfly* succumbs to the desire for ontological resolution by invoking Song's body as material evidence—a measure of authenticity against which to expose his transgender performance or masquerade.

By concluding its promising query into the powers of fantasy with an appeal for truth, recognition, and reconciliation, the play seems fixated on one question: "how could Gallimard have overlooked Song's penis?" Instead of pursuing this enigma more richly in relation to gender ambiguity and queer desire, Hwang seems content to resolve Gallimard's crisis of misrecognition with the "truth" of bodily identity. Significantly, a desire to establish bodily truths pervaded the real-life espionage trial, as well—which sparked avid scrutiny of, and heated debate regarding, the particularities of Pei Pu's Asian male body. Trial lawyers subjected Pei Pu to a battery of medical tests that produced abundant "evidence" in the form of medical reports, hormonal analyses, and anatomical diagrams of his genitalia. In this respect, Pei Pu's body, rather than the complicated allure of fantasy and misrecognition, emerged as the focal point of the trial and as an erotic object for public consumption. Hwang similarly display's Song's body as a privileged site of truth that is somehow sufficient to resolve the "spectacle" of transgender identification.

Yet this hunger for the "truth"—especially sexual truth—often authorizes brutal campaigns of pathologization and dehumanization.[105] The case of Brandon Teena, an American transgender individual murdered in 1993 in response to his "deviant" sexual practices, reveals the stakes of this conventional desire to establish sexual identity as a knowable and demonstrable truth of the body. In the United States, a broad array of social discourses enforces our belief in, and adherence to, rigid norms of gender and sexual identity. When medical practitioners assign a gender to intersexed infants, for example, their decisions force such children to identify and comply with cultural constructions of "appropriate" maleness and femaleness. Similarly, sex education classes often construct femininity and masculinity as inherently passive or aggressive—and the female body as particularly vulnerable to violation—by encouraging teenage girls to devise "preventive" strategies to avoid rape. The net effect of these discourses is to silence and, at times, to punish bodily configurations and performances that threaten to disrupt binary conceptions of sexual difference.

Although Hwang's call for truthful recognition is clearly grounded, like Fanon's, in humanist ethics rather than dehumanizing politics, I nonetheless regard it as an ambivalent goal for minority subjects. All too often, the desire to establish national, sexual, or cultural "truth" supports an unacknowledged, masculinist conception of the "universal" subject. Furthermore, a politics centered on truthful recognition presupposes the ability to neatly distinguish between fantasy and reality. Yet such a distinction is virtually impossible to sustain, and ignores the transformational potentials of their interdependence. Although Hwang sets out to explore fantasy's constitutive effects for subjectivity, his play concludes with a reductive vision of "true" identity—one that favors the recognition of bodily and cultural "truths" as a corrective to fantasy and misperception.

By dispensing with the notions of sexual truth and masculinist consensus, the film adaptation of *M. Butterfly* exceeds the play's modus operandi of recognition and identity politics. Most noticeably, Cronenberg's film omits the homophobic and sexist jokes that abound in Hwang's play. By refusing to presume a predominantly misogynist and/or heterosexual audience, the film proves more amenable to feminist appropriation.

Cronenberg's film asks questions about fantasy, image, and desire that Hwang initially alludes to, but ultimately seems to dismiss. For example, what is fantasy for Gallimard? How does his very identity depend upon it? How does his love for Liling sustain it? Cronenberg's *M. Butterfly* uses fantasy to stage multiple and, at times, conflicting identities—especially transvestite and queer subjectivity. Moving beyond the wounding potentials of fantasy and stereotypical imagery, the film imagines how masquerade and misrecognition might enable politically progressive narratives of identity, difference, and intersubjectivity. As feminist film critic Teresa de Lauretis points out,

> It is not the revelation of Song's maleness that causes Gallimard to lose his love object, but the *end of the masquerade*. With it comes the realization that what Gallimard loved was not Song, but Butterfly—the masquerade of femininity; that the object of his desire is a fantasy object, Butterfly, and that object alone can sustain his desire.[106]

By emphasizing the primacy of fantasy for Gallimard's identity, the film anticipates the complexities of the position occupied by real-life French diplomat Boursicot. When asked by a Parisian trial lawyer how he could have been unaware of his lover's true sex for so long, Boursicot replied: "My conviction remains unshakable that *for me, at that time, he really was a woman*, and the first love of my life."[107] For Boursicot, Pei Pu's masquerade of femininity, rather than his male body, effectively constituted the "truth" of his sexual identity. By his own account, Boursicot's only mistake, or tragic flaw, was to disavow a powerful erotic fantasy and thereby efface himself as a desiring subject. Likewise, the film portrays bodily "truth" and queer desire as less threatening to Gallimard than the curtailment of Liling's masquerade. Especially in its final scenes, the film posits the death of fantasy and desire—rather than romantic deceit or cultural misperception—as the catalyst for Gallimard's disintegration.

Boursicot's testimony provocatively reveals a man for whom recognition can neither compensate for, nor serve as the ultimate goal of, desire. Rather than desperately pursuing the "truth" of his lover's sexual identity, Boursicot deliberately defers and disavows that truth. Not only does he desire his lover as a cultural and sexual fantasy; he also needs to sustain this fantasy in order to consolidate his own identity. Within heteronormative society, Boursicot's hunger for—and reliance upon—the fantasy of "Butterfly" vitally supports his attempt to carve out a space for queer male subjectivity and sexuality. It is this productive space of fantasy that Cronenberg's film chooses to explore, rather than fixating—like the play—on Gallimard's errors of identification and sexual attribution. Notably, this is the same space investigated by Marguerite Duras in *The Lover*, and the one that I am most interested in navigating throughout this work.

In both versions of *M. Butterfly*, what Gallimard mourns most is the loss of an exotic cultural and sexual fantasy—or a "vision of the Orient"—that had authorized social and political transgressions including international espionage, drag, homosexuality, and romantic betrayal. Yet the play and film frame this mourning in dramatically different ways. As I have argued, the play places fantasy on a continuum with error and immorality. Consequently, it posits truth as the ultimate goal of human relations and desire, notwithstanding Boursicot's real-life testimony to the contrary.

Conversely, the question that most powerfully emerges from Cronenberg's film is not "how could Gallimard mistake a man for a woman?" but rather, who was Gallimard in relation to the persona of "Butterfly" and an exotic vision of the Orient? How did his very identity depend on fantasy, and what was made possible for both Gallimard and Liling in and through fantasy? Instead of advocating a corrective to cultural and sexual misperception, the film regards fantasy as the "very stuff that makes 'self' and 'self-story' possible."[108] By appropriating fantasy to its own ends,[109] Cronenberg's *M. Butterfly* complicates traditional conceptions of the subject and object of sexual and colonial exchange.

In the film's finale, Gallimard—languishing in a prison cell in Paris—treats his inmate audience to an aria of monstrous proportions. Setting the stage for a real-time suicide in drag, Gallimard assumes the costume and persona of a Japanese geisha and grotesquely resurrects his fantasy of "Butterfly" as a melancholic subject/object. By staging his death or "final act" as a confusion of subject positions (Gallimard and Butterfly), Gallimard dramatizes the melancholy that haunts minority identity.[110] He simultaneously identifies with and murders Butterfly, his Oriental fantasy. By so doing, Gallimard complicates facile distinctions between the creator, consumer, and victim of Orientalist representation.

Gallimard's prison performance enlists standard props of Chinese opera and Japanese kabuki theater, including a silk kimono, black wig, geisha makeup, and opera soundtrack. In this sense, it evokes the residual and polyvalent "otherness" of Song Liling relative to the process of cultural assimilation. In his final act, Gallimard physically embodies—and ritualistically enacts—an obsessive vision of racial, cultural, and sexual difference. His performance seems to predictably resolve the psychological crisis of identification: Gallimard appropriates or "consumes" the other in order to preserve his own sense of self, which has fully merged with the other in the realm of the Imaginary.

From a psychoanalytic perspective, Gallimard's suicide might be understood as an effort to colonize or appropriate cultural, racial, and sexual difference. Yet the film is careful not to portray Liling as a passive object of colonial incorporation. Instead, the closing scene depicts him comfortably seated in the first class cabin of a transatlantic flight to China, clad in an Armani suit. In this finale, Liling seems to occupy the position of the Western subject or colonizer. He emerges from the film not as the dehumanized "other" of colonial desire, but as the agent of a transgressive fantasy that powerfully sustains his identity as desiring subject.

I read Gallimard's cinematic suicide as a dramatic attempt to rethink the trafficking between fantasy and identity. The film imagines Gallimard's death not as punishment for his immersion in fantasy, but as an opening onto a radically new vision of the constitutive effects of fantasy and intersubjectivity. The following chapters will explore the aesthetic and political possibilities of this vision as imagined by postcolonial writers Leila Sebbar, Theresa Hak Kyung Cha, Hélène Cixous, and Assia Djebar. What does it mean to forge alternative relations between self and other, image and identity in the context of sexual and political trauma? How might the wounding effects of colonial representation spark dissonant visions and creative revisions of diasporic identity?

This book will consider these productive and disorienting potentials of fantasy, which are especially evident in feminist efforts to challenge masculinist ideals of correspondence and recognition. As I hope to show, the destabilizing tactics at play in transnational feminist art and literature enact a space beyond recognition—a space that resists an appeal to "truthful" identity as its stable foundation. Although postcolonial feminist literature conceives of social emancipation as a primary objective, it redefines emancipation in a language responsive to women's polyvalent experiences of transnational trauma, fantasy, and intersectional identity.

NOTES

1. Anne Anlin Cheng, *The Melancholy of Race: Psychoanalysis, Assimilation, and Hidden Grief* (Oxford: Oxford University Press, 2001), 105.

2. Frantz Fanon, *Black Skin, White Masks*, trans. Charles Lam Markmann (New York: Grove Press, 1967), 112–13, my emphasis.

3. See Homi Bhabha, "Foreword: Remembering Fanon," in Frantz Fanon, *Black Skin, White Masks*, trans. Charles Lam Markmann, 2nd ed. (London: Pluto Press, 1986), xi.

4. See Louis Althusser, *Lenin and Philosophy* (New York: Monthly Review Press, Reprint 1990).

5. For more on this see Mary Ann Doane, "Dark Continents" in *Femmes Fatales: Feminism, Film Theory, Psychoanalysis* (New York: Routledge, 1991), 224.

6. Fanon 1967: 109. His words also evoke the photographic process of "fixing" an image in fixative chemical solution.

7. Slavoj Žižek, *The Sublime Object of Ideology* (London: Verso, 1989), 113.

8. Alma Garcia, "The Development of Chicana Feminist Discourse, 1970–1980," in Vicki Ruiz and Ellen DuBois, eds., *Unequal Sisters: A Multi-Cultural Reader in US Women's History* (New York: Routledge, 1989).

9. Kimberlé Williams Crenshaw, "Mapping the Margins: Intersectionality, Identity Politics, and Violence Against Women of Color," 43 *Stanford Law Review* 1241 (1991). See also Mari Matsuda, "When the First Quail Calls: Multiple Consciousness as Jurisprudential Method," in *Where Is Your Body? And Other Essays on Race, Gender, and the Law* (Boston: Beacon Press, 1996).

10. Crenshaw, "Demarginalizing the Intersection of Race and Sex," *University of Chicago Legal Forum* 139 (1989).

11. See for example any or all of the following: Gloria Anzaldúa (1987), Anzaldúa and Cherríe Moraga, eds. (1981), Norma Alarcón in Anzaldúa, ed. (1990), Chela Sandoval (2000), bell hooks (1981), Trinh T. Minh-ha (1989), Gloria Hull, Patricia Bell Scott, and Barbara Smith, eds. (1982), Angela Davis (1981), Patricia Hill Collins (1990), and Deborah King (1988), among others. I use the term "U.S. third world feminists" here in the sense proposed by Chela Sandoval in *Methodology of the Oppressed* (Minneapolis: University of Minnesota Press, 2000).

12. See for example Kimberlé Williams Crenshaw, "Whose Story Is It, Anyway?: Feminist and Antiracist Appropriations of Anita Hill" in Toni Morrison, ed., *Race-ing Justice, En-gendering Power: Essays on Anita Hill, Clarence Thomas, and the Construction of Social Reality* (New York: Pantheon Books, 1992).

13. In a legal context, the reasonable person standard posits a certain pattern of behavior that should be expected from a prototypical "reasonable person" in any given situation. Battered woman's syndrome is a psychological and legal model for assessing women's responses to domestic violence. It assumes that women are most often passive victims who, because they are powerless to change their situation, become trapped in abusive relationships.

14. Bhabha 1986: xiii.

15. Gloria Anzaldúa, *Borderlands/ La Frontera* (San Francisco: Aunt Lute Books, 1987), 25.

16. Diana Fuss, *Identification Papers* (New York: Routledge, 1995), 14.

17. Fanon 1967: 109.

18. See Ernest Renan, *Qu'est-ce qu'une nation?* (Paris: Pocket, 1992), 41.

19. Fanon 1967: 179–80.

20. I borrow this phrase from Crenshaw (1989). For more on Fanon's erasure of black female subjectivity in the face of violence, see Doane 1991: 222. For a differing perspective, see Madhu Dubey, "The 'True Lie' of the Nation: Fanon and Feminism," in *differences* 10, no. 2 (Summer 1998). In her reading of Fanon's *The Wretched of the Earth* and *A Dying Colonialism*, Dubey agrees that Fanon fails to recognize gender differences as constitutive of his own categories of "native" and "nationalist." Yet she argues that Fanon's work can still be aligned with feminist critiques of nationalism in that it refuses to fix feminine or national identity with reference to either "tradition" or "modernity."

21. Daniele Djamila Amrane-Minne, *Des femmes dans la guerre d'algerie* (Paris: Karthala, 1994).

22. Fanon 1967: 217, my emphasis.

23. For more on this see Kaja Silverman, *The Threshold of the Visible World* (New York: Routledge, 1996), 202. Fanon evokes these resistant potentials of disidentification as well, but his work is primarily motivated by a desire to theorize the wounding effects of representation for colonized subjectivity.

24. Frantz Fanon, "Algeria Unveiled," in *A Dying Colonialism*, trans. Haakon Chevalier (New York: Grove Press, 1965).

25. Fanon 1965: 35–67.

26. Ibid. 112–14.

27. Djebar's first novel, *La soif*, provoked a scandal in Algeria because, although Djebar wrote it during the revolution, she chose to depict a female character's sexual awakening rather than her reflections on the anticolonial revolution. Djebar's choice of topics at that historical moment, and under the pressures of the nationalist movement, can be understood as an indication of the audacity of her commitment to the expression, politicization, and "liberation" of female sexuality in Algeria.

28. "Car je sais à l'avance—vieux préjugé?—que la guerre qui finit entre les peuples renaît entre les couples." Assia Djebar, *Les alouettes naïves* (Paris: Julliard, 1967), 481.

29. Fanon 1965: 66.

30. I do not mean to suggest that this would be the "consensus" of either Algerian women or Fanon's audience; but, rather, that it is one *possible* conclusion that Fanon fails to consider or draw from Algerian women's personal testimony.

31. Fanon 1967: 62.

32. Cynthia Enloe, *Bananas, Beaches, & Bases: Making Feminist Sense of International Politics* (Los Angeles: University of California Press, 1989), 42.

33. See for example a documentary directed by Jennifer Kawaja entitled *Under One Sky . . . Arab Women in North America Talk About the Hijab* (National Film Board of Canada, 1999) for its showcasing of several complex and engaging perspectives on the contemporary practice of *hijab*.

34. See Winifred Woodhull, *Transfigurations of the Maghreb: Feminism, Decolonization, and Literatures* (Minneapolis: University of Minnesota Press, 1993), 23.

35. Although only a minority of women explicitly identified veiling as a form of gender oppression, or unveiling as a feminist imperative, during and after the revolution,

Fanon's investment of the veil with unambiguously revolutionary implications should be contrasted with his more sophisticated treatment of male subjectivity.

36. Fuss 1995: 154, 160.

37. Marguerite Duras, *The Lover*, trans. Barbara Bray (New York: Harper Collins, 1985). Originally published as *L'amant* (Paris: Les Editions de Minuit, 1984).

38. *The Lover* is widely interpreted as autobiographical fiction. Here, I share this perspective by deliberately blurring the distinction between the narrator and "Duras."

39. That is, part of an expatriate, "colonial" administrative community (of French descent) living in Vietnam.

40. See Teresa de Lauretis, "Aesthetics and Feminist Theory: Rethinking Women's Cinema" in Sandra Kemp and Judith Squires, eds., *Feminisms* (New York: Oxford University Press, 1997), 33.

41. Ibid.

42. Trinh T. Minh-ha refers to "hyphenated identities" and the "challenge of hyphenated reality" in "Bold Omissions and Minute Depictions," a chapter of her book *When the Moon Waxes Red: Representation, Gender and Cultural Politics* (New York: Routledge, 1991), 155–66. I mean to suggest here that all of the above-listed writers explicitly address the interwoven histories and representations of France and Algeria (or Korea and the United States) in their work. Although not all of these writers identify with dual nationalities—Leila Sebbar, for example, identifies herself as simply "French"—all have spent their childhood and adulthood in various states of intersection between at least two countries and cultures. Of course, the terms "French," "Algerian," "Korean," and "American" should be understood to include various crossings of origin or mixed heritages, as well. By considering these women collectively, I do not mean to gloss over important differences in their personal and political locations. Rather, I will study their work as the variegated product of particular transnational and transcultural crossings.

43. Djebar 1967: 9, my translation.

44. As discussed earlier, my usage of "intersectionality" is based on the concept articulated by legal theorist Kimberlé Williams Crenshaw, which refers to the simultaneity of multiple facets of oppression that "intersect" to inform the subject positions of women of color. See Crenshaw 1991.

45. Rey Chow, "Where Have All the Natives Gone?" in *Writing Diaspora: Tactics of Intervention in Contemporary Cultural Studies* (Bloomington: Indiana University Press, 1993), 51.

46. Yves Bonnefoy, "Igitur and the Photographer," in *PMLA* 114, no. 3 (May 1999), 340.

47. Roland Barthes, *Camera Lucida*, trans. Richard Howard (New York: Hill and Wang, 1981), 87.

48. I should point out that Barthes readily admits that he is not a photographer, and has no experience as such. His "realist" approach toward the photographic image should be attributed, at least in part, to this personal lack of experience with the act of photographic composition and processing. For more on his conception of the photograph as an image without a code, see Roland Barthes, *Image-Music-Text*, trans. Stephen Heath (New York: Hill and Wang, 1978).

49. Barthes 1981: 102.

50. Roland Barthes, "The Photographic Message," in *Image-Music-Text*, trans. Stephen Heath (New York: Hill and Wang, 1978).

51. Barthes 1981: 11–12.

52. Gilles Deleuze and Felix Guattari, *Kafka: Toward a Minor Literature*, trans. Dana Polan (Minneapolis: University of Minnesota Press, 1986), 22; see chapter 9 for further definition of this term.

53. I refer here to an essential component of Irigaray's project as summarized by Gayatri Spivak in "French Feminism in an International Frame," in *In Other Worlds: Essays in Cultural Politics* (New York: Routledge, 1988).

54. See Michel de Certeau, *The Practice of Everyday Life*, trans. Steven Rendall(Berkeley: University of California Press, 1984), General Introduction and 25.

55. See Barthes 1978.

56. I am especially interested here in Fanon's usage of the term "fix." In *Black Skin, White Masks*, he refers to being "fixed" by the racist gaze in both subjective and aesthetic terms: "the glances of the other *fixed* me there, in the sense in which a chemical solution is fixed by a dye . . . I burst apart" (Fanon 1967: 109).

57. Diane Arbus, *Diane Arbus* (New Jersey: Aperture, 1972), 14–15.

58. Barthes 1981: 6.

59. See Barthes 1981: 79, in reference to photography as an art of identity. For more on time as elsewhere, see Bhabha 1986: xvii.

60. Barthes 1981: 10.

61. Ibid. 12.

62. Ibid. 12, my emphasis.

63. By this I mean to suggest the mechanism whereby a traditional camera—which is in essence a "light box"—registers an image.

64. Barthes 1981: 21.

65. Barthes 1978. Cited in Susan Sontag, ed., *The Barthes Reader* (New York: Hill and Wang, 1982), 209.

66. Barthes 1978. Cited in Sontag, ed. 1982: 210.

67. Consider, for example, virtual or online child pornography; or the manipulated fetal imagery that is a staple of antiabortion protests and web-sites.

68. Lacan first proposed the model of the mirror stage (*stade du miroir*) in 1936. Most infants experience this stage between the ages of 6–18 months.

69. Jacqueline Rose, *Sexuality in the Field of Vision* (London: Verso, 1986), 178–79.

70. I should point out here that chimpanzees are also able to recognize themselves in the mirror, hence to believe—like humans—in this correspondence between image and identity.

71. Jacques Lacan, *Ecrits*, trans. Alan Sheridan (New York: W. W. Norton & Company, 1977), 306.

72. Jacques Lacan, *The Seminar of Jacques Lacan, Book I: Freud's Papers on Technique 1953–1954*, trans. John Forrester (New York: W. W. Norton & Company, 1988), 167.

73. See Homi Bhabha for more on this peculiar ambivalence of colonial identification, which presumes that the colonized subject is "like me, but not like me." Homi Bhabha, *The Location of Culture* (New York: Routledge, 1994).

74. Žižek 1989: 106.

75. Ibid. 109.

76. Bhabha 1986: xxii.

77. I mean to evoke "subjectification" here as the passage to the Symbolic through which the subject is "produced" as an effect of discourse and the Law of the Father. Note that this sense of the term implies no agency on the part of the subject.

78. See Deleuze and Guattari 1986: 16–27.

79. Gilles Deleuze, "November 20, 1923—Postulates of Linguistics," in *A Thousand Plateaus*, originally published as *Mille plateaux: Capitalisme et schizophrenie* (Paris: Minuit, 1980), 95.

80. See for example Abdelkebir Khatibi, *Love in Two Languages*, trans. Richard Howard (Minneapolis: University of Minnesota Press, 1990), originally published as *Amour bilingue* (Paris: Editions Fata Morgana, 1983). See also Khatibi, *Maghreb pluriel* (Paris: Denoel, 1983).

81. See Karla Holloway, "The Body Politic," in Michael Moon and Cathy Davidson, eds., *Subjects & Citizens: Nation, Race, and Gender from Oroonoko to Anita Hill* (Durham, NC: Duke University Press, 1995), 493.

82. Michel Pêcheux, *Language, Semantics and Ideology* (New York: St. Martin's Press, 1982), 122.

83. Margo Jefferson, "The Tricks Mirrors Play," in "The Me Millennium,"(New York: *The New York Times Magazin*e special issue, October 17, 1999), 99.

84. Bhabha 1986: xii.

85. Gayatri Spivak, in Donna Landry and Gerald Maclean, eds., *The Spivak Reader* (New York: Routledge, 1996), 187. As Spivak points out here, "Isma" is colloquial Arabic for "she is called____(fill in the blank)." Hence this name signals the absence of the proper name, or its impossibility.

86. David Henry Hwang, *M. Butterfly* (New York: Penguin, 1989).

87. Although Boursicot originally met Pei Pu as a man, Pei Pu later convinced Boursicot that he was actually a woman who had adopted a male persona for artistic and political purposes. It is worth noting that Boursicot had previously enjoyed gay relationships, and has since the trial, as well. Thus, his claim to have been successfully "deceived" by Pei Pu is questionable. See Cheng 2001: 114.

88. Boursicot later learned that Pei Pu had adopted the child that she called their son with the help of the Chinese government.

89. Richard Bernstein, "France Jails Two in Odd Case of Espionage," *The New York Times*, May 11, 1986 (A7).

90. French president François Mitterand pardoned the two lovers a year later, in 1987.

91. For more on this, see Colleen Lye, "M. Butterfly and the Rhetoric of Antiessentialism: Minority Discourse in an International Frame," in Sucheng Chan, Josephine Lee, Michael Omi, and David Palumbo-Liu, eds., *Performing Asian-American Race and Ethnicity on the Contemporary Stage* (Philadelphia: Temple University Press, 1988).

92. See for example Dorinne Kondo, "*M. Butterfly*: Orientalism, Gender, and a Critique of Essentialist Identity," *Cultural Critique* 16 (Fall 1990); and Marjorie Gar-

ber, "The Occidental Tourist: *M. Butterfly* and the Scandal of Transvestism," in Andrew Parker, Mary Russo, Doris Sommer, and Patricia Yeager, eds., *Nationalisms and Sexualities* (New York: Routledge, 1992).

93. See especially Garber 1992.

94. Garber 1992: 141.

95. See, e.g., Hwang 1989: 66.

96. Lye 1988. Of course, the strength of the play derives from its general desire to pose the question of how fantasy might be strategically "played" to one's advantage.

97. Judith Butler, *Bodies That Matter* (New York: Routledge, 1993), 219.

98. Dir. David Cronenberg, *M. Butterfly* (1993).

99. Rey Chow, "The Dream of a Butterfly" in Diana Fuss, ed., *Human, All Too Human* (NewYork: Routledge, 1996).

100. Edward Said, *Orientalism* (New York: Vintage Books, 1978).

101. See Cheng 2001: 114.

102. See for example Maxine Hong Kingston, *Tripmaster Monkey: His Fake Book* (New York: Vintage Books, 1987), and Hanif Kureishi, *The Buddha of Suburbia* (New York: Penguin Books, 1990).

103. See for example Michel Foucault, *Discipline and Punish*, trans. Alan Sheridan (New York: Vintage Books, 1977); Thomas Laqueur, *Making Sex: Body and Gender from the Greeks to Freud* (Cambridge: Harvard University Press, 1990); Emily Martin, *The Woman in the Body: A Cultural Analysis of Reproduction* (Boston: Beacon Press, 1987); Evelyn Fox Keller and Helen Longino, eds., *Feminism & Science* (Oxford: Oxford University Press, 1996); Anne Fausto-Sterling, *Sexing the Body: Gender Politics and the Construction of Sexuality* (New York: Basic Books, 2000); and Suzanne Kessler, "The Medical Construction of Gender: Case Management of Intersexed Infants," in *Signs* 16, no. 1 (Chicago: University of Chicago Press, 1990).

104. Cheng 2001: 116.

105. See for example Friedrich Nietzsche, *Beyond Good and Evil*, trans. Walter Kaufmann (New York: Random House, 1966); Michel Foucault, *The History of Sexuality vol. I*, trans. Robert Hurley (New York: Random House, 1978); Judith Butler, "The End of Sexual Difference?" in Elisabeth Bronfen and Misha Kavka, eds., *Feminist Consequences* (New York: Columbia University Press, 2001); and Eve Kosofsky Sedgwick, *Epistemology of the Closet* (Berkeley: University of California Press, 1990).

106. Teresa de Lauretis, "Popular Culture, Public and Private Fantasies: Femininity and Fetishism in David Cronenberg's *M. Butterfly,*" *Signs* 24, no. 2 (Winter 1999), 313.

107. *The New York Times*, May 11, 1986, A7.

108. Cheng 2001: 123.

109. de Lauretis 1999: 325.

110. For more on this see Cheng 2001: 123.

Chapter Two

Disorienting Looks, *Ecarts D'Identité*[1]

Colonial Photography, Ownership, and Identity

> The act of representing others almost always involves violence to the subject of representation.
>
> —Edward Said, "In the Shadow of the West"

> To challenge the regimes of representation that govern a society is to conceive of how a politics can transform reality. As this creative struggle moves onward, it is bound to recompose subjectivity and praxis. More often than not, it requires that one leave the realms of the known, and take oneself there where one does not expect, is not expected to be.
>
> —Trinh T. Minh-Ha, *When the Moon Waxes Red*

> The "native" is not the defiled image, and not *not* the defiled image. And she stares indifferently, mocking our imprisonment within imagistic resemblance.
>
> —Rey Chow, *Writing Diaspora*

I. INTRODUCTION: OWNING IMAGES

Photography's invention in the mid-1800s as a "revolutionary means of reproduction" provoked a crisis of authorship in both law and art.[2] Especially in France, Britain, and the United States, photography raised a host of seemingly intractable problems for copyright law. If the invention of photography heralded a golden age of technological innovation and mass replication, it also prompted scrutiny regarding the precise meanings of creation and ownership. Given the interdependent roles of the camera, photographer, and photographed subject in the process of photographic creation, who could be rightly designated as the "author" of an image? Were photographs—like novels and scientific inventions—sufficiently "original" to warrant copyright protection, or did they merely record a preexisting reality? How important was the mark of human agency, or authorial trace, to a photograph?

Anxieties about how to establish the proper ownership of a photograph dominated Western copyright law in the mid-to-late nineteenth century. By 1880, the photograph had emerged as a highly contested legal object. Initially, the graphic design professionals at large printing presses regarded photographs as the products of mechanical intervention rather than artistic creation. Consequently, they reproduced images en masse without obtaining photographers' permission to do so. Fluctuating conceptions of authorship and creativity gradually challenged this practice, most notably in the landmark U.S. Supreme Court case *Burrow-Giles Lithographic Company v. Sarony* (1883).

In *Burrow*, a New York–based photographer named N. Sarony sued a local lithograph company for copyright infringement, based on the company's unauthorized reproduction of his portrait of Oscar Wilde. In accordance with existing legal custom, the respondent claimed that the photograph in question was an exact reproduction of Wilde's person, thus did not constitute a copyright-worthy work of art. In its ruling, the U.S. Supreme Court held that the two legally protected classes or beneficiaries recognized by existing copyright law—"authors" and "inventors"—should be more broadly construed to include photographers. Provided that the originality of a photograph could be established, photography constituted an "art" involving labors of "original mental conception," intellectual invention, and creativity. Accordingly, the Court found that the plaintiff in this case—who had created his image by posing the subject; eliciting a particular facial expression; arranging the costume, accessories, and backdrop; and manipulating available light to expose the image—should indeed receive copyright protection for his photograph.[3]

At issue in the legal debate surrounding photographic authorship was the question of how to properly define, classify, and attribute artistic creation, originality, and ownership. Also at stake was legal protection for the right to reproduce an image. As evident from the erratic weave of federal case law, most courts approached the camera as an industrial machine that significantly complicated traditional distinctions between the "subject" and "object" of artistic production.

The anxieties characterizing legal debates at the turn of the century reemerged in Western cultural and literary studies in the mid-twentieth century, when Roland Barthes initiated a "theory uprising"[4] that introduced one of the central preoccupations of postmodernism: the "death of the author."[5] Michel Foucault expanded on the themes of originality and authorship in his essay, "What Is an Author?"[6] while Andy Warhol raised similar questions in the 1970s American art world regarding the role of the artist in an age of mass production. For Walter Benjamin, the ambiguities of authorship in the mechanical age implied that exhibition sites and practices would supplant artistic "origins" as the most powerful shapers of aesthetic and political meaning.[7]

By the 1980s, U.S. minority studies scholars and feminist theorists began to question the political implications of the putative death of the author. What did it mean to proclaim this death—or the impossibility of unified subjectivity and authorship as such—just as the artistic works of previously marginalized groups, including women and minorities, were gaining visibility within the academy? On the other hand, how might a rejection of the traditional model of authorship complicate the static notions of creative agency and passive compliance (e.g., feminine muse and masculine source, seed, or origin) that had previously seemed to govern all transactions between producers and consumers of an image? These debates highlight exactly what the turn-of-the-century legal rush to establish proper photographic ownership seems to obscure: an understanding of the image as the product not only of mechanical reproduction, but also of a dynamic field of aesthetic and social relations and contestations.[8]

Postcolonial feminist literature often concerns itself with precisely this question of what it means to own or author an image, and how one might exist in creative and critical relationship to the other's gaze. Taking as a point of departure the notion that "reading and [remaking] pictures can be seen as forms of feminist resistance,"[9] I will study Leila Sebbar's reconfiguration of the relations between image and identity in her novel *Sherazade*. By so doing, I hope to illuminate a broader spectrum of women's experiences as consumers, creators, and manipulators of images.

This chapter begins with a reflection on Malek Alloula's study of French colonial postcards, *The Colonial Harem*. It goes on to assess wartime identity card portraits composed by the French photographer Marc Garanger, and their resurfacing in Leila Sebbar's novel *Sherazade (Missing: aged 17, dark curly hair, green eyes)*. I have chosen to focus on Garanger's photography primarily because Sebbar explicitly evokes it in her novel. Yet I also believe that Garanger's work as a war photographer yields fertile ground for debate regarding how colonial fantasies of "otherness" are photographically conceived, and how their orchestration depends upon a certain ambivalence that might permit creative forms of decomposition from within the photographic field.

Foregrounding the oppositional looks that abound in *Sherazade*, I will argue that Sebbar stages ambivalent yet highly productive encounters between women's "looks" and the photographic gaze. Instead of renouncing stereotypical imagery or reinforcing colonial desire, *Sherazade* asks the more compelling question of how Algerian-French women both participate in and misrecognize the melancholic racial and sexual fantasies at play within nationalist and colonial imaginaries.[10] In this sense, her work moves beyond Edward Said's paradigm of Orientalism to reimagine the relation between image and identity as one of creative negotiation.

My essay will develop an alternative framework for analyzing colonial photography by exploring how subaltern women "occupy" imagery in order to contest symbolic erasures and violations of difference. Within *Sherazade*, women's oppositional looks reconfigure hegemonic relations between power, sexuality, culture, and representation. Seizing on the ambivalence of colonial imagery, Sebbar creates powerful counterfictions of female sexuality and national identity.

My analysis of *Sherazade* will employ literary critic Marianne Hirsch's definition of the "feminist reader and creator of images":

> She is not just the collection of pieces of glossy paper on the floor, she is also the photographer who has subversively disassembled herself in them. As photographer and subject, she [locates identity] both in the collection of contradictory, incongruous, and discontinuous images, and in the act of reframing and rearranging them to trace a personal and collective history against their grain.[11]

As Hirsch emphasizes, the feminist reader of images does not only deconstruct representations of the feminine. She also invents an alternative aesthetic by appropriating the "powerful fantasies and anxieties that keep those images circulating"[12]—and that might be used to authorize other narratives and histories.

II. ALLOULA'S POSTCARDS: RETURNING THE LOOK TO ITS SENDER

In *The Colonial Harem*, Algerian writer Malek Alloula undertakes an ambitious study of French colonial representations of Algerian women, circa 1900–1930. He focuses on the aesthetic genre of the colonial postcard, whose erotic imagery has the power to circulate between eyes and cultures. Alloula identifies postcards as symptoms of a complex web of colonial and sexual domination that shaped the French national imaginary.[13]

In many ways, *The Colonial Harem* constitutes a groundbreaking inquiry into the enabling conditions and political effects of colonial visual culture.[14] Alloula demonstrates the efficacy of the erotic postcard, as a cheap travel relic, to disseminate Orientalist fantasies to an audience spanning colony and metropole. Taking up Said's analysis of Orientalism, Alloula approaches Oriental imagery not as the expression of dispassionate knowledge about another culture, but as a means of reinforcing hierarchical power relations between colonizer and colonized. As Alloula points out, the postcards' Orientalist subplot aided French political efforts to thwart Algerian independence via educational and religious reform and mandatory adoption of the French language.

The Colonial Harem especially scrutinizes the colonial gaze upon "native" women and the feminized trope of the Orient.[15] Alloula centers the postcard image of the veiled Algerian woman—most often posed in the photographer's studio—as a "cornerstone of Orientalist ideology and imperialist politics."[16] Building on analyses of the male gaze whereby "men act and women appear,"[17] Alloula identifies Algerian women—most of whom he presumes to be slaves and prostitutes—as sexualized objects of the obsessive French male gaze. The Oriental gaze peruses these women with an ambivalent sense of superiority and lecherous titillation.

Alloula outlines a visual and political economy in which Algerian women are desired and exchanged, yet ultimately effaced by the colonial gaze. Within this symbolic economy, images work on several levels to fabricate exotic otherness and to suppress female agency. Colonial postcards employ stereotypical props, spaces, and textures—including veils, lush fabrics, opium pipes, and ornate jewelry—that exoticize their subjects and emphasize intractable difference relative to European culture.

Posing is foundational to the colonial imaginary, and the colonized woman's gaze is typically averted rather than confrontational. Alloula contends that this gaze, directed inward or away from the camera, accentuates passivity and alienation, often suggesting the reverie of opiate sedation. Only when a woman is photographically staged as a prostitute or lesbian does her gaze meet the camera head-on, reinforcing Orientalist myths of the sexually promiscuous and deviant Eastern woman. Given widespread perceptions of photography as a documentary rather than aesthetic genre, the fantasies embedded in colonial photography had the power to circulate as evidence of Algerian lifestyles and identities.

For Alloula, the photographer's camera lens reduces Algerian women to a pornographic surface that it hungers to penetrate. Postcard photographs depict women in large groups and in varying states of undress—a mingling of skin, costume, and exotic jewelry, exposed behind the harem curtains and beneath the veil. If these photographic orchestrations betray a desire to sexually access Algerian women's bodies, Alloula argues that the reflective properties of the veil ultimately frustrate colonial dreams of trespass.[18] The veil, as an excessive trace and barrier to entry, shatters the "illusion of transparency upon which photography as a form of representation relies for its power of truth-telling."[19]

Because Alloula silences female resistance as well as the troubling gender dynamics within the Algerian nationalist movement, his text often reads like a sexually charged threat to French male surveyors of Algerian women. Amidst this flurry of words, women's bodies emerge as the titillating currency of a specular economy. A male battle for sexual access to Algerian women waged throughout the Algerian revolution, most notoriously by way of rape and "the battle of the veil."[20] Forced unveiling was a recurring colonial strategy during the revolution. Ostensibly a measure to enhance national security and identification, unveiling also served as a means of psychological warfare to thwart Algerian national and religious culture. In response to colonial unveiling imperatives, Algerian nationalist leaders proposed female veiling as an expression of Algerian identity and solidarity. At times, they encouraged women to exploit the veil's coverage in order to smuggle bombs onto enemy soil. Or conversely, they asked female nationalists to unveil and wear Western clothing in order to pass unnoticed through French security checkpoints. This ideological battle of the veil led many Algerian women to feel like pawns, doubly colonized by French and Algerian men. Of this, Assia Djebar remarks:

> as one nationalism after another is successful, one realizes that *inside that Orient* delivered unto itself, the image of the *woman* is no differently conceived: by the father, the husband, and in a way more troubling still, by the brother and the son.[21]

Strikingly, her words appear in the introduction to *The Colonial Harem*; yet Alloula does not seem to realize his own potential implication as a husband, brother, or son.[22]

By crafting a narrative of reversal, Alloula perpetuates this masculinist contest for Algerian women. In his rush to return the colonial gaze, Alloula often indulges in that voyeuristic gaze upon women's bodies—especially by reproducing the postcards in large, coffee-table format and lavish sepia tones.[23] *The Colonial Harem* seems oblivious to the nuanced meanings, negotiations, and subject positions that women might associate with their photographs, especially within a cultural context that has traditionally prohibited female photographic posing and the display of women's images.

Given the complex reception and role of photography within Algerian society, Alloula's reading of the Oriental postcard in terms of a sexual and racial contest between men is not entirely unjustified. Within decades of photography's debut as an artistic genre in 1839, Western scientists began to use anthropometric photography as a tool with which to support burgeoning theories of racial and ethnic hierarchy. Anthropometric photographs typically depicted frontal and side views of "native types," which were used to classify people "according to the 'evolution' of their physical features, head shape and size, and cranial capacity."[24] This scientific deployment of photographic "evidence" set the stage for racial and colonial conquest. Significantly, the identity card photographs that I will examine later in this chapter bear an uncanny compositional resemblance to earlier anthropometric images, in that both sets of photographs present stark headshots intended to facilitate classification.

During the colonial era that witnessed photography's invention, many Algerians felt threatened by what they perceived as the camera's ability to freeze or steal the soul. Rural inhabitants, in particular, regarded photography as an act of both aggression and possession. Images of women proved especially offensive to conservative Algerian men, whose patriarchal control depended to a large degree on their regulation of female visibility within society. Based on photography's complicated function within racial science and colonial culture, then, Alloula is right to suggest that Orientalist photographs may have inaugurated a racial and sexual contest of sorts between men—especially a battle for control over Algerian women.

Yet it is important to distinguish between the varied aesthetic histories of the photograph and the postcard. Colonial postcards represent a "distinctively modern visual genre" marked by its status as souvenir and collectible.[25] Noteworthy for its ability to travel, the postcard forces a somewhat different understanding of its gendered economy than does the photograph more generally. In this sense, Alloula's work presents a monolithic account of Orientalist imagery by conflating the histories of these two artistic genres.

Furthermore, by framing colonial postcards in terms of a heterosexual competition between men, Alloula advances a disturbingly homophobic reading of these images. Throughout *The Colonial Harem*, pictorial conceptualizations of female intimacy elicit "a vocabulary of disgust."[26] Perhaps overly eager to counter the characterization of Algeria as a hotbed of homosexuality, which was especially prevalent in nineteenth-century racial science and sexology, Alloula crafts a homophobic narrative discounting all but heterosexual, masculinist desire.

Ultimately, the questions *not* posed by Alloula are disturbing. As Cynthia Enloe asks:

> But what of the women themselves? Aicha and Zorah must have had their own thoughts about being posed unveiled and behind bars. Maybe they later saw the postcard on sale near a hotel. Maybe they were flattered; maybe they were humiliated. How were they persuaded to sit for the photographer in the first place? Were they paid?[27]

Alloula "seems remarkably uncurious about women's own thoughts" about image-making, and indifferent to the various meanings, negotiations, and subject positions that women might engineer *vis-à-vis* their photographs. He also fails to examine the varied relationships that women posers might have had with their photographers. As Graham Brown concludes in her study of Middle Eastern photographic archives, although the vast majority of postcard photographers were Western men, a small minority of photographers consisted of women, relatives, and indigenous men. Furthermore, not all women who posed for photographs were slaves or prostitutes. While most posers belonged to the lower classes, norms of respectability and female visibility varied greatly from place to place. Moreover, by 1900, the genre of photography had acquired social prestige. As a result, many wealthy women commissioned studio photographers to compose their portraits or *cartes de visite*. Thus, it is not entirely accurate to assume an asymmetric power relationship between the photographer and his or her photographed subject, although this relationship was certainly the norm.

Alloula seeks to "return this immense postcard to its sender" (Alloula: 5) by rejecting the phantasmic investments of colonial photography. He wants to "force the postcard to reveal what it holds back" in two ways: first, by uncovering the imperialist motivations of the photographic gaze; and second, by renouncing its stereotypical representations of Algerian women. Alloula's subversion consists of de-exoticizing Algerian women: although he acknowledges that there is a grain of truth to some of the photographic detail (Alloula: 52), he overwhelmingly identifies French postcards as fraudulent counterfeits of real Algerian women.

Unfortunately, Alloula's analytical gesture remains caught within an economy of *renversement* or reversal. Because his narrative is often complicit with the sexualized French gaze, readers of *The Colonial Harem* witness a double violation of Algerian women. Alloula's project to "rescue" Algerian women often reads like a masculinist heroic epic, or as a "homosocial discourse" in which women are the objects of exchange among men.[28] Within this economy, women's bodies function as "what is at stake in a usually rivalrous transaction between men,"[29] and become little more than dark mirrors that endlessly reflect endangered masculinity. Interestingly, tropes of actual or potential impotence abound within Alloula's male-centered discourse.[30]

The Colonial Harem culminates with a particularly unsettling vision of Algerian womanhood: a *hijab*-clad woman with her breasts strategically exposed. Since Alloula includes no critical commentary about this photograph, viewers are left to question authorial intent. Why close with this image, and for whose benefit? By reproducing this and similar images of women throughout his text, Alloula demonstrates a certain collusion with the colonizing gaze. As Rey Chow concludes:

> What results is neither a dismantling of the pornographic apparatus of imperialist domination nor a restoration of the native to her "authentic" history but a per-

> fect symmetry between the imperialist and anti-imperialist gazes, which cross over the images of native women as silent objects.[31]

For Alloula, what most powerfully emerges from the colonial postcard is an absence of oppositional looks—women are posed, he claims, as if surrendering themselves to French men. Immersed in the dynamics of male desire and voyeurism, *The Colonial Harem* ultimately erases women's looks. Alloula fails to imagine that Algerian women might ironically perform, "disarm,"[32] or subtly resist the stereotypical images that they help to construct on the surface of the colonial postcard. Instead, his commentary reduces women to: "ecstatic icons, passively submitting to their cosmetic make-over"; "pliable [. . . figures of the] dissolution of resistance"; "trophies offered up, body and soul"; and "puppets of a tedious and repetitious imagination" (Alloula: 62, 64, 122, 93).

Alloula assumes that Algerian women have no choice but to passively identify with their photographed images. In a passage of his text that examines "Sapphist" photographs, Alloula indirectly hints at, then dismisses the possibility of female agency. He remarks that

> Most often, the [woman's] facial expression is vague, distant, absent . . . *As if the models themselves had no illusion about the effect they would produce.* Or as if they understood that only their breasts could find favor with the photographer and his clients. Reduced to what is enticing about them, these women can only efface themselves behind their own breasts, which they push forward to earn better payment.[33]

In another passage, Alloula likens the female gaze to a camera lens that "takes aim at everything," and has the potential to "dispossess [the photographer] of his own gaze" (Alloula:14). Yet Alloula ultimately assimilates this disruptive potential into a masculinist nationalist allegory of sexual frustration. He first conflates the "feminine gaze" with the "feminine world" of Algerian society, then suggests that the colonial photographer doubly avenges himself in the photo studio, where "he will unveil the veiled and give figural representation to the forbidden" (Alloula:14). Alloula's reading of the female gaze ignores specific aspects of women's presentation that might suggest opposition to intended photographic messages. These include the details of facial expression, such as frowning mouths or curled lips, and eyes that either glare at the camera or refuse to acknowledge the photographer altogether by staring beyond the photographic frame. They also encompass effects of reluctance, resistance, and ironic mimicry that are often conveyed through the body language of photographed women.

By absorbing moments of potentially oppositional consciousness into a totalizing narrative of female passivity and colonial penetration, Alloula denies that women posing for Orientalist photographs could have a critical and/or creative relation to the clichéd images of femininity that they photographically portray. His account leaves no room for the challenge of a knowing gaze that might employ fantasy and stereotype to subvert an image, mimic a stereotypical identity, or resist identification altogether. As a result, Alloula minimizes possibilities for feminist infiltration and appropriation of images.

While they posed as "exotic types" for French colonial men, veiled Algerian women undoubtedly had limited potentials to interrupt the Orientalist fantasies underlying their images, especially given the characteristically unequal power relations between photographer and photographed subject. Yet it is important to acknowledge traces of resistance in the looks of photographed women. Often, women depicted on French postcards seem to achieve a critical distance from their audience by ironically mimicking Orientalist stereotypes, misrecognizing the colonial male gaze, and assuming protective or defiant postures. Given the social, spatial, and sexual restrictions imposed on women in Algerian society, photographic posing might have afforded some women a sense of creative authorship and agency.

My sense is that more harm may be done by blindness to this possibility than by its consideration. If a primary objective of postcolonial theory is to engage with both the silence and speech of the subaltern, what ends might the repression of women's critical and creative misrecognition serve? By emphasizing female display and male sexual penetration, Alloula presents "a voyeur's theory"[34] of colonial representation. He effaces the looks that might disrupt photographic composition and consumption, and puncture the surface of the image altogether. Because Alloula fails to imagine how Algerian women might misrecognize, interrupt, or refashion images of identity, his study remains available for reappropriation.[35] Without diminishing the profoundly wounding effects of Orientalist representation and split subjectivity, I want to suggest that creative and strategic practices of misrecognition might afford women the possibility to achieve critical distance *vis-à-vis* the scripted self. And it is in the photograph's effect of distance that one can challenge the image's totalizing power. I agree that a woman posing for a photograph

> does control the nature of her gaze—and that gaze can be read in different manners . . . The girl's look is not only an affirmation of her subjectivity, but also an interactive event: she responds to the men in front of her.[36]

Yet the female gaze cannot be construed as purely responsive. Women's looks are often active and resistant—gestures of creative rupture; refusals to identify according to aesthetic imperatives; and attempts to subversively deconstruct and re-vision the self. To be able to see this look requires new ways of reading photographs—methods that escape purely oppositional, specular, or voyeuristic frameworks.

Alloula's work silences one of the most pressing lines of inquiry with respect to colonial imagery: namely, how did Algerian women engage with the fantasies and stereotypes that they helped to create? Or more broadly, "what kinds of subjective negotiations must go on there,"[37] between image and identity? Whereas Alloula perceives photographed women as powerless players in an orgy of colonial exploitation, Leila Sebbar imagines chances for hidden transcripts of resistance in women's staging of these images. As women misrecognize their contradictory roles of exotic lure and colonized object, they construct creative and contesting relationships to the photographic gaze.

Unlike the charge of misrepresentation, an emphasis on fantasy and misrecognition acknowledges the represented subject not as frozen or fixed by the camera's eye, but as a playful and shifting composition able to scrutinize, to contest, and ultimately to position herself as "too much" for the lens. This concept of misrecognition also allows for the possibility that a photographer may be disarmed by unintended elements of his or her own images. As we shall see, the work of colonial photographer Marc Garanger powerfully attests to this potential.

III. MARC GARANGER: PHOTOGRAPHING "IDENTITY"

During the Algerian revolution, Algerians were required to carry identity cards that would render them "visible and 'legible'"[38] to French colonial authorities. Soldiers rounded up entire communities of Algerians, and forcibly unveiled Algerian women, to take portraits for their ID cards. Although the French policy of unveiling was nominally intended to render Algerian women identifiable to colonial authorities, it also blatantly violated local custom and religious practice.[39]

Symbolically, identity cards helped to formalize the French fantasy of empire, and functioned within a broader discursive network to deny citizenship rights to colonial Algerians who were not of French descent. As a final attempt at French signature or authorship within the receding colony, Algerian identity cards marked an effort to both defer and compensate for impending national loss on the dawn of a traumatic rupture within *l'empire français*.

Within this context, the Algerian identity portraits composed by French army photographer Marc Garanger can be read as ambivalent performances of national fantasy. Photography enlists Garanger and his subjects in arduous negotiations with popular narratives of racial, sexual, and national identity. In a sense, their fraught subject positions bear out the psychoanalytic understanding of subjectivity as an ongoing struggle to negotiate ambivalent identifications—or as the history of those shifting affiliations.[40] Yet the asymmetric positions occupied by Garanger and his photographic subjects highlight the need for a critical vocabulary with which to address a broad range of national traumatic experience. Colonial representation and identification, in particular, need to be rethought in terms not only of epistemic violence, but also of the negotiations between fantasy and identity that they may permit relative to visual stagings of race, gender, and ethnicity.

In the context of forced unveiling, Algerian women's identity card photographs can be understood as uniquely staged. Although they are military rather than studio photographs, they bear some resemblance to the posed images exhibited in Malek Alloula's study of French colonial postcards. Both sets of photographs suggest a latent history of colonialist intervention into the image or self-presentation of women, especially efforts to refashion or redress Algerian women's bodies according to divergent political objectives. Aesthetic investments in the fantasy of the unveiled Algerian woman—and in the veil itself as the primary trope for the "Oriental feminine"—haunt the surface of colonial postcards and identity photographs alike.

Marc Garanger, a French photographer born in Normandy, helped to orchestrate women's images during the revolution. Garanger served as a photographer in the French army from 1960–1962, where he was assigned to photograph Algerians for their *cartes d'identité*. Yet his photographic encounters ultimately converted Garanger to a staunch critic of colonial policy and practice. He especially opposed the campaigns of torture conducted by the French Organisation de l'Armée Sécrète (OAS), as well as the forced unveiling of Algerian women prior to their portraiture.

An evolving consciousness spurred Garanger to work feverishly during his two-year tenure to create a portfolio of images that would memorialize colonial injustice and record the agency of the colonized "look." Although photography constituted Garanger's official duty relative to the French nation, it also offered a tool with which to record his opposition to colonial practice:

> To express myself with my eye, I took up my camera. To shout my disagreement. For twenty-four months I never stopped, sure that one day I would be able to testify, to tell stories with these images . . . All of this I did with more force than the dominant military ideology of the era that surrounded me with hatred and violence. My spirit's revolt was proportionate to the horrors that I witnessed.[41]

Driven by this spirit of revolt, Garanger exploited photography's capacity to shape the national imaginary. He tried to create images that would question the authoring (and authorizing) functions of the colonial gaze. In light of Garanger's ambivalent position *vis-à-vis la mission civilatrice*, his work opens up multiple spaces for disidentification with the racial and sexual politics embedded in colonial imagery.

Garanger's photography foregrounds tense encounters between colonial desire and the disarming looks of photographed subjects. During his tour of duty in Algeria, Garanger was repeatedly struck by the violence in Algerian women's eyes as they met his camera's gaze. His work registers profound ambivalence about the objectifying function of colonial photography—ambivalence that frequently erupts on the surface of his images. Garanger's most provocative images record not only the violence of colonial representation, but also the destabilizing potential of Algerian women's looks back at the camera.

But how can we evaluate the disruptive potentials that, as I have argued, haunt the surface of Garanger's photographs? On one hand, the gazes of Garanger's photographed subjects can only be understood with respect to the plurality of gazes that intersect in each image.[42] For example, women's looks cannot be completely disentangled from the photographer's eye, or from the varied lenses of their viewers. Nor can women's looks be interpreted without reference to the social and historical context of Garanger's images. As I have noted, Garanger's photography records particularly loaded moments of colonial encounter—moments orchestrated to produce identity card portraits for purposes of colonial classification, control, and surveillance. In this sense, the sociohistorical backdrop in which Garanger's images are embedded must be understood as one of the many gazes that converge on their troubling surfaces. Collectively, these gazes are

> the source of many photographic contradictions, highlighting the gaps and multiple perspectives of each person involved in the complex scene. [They] are the root of much of the photograph's dynamism as a cultural object, and the place where the analyst can perhaps most productively begin to trace the photograph's connections to the wider social world of which it is a part.[43]

As a reader of Garanger's images, it is crucial to attend to the colonial and voyeuristic encounters that inevitably frame the photographic scene.

Yet as I have argued, it is equally important to note the resistant potentials of what Homi Bhabha has referred to as "the threatened return of the look."[44] Photographs often create unintended effects, including misrecognition on the part of the photographed subject, and viewer identification with the subject by way of eerily familiar details. These unauthorized readings flow from the internal ambivalence of representation, and radically unsettle the boundary between self and other that Orientalist imagery works to preserve.

The women photographed by Garanger unambiguously return his gaze. But exactly how and where do they look, and how do their looks gesture toward resistance? The "threatening" potentials of Garanger's images are most productively analyzed in relation to the photographed women's posture and gesture, facial expression, and gaze.

Before engaging in a closer reading of Garanger's photographs, it is worth noting the specific constraints of his medium. As a military identity card photographer, Garanger was permitted less creative license, on average, than conventional portraitists. Furthermore, since identity portraits had to conform to uniform specifications governing size, content, and angle, Garanger's aesthetic techniques do not necessarily correspond to personal sociopolitical objectives. As a result, the traditional photographic principles of design—including lighting, depth of field, point of view, composition, focus, graininess, exposure, and paper contrast—are not particularly instructive guidelines for a critique of his work.[45]

For example, Garanger was required by the French army to take individual rather than group portraits. As a result, his work specifically enlisted him in one-on-one encounters with Algerian women—meetings that, at first glance, would seem to yield purely exploitative exchanges between a male "colonizer" and his "native" female subjects. Yet the implications of such individual confrontations between photographer and photographed subject prove, on further analysis, to be highly ambiguous. On one hand, as Catherine Lutz and Jane Collins suggest, the photographic genre of the individual portrait is less likely to reproduce stereotypical or Orientalist constructions of "third world" or "native" subjects. On the other hand, the nature of Garanger's portraiture also required that it be somewhat forced or posed, which ordinarily affords the photographer a greater degree of control over the image.[46]

Similarly, the political objectives of the identity card—which served to classify and identify all Algerians to the French military—required Garanger's photographed subjects to directly face the camera in full frontal view. This political and aesthetic mandate significantly limited the potentials for how and where Algerian women might look *vis-à-vis* the photographer. Ordinarily, the photographed subject has several choices regarding how and where to look. He or she might choose to directly confront the camera; to look at something else within the photographic frame; to look off into the distance; or not to look at anything at all—perhaps even to close his or her eyes. For Garanger's subjects, however, these fields of vision were restricted. Because their portraits had to be clearly recognizable to colonial authorities, women were obliged to meet the camera's eye.

With these constraints in mind, I want to briefly consider some of the ways in which Algerian women attempted to transform the photographic space of Garanger's images from within. As described above, these women were required to confront the camera in full frontal posture for purposes of identification. Yet many of them managed to customize this posture, especially by way of hand positioning and gestures. For example, some women use their hands to draw their clothing more closely or tightly toward them in a self-protective gesture. Others position their arms either on or just below their chests, with tightly closed fists aimed at the camera. Several of Garanger's subjects conceal their arms beneath their veils, whereas one woman drapes her arm across her chest and knees in a posture that seems to signal audacity and defiance.

The women photographed by Garanger most strikingly communicate resistance with their eyes and facial expressions. As one might expect, none of these women opt to smile for the camera. This is important to note since, as Lutz and Collins point out with respect to Western images of non-Western people, the smile typically serves a "mitigating" function to mute the potentially disruptive or confrontational role of the "other's" return gaze.[47] Instead of smiling to efface or palliate the asymmetrical power relations between colonizer and colonized captured in these photographs, Algerian women confront Garanger's camera with lips tightly pursed, their mouths conveying resolve and a preference for confrontation. Most women dramatically scowl or frown at the camera.

The women in Garanger's images also communicate an explosive mix of indifference, curiosity, indictment, and hostility with their eyes. Some women gaze directly at the camera with fully opened eyes in a spirit of challenge, inquisition, and confrontation. Others pointedly look downward at the camera lens to convey disdain for the colonial photographic enterprise. Still other women glare sidewise at the camera in gestures of disgust and dismissal, or concentrate their stares slightly upward to escape the photographer's gaze—and the confines of the photographic frame—altogether. One woman narrows her eyes and furrows her brow accusingly at the camera, whereas another lowers her eyelids to express resolution, determination, and a desire for confrontation.

Women's looks communicate an undeniably aggressive and hostile presence throughout Garanger's work. They especially destabilize the intended colonial position of mastery and domination *vis-à-vis* the image. Consequently, it is important to recall that although women's looks "may be difficult to discern [amidst] the traffic of the more privileged gazes of image-producers and consumers, stories of contestable power are told there nonetheless."[48] The defiant postures and expressions that haunt Granger's imagery locate possibilities for rupture within the very processes of photographic composition and interpretation.

After fulfilling his military duty, Garanger sought to highlight these scenes of resistance to the colonial gaze by publicly displaying his work in explicitly anticolonial settings. Beginning in 1961, one year before the war's end, Garanger organized a series of photographic exhibits in France to spark public debate about French military practices in Algeria. He also published photo-essays to raise awareness regarding the brutalities of colonial occupation, and to memorialize Algeria within the French national imaginary. By pursuing these venues, Garanger hoped to shatter French silence regarding the Algerian revolution.

Yet Garanger also sought to challenge the presumed "mastery" of the colonial gaze. In the introduction to his published collection of identity card portraits entitled *Femmes algériennes 1960*, Garanger recalls that while photographing Algerian women, he was repeatedly "hit by their look at pointblank range."[49] As he elaborates in a subsequent publication:

> The gaze is a means of communication and knowledge, and I don't think that the people who I photographed had any illusions about that. Women's violent protestation of colonial aggression [especially forced unveiling and portraiture] is visible in every one of their gazes. *It is this gaze to which I want to bear witness*.[50]

During one of his identity card expositions at a French art gallery, Garanger was startled by the reaction of a group of young Algerian girls viewing the exhibit with their mothers, survivors of the revolution. He notes that the women's gazes seemed to "cross" or intersect at the surface of his images,[51] serving like Barthes' *punctum* to disrupt photographic composition.

I want to explore the productive capacity of these crossed glances, as contentious meetings between women's looks and the photographic image. What becomes possible when women critically engage with their images—especially when their looks collide with colonial fantasies? How do these moments of disidentification resist absorption into the specular economy of masculinist nationalist, and Orientalist, vision? How do women's looks destabilize photographic composition, and challenge binary constructions of creation and consumption? And how does Leila Sebbar creatively mobilize this gap between the intended photographic gaze and the resistant look throughout her work?

Because he pictorially foregrounds and retrospectively attends to the critical significance of women's defiant looks, Garanger might be said to resist a male-centered, voyeuristic gaze. Literary critic Winifred Woodhull subscribes to this view of Garanger's work by reading his imagery as a record of women's contempt and defiance rather than passive subordination.[52] Conversely, by virtue of Garanger's role in the French army, his images might be considered to perpetuate colonial exploitation. Cultural theorist Kaja Silverman adopts the latter premise when analyzing Garanger's photographs.[53] For Silverman, Garanger's photography is enabled and circumscribed by the violence of forced unveiling, coupled with Algerian women's "horror of being photographed for the first time."[54] Emphasizing the exploitative origins of colonial photography, Silverman understands Garanger's identity portraits to exist on a continuum with Orientalist imagery of the sort analyzed by Alloula.

For Silverman, both forms of colonial photography help to construct sexual and cultural otherness, and to promote social hierarchy. She approaches the Orientalist trope of woman-as-spectacle as always "complicated by other kinds of culturally constituted differences," especially race.[55]

Yet Silverman fails to acknowledge the ambivalence of Garanger's self-described position as both a critic and executor of the material practices of colonization. Clearly, Garanger's attentiveness to moments of tension and contradiction within the process of colonial image-making allows for feminist recuperation of his images, however conditional. Sebbar's decision to write the textual accompaniment to *Femmes des Hauts-Plateaux* attests to this potential, as does her creative engagement with Garanger's photography in *Sherazade*.

In their respective works, Garanger and Alloula present opposing views of Algerian women as either passive icons or critical agents of photographic representation. Whereas Alloula "reads" Algerian women's images in terms of impotence and subjugation, Garanger understands the Algerian women that he photographed as critical agents of photographic representation. From his perspective, their looks express a scathing critique of colonialism and, especially, an astute awareness of the role played by colonial representation in political conquest and the transmission of fantasy.[56]

The conflicting viewpoints of Garanger and Alloula partly stem from their opposing status as members, respectively, of the French empire and the Algerian resistance. They provide a compelling backdrop against which to read women's own formulations of identity *vis-à-vis* the photographic image, especially because it was precisely in the troubled interstices between Algerian nationalism and French colonialism that Algerian women were forced to carve out their identities during the anticolonial revolution. The burden of women's double marginalization relative to these discourses is perhaps most apparent in the battle of the veil, but it also emerged in relation to the sexual division of labor and campaigns of rape during the revolution. The divided loyalties and ambivalent identifications necessitated by the competing ideologies of nationalism and colonialism resurface today as contemporary Algerian women writers attempt to negotiate the images of "Algerian womanhood" that found nationalist and Orientalist symbolism.[57]

To choose between the models of female submission and agency offered by Alloula and Garanger is not the intent of my analysis. Indeed, this is exactly the kind of "choice" that Sebbar cautions against and, ultimately, presents as impossible in her novel *Sherazade*. For Sherazade, Sebbar's protagonist, the image is most productively explored as a fantasy that encapsulates both the seeds and limits of subjugation and contestation. As a result, Sherazade's trafficking between fantasy and identity, which plays out along a continuum of complicity and resistance, proves an endlessly ambivalent enterprise.

III. UNMAPPING OWNERSHIP, IDENTITY, AND THE *CARTE D'IDENTITÉ* IN *SHERAZADE*

> I don't think that Algerian women ever interiorized the image offered by the colonizers. I, an Algerian-born, have *never* met an Algerian woman who did not resist the use or appropriation.
>
> —Hélène Cixous, unpublished notes, December 1996

> To create an image, do you have to destroy madly?
>
> —Leila Sebbar, *Le fou de Sherazade*

Leila Sebbar provocatively intervenes in the debates about ownership and agency that simultaneously haunt theoretical formulations of the subject and object of representation; the legal and colonial histories of photography; and the relentless mappings of the national identity card. By constantly reproducing and reassessing Orientalist images throughout her work, Sebbar frustrates the visual economies of agency and submission that appear to "fix" the identities of artist, subject, and viewer in an unwilling embrace with the violence of colonial imagery. Not only do Sebbar's protagonists radically interrogate the mise-en-scène of representation; they actively participate in the violence of image-creation.

Born to a French mother and Algerian father, Sebbar inhabits the interstices between French and Algerian national identity. Although she does not precisely fit the definition of a Beur, or a second-generation Maghrebian immigrant living in France, her work shares the primary preoccupations of Beur literature including race, sexuality, multiculturalism, nationality, immigration, and diaspora. A prolific writer, Sebbar began to explore the possibilities of semiautobiographical fiction in the 1980s. Her efforts culminated in a trilogy of novels chronicling the urban exploits of a female Beur protagonist named Sherazade. Sebbar's trilogy is composed of the following three volumes: *Sherazade: 17 ans, brune, frisée, les yeux verts* (1982), *Les carnets de Sherazade* (1985), and *Le fou de Sherazade* (1991).

Sherazade (Missing, aged 17, dark curly hair, green eyes), the first volume of Sebbar's *Sherazade* trilogy, constitutes a prolonged attempt to unmap the symbolic and colonial politics of the identity card.[58] We first meet Sherazade after she has fled her family's home in the HLM, or suburban housing projects, in search of a better life in Paris. A teenager with scarce financial resources, Sherazade shares a squatter's apartment with an eclectic group of Beurs and post-1968 leftists. Lively, conversational, and irreverent in tone, the novel describes Sherazade's adventures as she roams the Parisian streets with her newfound friends. Her nomadic wanderings spark constant confrontations between "high" and "low"—which roughly correspond to French and Algerian—cultures. Endless warring between Sherazade's two main cultural spheres of influence fosters a somewhat romantic longing to return to native origins—a desire that ultimately proves impossible to sustain or fulfill throughout Sebbar's trilogy.

Sherazade is consumed with the relationship between image and identity, especially as it is resolved in official documents like the identity card and the missing person report. Leitmotifs throughout the novel include the proper name, map, and photograph. To highlight the national identity card's primary function of mapping the coordinates of name and place, Sebbar names her chapters after people or geographic places. Yet despite the illusion of clear identification and cartographic precision, *Sherazade*'s chapter titles and content do not always correlate or help to orient the reader.

Proper names are at issue in *Sherazade* from the title page forward. Although the protagonist's name, Sherazade, evokes a character from the Arabic narrative *The Thousand and One Nights*, this evocation is partial and flawed. Rather than a double or mirror image of this character, Sherazade remains a distant echo. Crucially missing from Sherazade's name is the extra syllable, "*her*," that would signal a perfect correspondence between her and the fabled Sheherazade.[59] In oral English, the omitted syllable is doubly evocative of "*her*," the missing woman. This elided syllable—or unresolved reference to Sheherazade—functions as a phantom limb of sorts, suggesting mispronunciation, a missing cultural narrative, and the peculiar loss sustained by any act of translation.

In a similar case of foiled identity or nominal disjunction within the text, Sebbar gives the name "France" to a friend of Sherazade who is openly critical of French national policy, and who instead adopts an Afrocentric feminist perspective. France's self-appointed nom de plume is Zingha, after the seventeenth-century warrior and queen of Angola. Interestingly enough, when white acquaintances interrogate her as to the origins of the name Zingha, France relays Zingha's legend without revealing any personal details about herself (*Sherazade*: 129).

Sherazade and her friends roam the streets of Paris in search of any mention of, or link to, Algerian history. Yet they constantly fall short of this goal. On one hand, their wanderings envelop them in a flurry of images endemic to French society. These representations span the gamut from "high art" (the tableaux of Fromentin, Matisse, and Delacroix; classical opera; the Nouvelle Vague cinema of Jean-Luc Godard), to "low art" (Western cultural icons including Coke, comics, graffiti, and the Walkman). On the other hand, Sherazade and her pals encounter scant references to the Algerian revolution. Sherazade's inability to access Algerian history is symbolized by French library bookshelves that are perpetually understocked with Algerian texts. Sherazade helps to fill these shelves—and the epistemological lacuna they represent—by filing requests with a local librarian sympathetic to her plight.

By collecting scraps of Algerian culture and history from the subaltern sources of oral culture and public graffiti, Sherazade attempts to counter the silence that obscures Algeria from French historical record and collective memory. When she encounters Beur-authored graffiti on her subway sojourns throughout Paris, Sherazade obsessively transcribes their Arabic characters onto the pages of a reserved notebook as if they were cultural artifacts. The cover of this notebook is decorated with Chinese calligraphy, thus serving as a third level of cultural overlay within the text. Sherazade also gleans fragments of cultural and historical knowledge from her Algerian grandfather, and from other Algerian immigrants whom she occasionally meets on the streets of Paris.

Sherazade's quest to learn about Algerian history is shared by her friend Julien. Another Beur, or second-generation Algerian immigrant living in France, Julien spent a year in Aix-en-Provence conducting research at Le Centre des Archives d'Outre-mer (CAOM). Renowned for its French colonial, especially Algerian, holdings, the CAOM also houses an impressive iconography section of maps, odalisque postcards, and colonial photographs. Despite his opportunity to do archival research on colonial history, Julien hungers to learn more about his Algerian roots and their resurfacing in Orientalist art.

Sherazade and her friends suffer not from national trauma per se, but from their inability to properly mourn and memorialize Algeria's traumatic past. Denied access to the past, Sherazade is both limited to, and freed by, her imagination. She must invent the community of Algeria and its implications for her identity.

Along with historical absence, the loss of identity—especially the proper name—remains at stake throughout *Sherazade*. Protagonists attempt to overcome this loss by piecing together shards of information in a multimedia pastiche or assemblage. Sherazade's friends and family incessantly scan the personal ads of local newspapers (*Sherazade*: 2, 55, 71, 272) for clues to her whereabouts. Her sister broadcasts pleas for information on local Parisian radio stations, and her father conquers his fear of racist police practices in order to file a missing person report for Sherazade. Ironically, the identity photo that he affixes to his official report is the product of Sherazade's laughter-filled rendezvous at a local Photomaton booth.

All of *Sherazade*'s main characters but one, Julien Desrosiers, remain surname-less throughout the novel (*Sherazade*: 118, 242). Sherazade herself assumes two pseudonyms (noms de plume or noms de guerre) depending on context. While awaiting the arrival of forged identity papers that will identify her as "Rosa," she refers to herself as "Sherazade." Yet she also adopts the name "Camille" in the company of unscrupulous men. She explains that her name "depends [on] who I'm with" (*Sherazade*: 193).

Sherazade's playful deployment of pseudonyms highlights the protean and fluid potentials of transnational identity. Yet it also calls attention to the adaptability necessitated by a society founded on panopticism.[60] Sherazade lives out her identity under the watchful eyes of the police and immigration officials, and in relation to surveillance as both a limit and condition of possibility (*Sherazade*: 192). By creatively violating the sanctity of the proper name, Sherazade resists the discursive imperatives of the identity card and the national belonging that it purports to represent. Approaching the self as a playground of perpetual transformation, she fashions a fluid sense of identity that, although it does not completely evade surveillance, routinely finds loopholes in the tightly woven fabric of state regulation.[61]

The first installment of Sebbar's *Sherazade* trilogy especially brings to life the "fierce looks" evoked by Marc Garanger's photo-essays. *Sherazade* traces historical loss, and anxieties about identity, as they impact personal efforts to subvert Orientalist imagery. Hungry to explore the national, sexual, and ethnic politics that coalesce in the identity portrait, the novel constitutes a literal and figurative attempt to file a missing persons report of sorts.

By staging feminist interventions into Orientalist visual culture, Sebbar offers an ambivalent meditation on the role that fantasy might play to "unsuture" the relations between image and identity.[62] In the following discussion I will explore the varied subject positions engineered by Sherazade *vis-à-vis* Garanger's identity card photographs in order to show how *Sherazade* uses colonial imagery as a point of departure to misrecognize sexual, racial, and cultural identities.

IV. READING GARANGER'S PHOTOGRAPHS

In her introduction to a collection of Marc Garanger's photography, Leila Sebbar describes Garanger as "a young French soldier, a man, a foreigner, who wanted to preserve the memory of years of violence in the gazes and gestures of women of the Hauts-Plateaux of Algeria."[63] Sebbar imagines the defiant voices that might have accompanied women's "pointblank" looks at Garanger:

> They say *no*, they don't want to be regarded as primitive in their traditional African dress. No, they refuse here . . .[64]

She suggests that Algerian women refuse identification by either targeting or withholding their gaze from the soldier-photographer who attempts to fix their images.

During the Algerian revolution, sexual and colonial aggression against women converged in campaigns of rape by French colonial and Algerian nationalist men. Sebbar discusses wartime rape as a strategy of sexual violation and genealogical deprivation:

> It's not enough to destroy the body; houses must be beaten to their very foundations until life's site of production is destroyed. To rape women is precisely that kind of destruction: it is to insinuate the enemy in the most profound place of the female body. To destroy forever the possibilities of *jouissance* and motherhood, to prevent descent, to sever filiation.[65]

By emphasizing rape as a genocidal tool, Sebbar conceives of feminist resistance not only in aesthetic terms—as hostile looks that deflect colonial violence—but also as integral to national political survival. In effect, she understands the French colonial mission as an effort to thwart Algerian cultural transmission:

> Transmission is impossible. Who are the Ancestors? Who will be the descendants? Although deprived of genealogy, women are rediscovering fragments of memory in everyday objects and domestic rituals.[66]

Although women are similarly evoked as the "transmitters of culture" in masculinist nationalist discourse,[67] Sebbar works this affiliation to slightly different ends. While she references a nationalist rhetoric of lost origins, she also emphasizes the provisional status of national, ethnic, and sexual identities. For Sebbar, resistance is possible in the gap between women's looks and coercive identifications—a space born of memory, critique, and hope.

For Sebbar, identity is at once indebted to, at war with, and inextricable from the image. To navigate the charged intersections between image and identity, Sebbar investigates the strategic possibilities of "disidentification," which is not reducible to a desire to reject representation. Instead, it is a "strategy that works on and against dominant ideology"[68]—one that involves at least partial incorporation of, and negotiation with, dominant fictions. Sebbar challenges facile notions of identity politics by suggesting that the self is always infused with the potential for other identifications. Her *Sherazade* trilogy bears out Diana Fuss' claim that "even our most impassioned identifications may incorporate nonidentity, and our most fervent disidentifications may already harbor the very identity that they seek to resist."[69] Sherazade's self-fashioning involves multiple processes of identifying with and against.[70]

By unmapping colonial projects of identification, Sherazade echoes Sebbar's own refusal to identify with exclusionary categories of racial or national affiliation. As the child of a French mother and Algerian father, Sebbar locates herself at a peculiar "crossing" that defies categorization. As she explains in a letter to a friend:

> I am neither a Maghrebian writing in French nor a Frenchwoman with French roots . . . If I talk about exile, I am also referring to cultural crossings. It's at these points of junction or disjunction where I live and write, and contest simplistic notions of identity.[71]

Highlighting the various crossings at play in her genealogy—"*mon histoire de croisée*"—Sebbar rejects exclusionary constructions of French or Maghrebian identity, much like her protagonist Sherazade. She formulates instead an intersectional model of identity, one that takes into account the nuances of geography, language, and history to forge a feminist politics of location. Sebbar conceives of identity as, above all, a contested and negotiable territory of intersection, fantasy, selective affiliation, and disjunction.

Most strikingly, Sebbar's literature amplifies the violence and productivity of Algerian women's crossed glances. In an exemplary passage within *Sherazade*, the protagonist fortuitously discovers the wartime photography of Marc Garanger. As Sherazade leafs through a coffee-table copy of Garanger's *Femmes algériennes 1960*, her sentiments recall Sebbar's photographic commentary accompanying the text:

> These Algerian women all faced the lens [*l'objectif-mitrailleur*] as if they were facing a machine-gun, with the same intense, savage look—a fierceness that the image could only record without ever mastering or dominating. (*Sherazade*: 237–38)

Like Sebbar, Sherazade emphasizes the resistant potentials of the female gaze *vis-à-vis* Garanger's imagery.

Interestingly enough, Sherazade's encounter with these images immediately follows an experience of seeing herself on screen for the first time. A few minutes prior to her photographic discovery, Julien's friend, a film director, had heralded Sherazade as the perfect girl to play the lead role of Zina in his upcoming film:

> That's her! That's Zina! I've been on the lookout for ages, I've had the idea of a girl like this. I [wanted] to find the girl who got away from all of the stereotypes . . . And then Julien showed me some photos. I don't trust photos, unless I've taken them myself. But there you are, I can see with my own eyes, Sherazade in person . . . Zina. (*Sherazade*: 233–34)

Sherazade is taken aback by the mixture of enthusiasm, fantasy, and projection with which Julien's friend greets her. After shooting a few scenes for his film, she reviews a videotape of her performance in a state of detachment:

> Sherazade could see and hear herself for the first time on a screen. It was curious, as if it didn't concern her. The girl she was seeing wasn't her. (*Sherazade*: 237)

By the tape's end, Sherazade remains noncommittal and unconvinced about her identity *vis-à-vis* the fictional Zina.

In the wake of her performance as Zina and the feelings of alienation or misrecognition that it occasions, Sherazade catches sight of Garanger's photographic collection. She views his identity card photographs with a mixture of anger, sadness, resistance, and solidarity. As she turns the pages of the book, tears stream down her face: she is powerfully moved by the images, and seems to identify with the plight of their female subjects. The narrator describes Sherazade as "weeping like one who has taken leave of her senses—softly, silently, ceaselessly" (*Sherazade*: 238). The photographs awaken in Sherazade an unexpectedly profound mix of estrangement, loss, and connection. Through her tears, she notes that the photographed women "all spoke the same language, her mother's tongue" (*Sherazade*: 238).

Leafing through Garanger's wartime identity portraits, Sherazade employs a Barthesian "remembering look"[72] that puts each image in contact with the historical past. For Sherazade, Garanger's photography triggers a painful act of re-membering: "a putting together of the dismembered past to make sense of the trauma of the present."[73] Born after the revolution, Sherazade did not witness firsthand the ravages of war and colonization. Instead, a persistent inability to access the past traumatizes her life as a Maghrebian immigrant in France, and precludes successful mourning. Sherazade's ability to mourn her lost homeland is partially restored by Garanger's photographs. Because they equip Sherazade with a supplemental shortcut to the past, they allow her to temporarily mourn her (lack of) Algeria.

Given its melancholic undertones and timing immediately following her alienating cinematic debut, Sherazade's perusal of Garanger's photographs would seem to trigger a staunch rejection of fantasy.[74] Perhaps Sherazade's encounter with these images will preface a realist turn to the restorative potentials of the photograph as "certificate of presence"? After all, the photographed women refuse to comply with colonial and Orientalist fantasies, and Sherazade is openly moved by their defiance. Her connection with Garanger's photographs seems to reveal, at least in part, a longing to dispense with the imagined communities and phantasmic identities that she has been forced to construct, in order to resurrect the "real" Algerian people and nation.

Yet Sherazade's rejection of fantasy proves as fleeting and unstable as her geographic coordinates within Paris. Elsewhere in the novel, she strategically indulges Orientalist stereotypes to highlight the potential for entrapment and disjunction that coheres in any effort to "fix" image, identity, and identification. Although Sherazade's resistant practices repeatedly derail the creation of fantasy-based photographs within the text, they also enlist her in highly stereotypical, albeit ironic, performances of the very same brand of Orientalist fantasy. As a result, Sherazade's opposing tactics—on one hand, to frustrate or deny the production of fantasy-based images, and on the other, to playfully embody Orientalist fantasies of identity—demonstrate the complexity, polyvalence and mutability of her negotiations between image and identity.

Ultimately, Sherazade's reaction to Garanger's photography moves beyond a tearful rejection of fantasy. Sherazade confronts these images as, above all, homeless—"melancholic objects"[75] that fail to resurrect the Real precisely because they can "never fully supplant the lack of history."[76] Most importantly, Sherazade does not read Algerian women's images as symptomatic of absolute domination. Instead, she apprehends "the severity and violence of people who submit to arbitrary treatment, knowing they will find the inner strength to resist" (*Sherazade*: 237). While viewing Garanger's photography, Sherazade compounds the photographic point of view in order to envision the plural positionings, relationships, and incongruities that converge in the identity photograph.

Because Sherazade's look promotes dispersal and "preserves and intensifies the violence"[77] of relations between self and world, it functions as glance rather than gaze. Acting as saboteur or trickster, Sherazade's glance conveys "unofficial messages of hostility, collusion, rebellion, and lust. Against the Gaze, [it] proposes the body and desire."[78] Throughout the novel, she deploys this subversive glance to disidentify with composed or intended images. Ultimately, Sherazade's glance upon images of women reinforces the violent looks of the women photographed in *Femmes algériennes 1960*.

Reframing Garanger's photographs from a postcolonial feminist perspective, Sherazade identifies with their female subjects not as a fellow victim, but as a comrade-in-arms. She decenters male authorship by highlighting the critical distance between women's looks (or glances) and the camera's gaze. Just as strikingly, she counters the seemingly fixed photographic image with an understanding of identity as precarious and unstable. In this sense, Sherazade reconfigures the identity card photograph as a work of art rather than a certificate of presence or an immutable mapping of national belonging. She also resists the presumed passivity of image consumption by using her own look to destabilize relations between image and identity.

Sherazade situates the identity card at the crossroads of sexual, class, racial, national, and cultural politics. By displacing the voyeuristic gaze, Sherazade imaginatively dislodges a coercive network of names, faces, and places. Her alternate framing of Garanger's photography allows for the possibility of other desires and spectators to emerge *vis-à-vis* the image—a possibility that, as bell hooks points out, is often foreclosed:

> When I asked a black woman in her twenties, an obsessive moviegoer, why she thought we had not written about black female spectatorship, she commented: "We are afraid to talk about ourselves as spectators because we have been so abused by 'the gaze.'"[79]

Sherazade's desire to move beyond the wounding potentials of the gaze is evident in her orchestration of the look as a tool for both aesthetic and political transformation. Like Sebbar, Sherazade imagines the unruly look not in the binary terms of subject and object, but as the basis for a politics of desire that might disrupt hierarchical relations between colonizer and colonized, self and other. Rather than assimilation, nostalgia, or identification, women's looks in *Sherazade* provoke misrecognition. Sherazade's reception of—and receptivity to—Algerian women's contumacious looks betrays a creative commitment to feminist confrontation and empowerment.

This explains why, immediately following Sherazade's tentative agreement to play the fantasy role of Zina in Julien's screenplay—"gang leader, rebel, poet, adept with a knife, fearless, unruly, as illusive and frightening as a war leader" (*Sherazade*: 236)—she eagerly enlists in another war of sorts with the colonial gaze and image. Her gesture can be understood as an expression of solidarity with the unruly subjects of Garanger's work, and as an attempt to disorient the hegemonic constellations of name, face, and place at stake in national identity photographs.

It is precisely at the moment of her encounter with Garanger's photography that Sherazade's look becomes "productive." The "productive look"

> necessitates the struggle, first, to recognize our involuntary acts of incorporation and repudiation of the dominant aspects of visual culture; and then, to see *differently*.[80]

Sherazade's introduction to Garanger's portraiture marks the moment at which her remembering gaze—or her gaze upon Algeria's traumatic, colonized past—becomes both disjunctive and productive. Her look does not simply return or reverse the gaze, but displaces conventional ways of seeing. In the space of parallax between look and gaze, Sebbar elaborates an iconography of sexual and racial misrecognition premised on "productive looking."

The "productive look" creates "opportunities for re-cognition," and offers her "something else to be" *vis-á-vis* the colonial image.[81] As Silverman suggests, "the look is not truly 'productive' until it effects one final displacement: the displacement of the ego. It does not fully triumph over the forces that constrain it to see in predetermined ways until its appetite for alterity prevails over sameness and self-sameness."[82] Sherazade's look at Garanger's imagery can be seen in this light—as an opening up of the consciousness to otherness, and as a realization of the mutually embedded nature of self and other, fantasy and identity.

V. RE-VISIONING THE PHOTO-SHOOT

Following her encounter with Garanger's photography, Sherazade parlays sexual fantasy and the loss of ethnic origins into a strategy of subversive engagement with the camera lens. Interestingly, it is in response to the fantasy of Orientalist images—rather than the presumed reality-effect of photographs—that Sherazade authors the creative performances that most compellingly define her identity. *Sherazade* mobilizes an insurgent female look that actively negotiates with Orientalist stereotypes. To highlight the productivity of this look, Sebbar repeatedly places her protagonist at the site or mise-en-scène of representation. She "complicates the projective thrust" of the camera gaze by explicitly positioning Sherazade in relation to both the technological apparatus of viewing (the camera), and the intersubjective relations that constitute her as a raced and gendered subject.[83] Sherazade's presence is most noteworthy at photo-shoots, where she stages provocative frame-ups between image and identity.

By inserting herself at the sites of representational inscription, such as the photo-shoot, Sherazade "violently decenters the photographic place of mastery."[84] Not content to define herself as the subject or object of representation, Sherazade's performances highlight the critical distance between the photographed *look* and the photographic *gaze*. As Kaja Silverman explains:

> The look has all along possessed the capacity to see otherwise from, and even in contradiction to, the gaze. The eye is always to some degree resistant to the discourses which seek to master and regulate it, and can dramatically oppose the representational logic and material practices [underlying particular visions].[85]

Yet it would be misleading to suggest that Sherazade's look is simply opposed to the camera's gaze in a sort of "reverse voyeurism";[86] rather, Sherazade seizes upon the incongruence between look and gaze. She acknowledges the inevitability of partial complicity with the other's gaze, but foregrounds the unruly potential of women's looks. By disturbing visual economies of projection, resemblance, and identification Sherazade invents feminist tactics of découpage and reassemblage.[87] Yet she does not reject her visual inheritance;[88] instead, she conceives of identity as a patchwork of interwoven representations, and locates power and knowledge in the very acts of reading and remaking images.

Sherazade's resistant look at the camera unsutures the bond between image and identity. It inaugurates an alternative economy of identity, wherein Sherazade mimetically embodies Orientalist fantasy to fulfill personal ambitions. Through her witty disruptions of several photo-shoots, for example, Sherazade recasts the voyeuristic gaze in terms of recalcitrant exhibitionism.[89] She does not oppose Orientalist imagery, but simultaneously integrates and destabilizes its embedded fantasies of racial and sexual identity. By so doing, Sherazade interweaves complicity and resistance, and dismembers the Oriental gaze.

In one particularly amusing scene of the novel, Sherazade disrupts a pornographic photographer's attempt to take her picture without permission. Playfully rewriting the photo-shoot, Sherazade stages this encounter as an occasion for both fantasy and violence. Unlike the passive icons or trophies on display in Alloula's text, Sherazade and her female accomplices reengineer the ideological and technological apparatuses of the photo-shoot. Rather than allow the licentious photographer to take unsolicited photographs of her and her friends, Sherazade grabs his camera and throws it so forcefully to the ground that it shatters on impact. By so doing, she denies the photographer's usual mastery of the gaze and damages his prized equipment.

Bereft of his camera, the famous photographer curses the agent of his symbolic castration: "I'll make her pay for it . . . And the little sluts can go back to their own country" (*Sherazade*: 134). He invokes sexual and racial epithets in a desperate bid to regain control over the scene of representation. By referring to Sherazade and her friends as sexually depraved immigrants who do not belong in "his" country, the photographer hopes to deauthorize their appropriation of the camera and, by extension, the entire representational economy that he had hoped to establish.

In another creative revamping of the photo-shoot, Sherazade contests masculinist nationalist symbolism during a discussion with two friends, Basile and Pierrot. Basile—a self-proclaimed feminist and revolutionary—extols female terrorist activities during anticolonial revolution. If women were admitted to positions of power and authority within nationalist movements, he contends, they would enjoy feminist as well as national liberation.

Rebutting Basile's position, Pierrot notes that female revolutionaries in Algeria and Vietnam experienced lingering sex inequality once national independence was won. To insert a differently feminist emphasis, Sherazade dramatically punctuates their talk with gunfire. She aims Basile's .38 at a faded poster of Che Guevara, hitting his left eye and shocking her friends. In this literal photo-shoot, Sherazade indirectly participates in her male friends' debate about the potential compatibility of feminist and national liberation by symbolically wounding the image/eye of a male revolutionary icon whose nationalist movement famously alienated women.[90]

In a third photo-shoot within the novel, Sherazade and her friends, Zouzou and France, foil a famous fashion photographer's plan to cast them as the stars in a jungle scene of exotic female sexuality that he has arranged in his studio. The photographer had pitched the image to them in the following terms:

> He had spoken in a roundabout way of daring pictures which were nice little earners, especially of three girls together—exotic beauties—It'd be a lark for them and they'd earn a pile for doing more or less nothing . . . They just had to listen to him, do what he asked. (*Sherazade*: 163)

Although Sherazade and her friends agree to pose for the photograph, they quickly devise a "collective countermeasure" (*Sherazade*: 163) with which to misrecognize the photographer's vision. When they arrive at the studio, Sherazade and her friends manage to secure a pay advance. Soon after, they change into their scantily clad alter egos of tigress, leopard, and zebra for the photo-shoot:

> Everything was set up. Heavy red and gold velvet curtains were everywhere, and Chinese screens. France was a tigress in a striped mini-skirt; Sherazade a zebra in hot pants; both wore black fishnet stockings and off-the-shoulder tops. Their hair was teased to look like a mane . . . Zouzou put on a leopard outfit consisting of split shorts and a top that barely covered her breasts. The photographer approached them and with a professional touch bared a breast here, a buttock there, and pulled Sherazade's *décolleté* a bit lower. (*Sherazade*: 164–65)

After surveying the women's bodies, the photographer decides that Sherazade and her friends should carry real, unloaded submachine guns to more closely approximate third world guerrillas. He also arranges for pseudolesbian encounters between the women, reminiscent of those staged on the colonial postcard:

> Here's what you do, first you kiss on the lips, then as soon as I say "Now" you change partners and lie down one on top of the other, it's quite simple. But see

> that your tits and bums are visible, you mustn't be prudish. If you were in a sauna or a Turkish bath since that's the thing now, you'd be starkers and it wouldn't worry you. (*Sherazade*: 166)

As the photographer waits for Sherazade and her friends to assume their positions, they whip out .38 pistols instead and point them ominously at the photographer, demanding that he let them go or face charges of inciting prostitution. Unable to discern that the guns are toy replicas, the photographer fearfully succumbs to their demands. In this scene, Sherazade and her friends "engage in an act of photographic self-creation by first positioning themselves as camera objects, and then deliberately transforming that stance into an effort to gain control through photographic re-framing and manipulation."[91] In this respect, they trick the photographer by "turning to their own advantage the very techniques he enjoins them to use."[92] At once the manipulators of the camera's eye and the agents of their own creation, Sherazade and her friends deploy French stereotypes of Arabic behavior—eroticism, trickery, and theft—to author subversive self-portraits in the flesh. Moreover, Sherazade subversively rewrites what feminist theorist Sharon Marcus has referred to as the "rape script" by disturbing masculinist expectations of female passivity, exoticism, and compliance.[93] Partially indulging the photographer's fantasies, they ultimately beat him at his own game, and create a legend of "antirape" resistance that lives on in their friends' oral culture long after the derailed photo-shoot (*Sherazade:* 167).

By inserting unruly subjects and confrontational glances into the photo-shoot, Sebbar challenges the erotic premise of the photographer's projective gaze. Sherazade and her friends stage the representational scene "otherwise" by interrupting its proposed grammar of race, sex, and class; and by simultaneously embodying and destabilizing the racial and sexual fantasies underlying the photographic gaze. By so doing, they pursue a creatively deconstructive politics of retouching and re-membering the scene of representation that I have alternately called disidentification or misrecognition. Their irreverent play inserts "the consciousness of a break," or a stammer, into the photographic scene.[94] It foils the intended message of the Orientalist image, and radically reconfigures racial and sexual economies of looking.

Sherazade's photographic play denies suture, which would seal the image and its referent in an embrace of mutual recognition. Instead, Sherazade "fissures the process of identification, defeats the closure of meaning, and opens up points of intrusion"[95] at the scene of photographic composition. Significantly, Sebbar evokes women's looks as catalysts for photographic decomposition. Recalling her description of the women in Garanger's photographs, Sebbar evokes women's "looks" as the driving force behind this scene of photographic decomposition: "Sherazade, Zouzou and France often heard people say of them, 'They've got the most incredible *look*'" (*Sherazade*: 163). Throughout *Sherazade*, women's looks testify to the complexities of the visual as a theatrical flurry of fantasy, assimilation, and creative self-fashioning.[96]

By lingering in the ambivalent space between complicity and resistance, viewer and viewed, Sherazade imagines an alternative iconography of sexual and racial disidentification. Her reading of Garanger's identity card photographs, as well as her playful restagings of the very scene of image-making, frame identity formation as a complicated and painful journey encompassing "fractures, splits, contradictions, and incomplete suturings."[97] In place of a passive model of femininity, Sherazade substitutes a feminist reader and "meaning-maker-contributor" able to invent new forms of subjectivity and pleasure relative to colonial imagery.[98] For Sherazade, the traffic between image and identity constitutes a "hot zone"[99] of ownership and dispossession, assimilation and misrecognition. Most at stake in this relationship are women's "productive looks," which enable them to forge alternative aesthetic and political possibilities.

Rather than neatly mapping the coordinates of name, face, and place à la the national identity card, Sebbar highlights the complexity and, finally, the impossibility of charting one's position *vis-à-vis* the image and its site of production. Ultimately, *Sherazade* records neither the "death of the author," as such, nor the birth of the sovereign subject. Instead, the novel both elicits and lingers in parallax, allowing Sherazade to "read" women's images with a creatively intersubjective model of authorship and appropriation. As she surveys Orientalist representations of women, Sherazade seems to ask of their subjects: "who are you?" and "who am I in relation to you?" In this sense, she richly exploits photography's potential to blur the lines between the subject and object of the gaze.

Sebbar's novel enacts a feminist politics of deterritorialization that both participates in and decomposes the violent subtexts of colonial history and Orientalist aesthetics. For Sherazade, "fantasy, melancholic incorporation, and creative disintegration are *constitutive* of, and fundamental to, the formation of any racialized body."[100] But *Sherazade* figures representation—especially images of the female body—as the site of inscription for sexual, national, and racial fantasies. Transnational feminist subjectivity is at once haunted by, enamored of, and at war with the image—especially its violations and fixations on the other, and its potentials for transgression.

By productively viewing or actively negotiating with inherited images, Sherazade constructs a sense of self that both assumes and subverts the other's gaze. For Sherazade, the mobile contours of the "I" come into play through projects of seeing, which encompass self and other, complicity and resistance. In this sense, *Sherazade* blurs binary visions of the subject and object of representation, and contributes to longstanding interdisciplinary debates about what it means to own or author an image.

Saber's violent manipulation of the gaze helps to produce a new eye—one that sees, for example, from the perspective of the torn aperture with which Marcel Duchamp stages his female nude series *Etant données* (1946–1966), or the kaleidoscopic lens through which contemporary American photographer Cindy Sherman ironically performs her "self." The disturbing glances that abound in *Sherazade* can be read as resistant efforts to jam the machinery of recognition, identification, and colonial representation. They also constitute efforts to recast women as historical agents, and as catalysts for destructively creative politics and poetics of disidentification. Sherazade bruises Oriental images and reworks them to disjunctive ends. By crafting productively feminist readings of the image, Sebbar approaches visual culture not as a static inheritance to be accepted or rejected, but as a difficult benefactor that requires constant acknowledgment and strategizing.

NOTES

1. "*Ecarts d'identité*" is a play on the French *carte d'identité* (ID card), by which I mean to evoke a distancing from, or unmapping of, fixed images of identity. Beur writers Azouz Begag and Abdellatif Chaouite have similarly evoked this concept in their book, *Ecarts d'identité* (Paris: Seuil, 1990). They define "*ecart d'identité*" as a misuse or movement away from identity, or, more particularly, as the difference in color between a green passport and a yellow ID card (10).

2. See Walter Benjamin, "The Work of Art in the Age of Mechanical Reproduction," in *Illuminations*, trans. Harry Zohn (New York: Schocken Books, 1968), 224.

3. *111 U.S. 53*, decided March 17, 1884.

4. Chela Sandoval coins this term in *Methodology of the Oppressed* (Minneapolis: University of Minnesota Press, 2000), 1.

5. Roland Barthes, "The Death of the Author," in *Image/Music/Text*, trans. Stephen Heath (New York: Hill and Wang, 1978).

6. See Michel Foucault, "What Is An Author?" in Paul Rabinow, ed., *The Foucault Reader* (New York: Pantheon Books, 1984), 101–20.

7. Benjamin 1968: 224–26.

8. See Silverman 1996: 136.

9. Marianne Hirsch, *Family Frames: Photography, Narrative, and Postmemory* (Cambridge: Harvard University Press, 1997), 215.

10. For more on the notion of stereotypes as melancholic racializations, see Anne Anlin Cheng, *The Melancholy of Race: Psychoanalysis, Assimilation, and Hidden Grief* (Oxford: Oxford University Press, 2001), 106.

11. Hirsch 1997: 213–14.

12. Ibid. 211.

13. Malek Alloula, *The Colonial Harem*, trans. Myrna and Wlad Godzich (Minneapolis: University of Minnesota Press, 1986).

14. Another key work in this field is Sarah Graham Brown, *Images of Women: The Portrayal of Women in Photography of the Middle East, 1860–1950* (New York: Columbia University Press, 1988).

15. Anne Maxwell, "'Native' Women and Tourism: A Contested Site of Orientalism," in *Third Text*, vol. 25 (London: Kala Press, 1993–1994), 22.

16. See Cynthia Enloe, *Bananas, Beaches & Bases: Making Feminist Sense of International Politics* (Los Angeles: University of California Press, 1989), 44.

17. John Berger, *Ways of Seeing* (London: Penguin Books, 1972). For Mulvey's theorization of the male spectator (or "woman as image, man as bearer of the look"), see Laura Mulvey, "Visual Pleasure and Narrative Cinema" in *Visual and Other Pleasures* (Bloomington: Indiana University Press, 1989).

18. I borrow this expression from Fatima Mernissi's memoir, *Dreams of Trespass* (Cambridge: Perseus Books, 1994).

19. Maxwell 1993–1994: 22.

20. Frantz Fanon, *A Dying Colonialism*, trans. Haakon Chevalier (New York: Grove Press, 1965), 35–68.

21. Assia Djebar, *Women of Algiers in Their Apartment*, trans. Marjolijn de Jager (Charlottesville: University Press of Virginia, 1992), 138.

22. In fact, Alloula and Djebar were married for several years.

23. For more on this see Mieke Bal, "The Politics of Citation," *Diacritics* (Spring 1991), 26–27. See also Mieke Bal, *Double Exposures: The Subject of Cultural Analysis* (New York: Routledge, 1996).

24. Brown 1988: 48.

25. Saloni Mathur, "Wanted Native Views: Collecting Colonial Postcards of India," in A. Burton, ed., *Gender, Sexuality, and Colonial Modernities* (London: Routledge, 1999), 95–115.

26. Mathur 1999: 115.

27. Enloe 1989: 44.

28. Taking up Eve Sedgwick's formulation of homosocial discourse, Mieke Bal makes this observation in *Diacritics* (1991).

29. Luce Irigaray, *This Sex Which Is Not One*, trans. Catherine Porter (Ithaca, NY: Cornell University Press, 1985), 157.

30. W. J. T. Mitchell, *Picture Theory* (Chicago: The University of Chicago Press, 1994), 307–11.

31. Rey Chow, *Writing Diaspora: Tactics of Intervention in Contemporary Cultural Studies* (Bloomington: Indiana University Press, 1993), 41.

32. See Maxwell 1993–1994: esp. 30.

33. Alloula 1986: 98, my emphasis.

34. Hélène Cixous, "Sorties: Out and Out: Attacks/ Ways Out/ Forays," in Cixous and Catherine Clement, *The Newly Born Woman*, trans. Betsy Wing (Minneapolis: University of Minnesota Press, 1986), 82. Originally published as *La Jeune Née* (Paris: Union Generale d'Editions, 1975).

35. See Ann Laura Stoler, *Race and the Education of Desire: Foucault's* History of Sexuality *and the Colonial Order of Things* (Durham, NC: Duke University Press, 1995), 175 fn. 40.

36. Bal 1991.

37. Cheng 2001: 230 n. 18.

38. Silverman 1996: 147.

39. For more on this see Frantz Fanon, "Algeria Unveiled," *A Dying Colonialism*, trans. Haakon Chevalier (New York: Grove Press, 1965).

40. For a succinct discussion of Freud's elaboration of subjectivity, for example, see Diana Fuss, *Identification Papers* (New York: Routledge, 1995), 34.

41. Marc Garanger, *La guerre d'Algérie vue par un appelé du contingent* (Paris: Seuil, 1984), 13, my translation.

42. For more on this, see Catherine Lutz and Jane Collins, *Reading National Geographic* (Chicago: University of Chicago Press, 1993), esp. ch. 7.

43. Lutz and Collins 1993: 216.

44. See Homi Bhabha, "The Other Question: Stereotype, Discrimination, and the Discourse of Colonialism," in Bhabha, ed., *The Location of Culture* (New York: Routledge, 1994).

45. For more on the principles of photographic design see Terry Barrett, *Criticizing Photographs: An Introduction to Understanding Images* (California: Mayfield Publishing Company, 2000).

46. For more on this, see Lutz and Collins 1993.

47. Lutz and Collins 1993: 198.

48. Ibid. 216.

49. Marc Garanger, *Femmes algériennes 1960* (Paris: Contrejour, 1982), 3, my translation.

50. Marc Garanger, *Femmes des Hauts-Plateaux: Algérie 1960* (Paris: La Boite à Documents, 1990), 7, all translations mine.

51. Ibid. 8.

52. Winifred Woodhull, *Transfigurations of the Maghreb* (Minneapolis: University of Minnesota Press, 1993), 43. I mean to evoke "voyeurism" here in its broad aesthetic sense, and also in light of its Freudian connotations as a psychological inclination to take a sadistic pleasure in exposing the "other." For more on this, see Kate Linker, "Representation and Sexuality," in Brian Wallis, ed., *Art After Modernism: Rethinking Representation* (New York: The New Museum of Contemporary Art, 1984).

53. Silverman analyzes the photographs by Garanger that are showcased in a film by Harun Farocki entitled *Images of the World and the Inscription of War* (1988).

54. Voice-over in Farocki's film. Cited by Kaja Silverman, *The Threshold of the Visible World* (New York: Routledge, 1996), 148.

55. Silverman 1996: 147.

56. As in most colonial endeavors, artists accompanied soldiers to Algiers on their *mission civilatrice*. See Deborah Cherry, *Beyond the Frame: Feminism and Visual Culture, Britain 1850-1900* (London: Routledge, 2000); Gerard-Georges Lemaires, *The Orient in Western Art*, trans. Harriet de Blanco (Cologne: Konemann, 2001), originally published as *L'univers des Orientalistes* (Paris: Edition Menges, 2000); and Assia Djebar, *L'amour, la fantasia* (Paris: Edition Jean-Claude Lattes, 1985, trans. 1993).

57. For more on the sexual politics of nationalism and colonialism, see Susan Pedersen, "National Bodies, Unspeakable Acts: The Sexual Politics of Colonial Policymaking," *Journal of Modern History*, 63, no. 4 (December 1991).

58. Leila Sebbar, *Sherazade (Missing: aged 17, dark curly hair, green eyes)*, trans. Dorothy Blair (London: Quartet Books, 1982).

59. It is worth noting here that—in a dramatic coupling of death and narration—the character of Sheherazade was forced to tell stories in order to save her life.

60. See Michel Foucault, *Discipline and Punish*, trans. Alan Sheridan (New York: Vintage Books, 1977).

61. My reading of Sebbar's attempts to escape the "identity check" differs slightly from that of Jared Hayes, who provocatively asserts that Sherazade "thwarts all attempts to control her identity." Hayes regards Sherazade as an "urban feminist guerrilla" who "queers the nation" by simultaneously resisting and opposing male heterosexual, ethnographic, and Oriental gazes. See Jared Hayes, "Escaping the Identity Police: Leila Sebbar," in *Queer Nations: Marginal Sexualities in the Maghreb* (Chicago: University of Chicago Press, 2000), 215–38.

62. For more on suturing, see Linker 1984.

63. Leila Sebbar in Marc Garanger, *Femmes des Hauts-Plateaux: Algérie 1960* (Paris: La Boite à Documents, 1990), back cover, all translations mine.

64. Sebbar in Garanger 1990: 34.

65. Ibid. 64.

66. Ibid. 70.

67. See for example Floya Anthias and Nira Yuval-Davis, *Woman-Nation-State* (London: Macmillan, 1989).

68. Michel Pêcheux, *Language, Semantics, and Ideology* (New York: St. Martin's Press, 1982).

69. Fuss 1995: 10.

70. For an overview of Sedgwick's analysis, see Jose Esteban Muñoz, *Disidentifications: Queers of Color and the Performance of Politics* (Minneapolis: University of Minnesota Press, 1999), 8.

71. Leila Sebbar and Nancy Huston, *Lettres parisiennes: Histoires d'exil* (Paris: Barrault, 1986), 133–34, my translation.

72. See Silverman 1996.

73. Homi Bhabha, "Foreword: Remembering Fanon," in Frantz Fanon, *Black Skin, White Masks* (London: Pluto Press, 1986), xxiii

74. For example, Winifred Woodhull and Anne Donadey have interpreted Sherazade's encounter with Garanger's photography as a rejection of, or turning away from, fantasy. See Donadey, *Recasting Postcolonialism* (Portsmouth, NH: Heinemann Press, 2001), 132; and Woodhull 1993: 121–22. Woodhull understands Sherazade not to share in the resistant look of the women in Garanger's photographs, but to tearfully identify with the critical documentation of their oppression and, as a result, to reject all forms of photographic fantasy. She approaches Sherazade's sense of divide between image and identity as less an effort to "denounce all representation as repressive than to signal the need to use representation to bring the history of colonialism into the present in critical and productive ways" (122). I agree with Woodhull's distinction here. However, I also view Sherazade's behavior as participating in the violently resistant "looks" of the women in *Femmes algériennes 1960*, all of which serve to misrecognize or disidentify with the composed image.

75. Susan Sontag develops this understanding of photographs as "melancholic objects" in *On Photography* (New York: Farrar, Straus, Giroux, 1977).

76. Cheng 2001: p.146.

77. Norman Bryson, *Vision and Painting: The Logic of the Gaze* (New Haven, CT: Yale University Press, 1983), 93.

78. Ibid. 94.

79. bell hooks, "The Oppositional Gaze: Black Female Spectators," in *Black Looks: Race and Representation* (Boston: South End Press, 1992), 126.

80. Silverman 1996: 184.

81. See Sandoval 2000: 35.

82. Silverman 1996: 183.

83. For more on this understanding of photography, see Amelia Jones, "Tracing the Subject with Cindy Sherman," in The Museum of Contemporary Art, *Cindy Sherman: Retrospective* (New York: Thames & Hudson, 1997), 47.

84. Silverman 1996: 127.

85. Ibid. 156.

86. Rafika Merini deploys this term in *Two Major Francophone Women Writers, Assia Djebar and Leila Sebbar* (New York: Peter Lang, 1999), 43.

87. I borrow this concept from Trinh T. Minh-Ha's film of the same name, *Reassemblage* (1982).

88. Denise Brahimi makes this observation in "Orientalisme et Conscience de soi," cited in Rafika Merini, *Two Major Francophone Women Writers, Assia Djebar and Leila Sebbar* (New York: Peter Lang, 1999), 49–50.

89. For more on the distinction between voyeurism and exhibitionism, and a summary of the notion of suturing, see Linker 1984. Sherazade disrupts the voyeuristic gaze in a literal sense, since she explicitly interrupts photo-shoots within the novel. Yet she also figuratively disrupts the voyeuristic gaze of theorists like Alloula, who underestimate women's resistant looks by reading the politics of women's representation as, first and foremost, a narrative of male sexual frustration and impotence.

90. It is worth noting here that Freudian psychoanalysis equates the act of blinding, or blindness more generally, with castration.

91. Hirsch 1997: 211.

92. Woodhull 1993: 119.

93. See Hayes 2000: 218–19. Sharon Marcus articulates her concept of the rape script in "Fighting Bodies, Fighting Words: A Theory and Politics of Rape Prevention," in Butler and Scott, eds., *Feminists Theorize the Political* (New York: Routledge, 1992).

94. Hirsch 1997: 214.

95. Linker 1984: 414.

96. Deborah Cherry similarly interprets the visual as an important arena of intervention and definition. See Cherry 2000: 7.

97. Hirsch 1997: 215.

98. Trinh T. Minh-Ha 1991: 19, 93.

99. With this term I mean to evoke ecological "hot zones": geographic regions that are home to a rich variety of species, yet whose species are at the same time at perpetual risk of endangerment or extinction.

100. Cheng 2001: 107.

Chapter Three

Misrecognizing the Family Album

Blood, Fantasy, and Nationality in the Works of Hélène Cixous and Theresa Hak Kyung Cha

> If we keep on speaking the same language, we're going to reproduce the same history.
>
> —Luce Irigaray, *This Sex Which Is Not One*

> Why resurrect it all now. History, the old wound. To name it now so as not to repeat history in oblivion. To extract each fragment by each fragment from the word from the image another word another image the reply that will not repeat history in oblivion.
>
> —Theresa Hak Kyung Cha, *Dictée*

> The pleasure of resemblance and repetition produces both psychic assurance and political fetishization. Representation reproduces the Other as the Same. Performance, insofar as it can be defined as representation without reproduction, can be seen as a model for another representational economy, one in which the reproduction of the Other as the Same is not assured.
>
> —Peggy Phelan, *Broken Symmetries*

I. INTRODUCTION: AUTOBIOGRAPHY AS BLINDNESS

In *First Days of the Year*, Hélène Cixous provocatively imagines autobiography as the "self-portrait of a blind woman."[1] What exactly does this mean, and how might a blind woman accomplish her self-portrait? Cixous often discusses her own farsightedness, which she associates with both blindness and prophetic vision. In a public lecture at Northwestern University entitled "Writing Blind,"[2] for example, Cixous explored the nonvisual, embodied potentials of writing. Her address conjured the image of a blind woman who engages in the art of self-portraiture by enlisting all of her senses in a creative pursuit that at once emerges from, yet exceeds the limits of, the body.

For Cixous, autobiography is above all an artistic pursuit: a bricolage of fantasy, imperfect memory, and the limits of self-knowledge. By evoking autobiography as a blind person's art, Cixous establishes self-representation as necessarily mediated by a partial lack of access to the self. Like the blind woman whose self-image is shaped partly through the other's gaze, Cixous anticipates the "I" as recognizable only in passages between self and other, intimacy and alienation.

This chapter considers the autobiographical practices of two Francophone women writers, Hélène Cixous and Theresa Hak Kyung Cha.[3] Both Cha and Cixous creatively rework autobiography—particularly the trope of the family album—by staging unexpected meetings between fantasy, identity, and nationality. Although they hail from distant geographic coordinates, both writers fundamentally challenge what it means to represent the self *vis-à-vis* the national family, collective memory, and transnational trauma. Most significantly, they envision home "not as a comfortable, stable, inherited, and familiar terrain, but instead as an imaginative, politically charged space [that necessitates] an analysis of social injustice, as well as a vision of radical transformation."[4]

By foregrounding their efforts to reimagine identity relative to the family album, I will ask how Cixous and Cha misrecognize traditional understandings of the nuclear and national family. Throughout my analysis, I hope to pose a series of questions: first, how might women's traumatic experience be differently conceived within the national imaginary? What are the limits of representation and recognition? And to what extent might the strategic use of fantasy and misrecognition allow for feminist reformulations of home and identity? I will devote most of my attention to Theresa Hak Kyung Cha, who deliberately frustrates our expectations of how fantasy, memory, and intimacy collide in artistic self-presentation. But I will open with Cixous' family album, which offers a compelling framework and point of departure for my analysis of Cha's creative orchestrations.

II. FANTASIZING NATIONALITY: HÉLÈNE CIXOUS' FAMILY ALBUM

> In my mother's room there are several photos of the author. The author is smiling broadly, baring all her teeth. I detest these photos. I am convinced they never look like me.
>
> —Hélène Cixous, *First Days of the Year*

> No imagination without memory; no memory without imagination.
>
> —Denis Diderot, *Elements de physiologie*

No document certifies our existence more intimately than a book of photographs. An invitation to indulge the past, the photo album welcomes us into "a network of looks that dictate feelings of recognition across miles and generations."[5] Family albums, in particular, are crafted to instill a sense of belonging, spur memory, and promote recognition, despite our changing lives and relationships. Indeed, it has been argued that the family as such exists only in and through the group photograph and family album, which "confer upon [the family] a coherence which it would otherwise lack."[6] Through its "family function," photographic practice immortalizes the high points of family life and imposes a fictional sense of unity.[7]

Putting together a photo album is a highly personal effort to come to terms with the past by memorializing the most significant people, occasions, and places in one's life. As the visual alphabets with which we tell stories about ourselves, photo albums entail loving efforts of commemoration. To arrange photographs in a cherished album is an act of hope for the future—an imagined future in which I expect to recognize meaningful faces and to reconnect with my past in all of its wonder, pain, and pleasure.

Designed to showcase the highlights of family life, family albums are ultimately exercises in selective memory and interpretation. Overflowing with images of happy occasions and extraordinary moments, family albums typically omit snapshots of misfortune, illness, failure, despair, or the myriad ordinary details that compose the fabric of *le quotidien*. From this perspective, the family album can be understood not as a record of the Real, but as a tome of fantasy and legend that permits, at best, only partial identification or recognition.

Acutely aware of the fictional potentials of photography and self-representation, Hélène Cixous pieces together a folkloric family album in *Rootprints,* her most explicitly autobiographical work to date.[8] In a chapter entitled "Albums and Legends," Cixous assembles what initially appears to be a standard family album by pairing childhood photographs with narrated memories of youth. Yet, while Cixous' album occasionally succeeds at memorializing genealogical detail, it more often confronts the past as a protean mosaic of loss, fantasy, conjecture, and omission. Although "Albums and Legends" delights in the nostalgic pleasures of recollection, it also ripples with the impossibility of locating a precise geographic home, or of tracing national belonging and familial identity to a singular origin.

For Cixous, autobiography is both a creative and physical emergence made possible through the act of writing. Cixous had written only a few autobiographical passages—notably in *Sorties*, *Les rêveries de la femme sauvage*, and *First Days of the Year*—before she officially broached the subject of identity in *Rookeries*. Yet life-writing is inseparable from her broader corpus, which distinctively blends poetry, theory, and personal reflection. In "Laughter of the Medusa," a manifesto widely regarded as a cornerstone of French feminist thought, Cixous contends that the very process of writing opens up to women the possibilities of political empowerment and self-invention, or *autopoeisis*.

Cixous' reference to *autopoeisis* draws upon the Greek notion of creating oneself as a work of art. Yet her appropriation of the term bears a distinctly feminist resonance. In *Sorties*, Cixous suggests that woman, or more broadly the feminine, has been conceived throughout Western history only in negative relation to the masculine. She cites a recurrent tendency in philosophical and psychoanalytic discourse to construe the feminine as dark, exotic, contagious, and material. By contrast, masculinity is associated with light, intellect, and transcendence. For Cixous, this binary construction of sexual difference demands feminist self-invention: it is not a luxury, but a matter of survival. Consequently, she approaches autobiography as not only a personal rendering of identity, but also as a subversive engagement with the founding images of sexual difference. She envisions herself as a mole—*topoi*, ground mole or land mine—capable of burrowing underground to creatively unsettle the sexual politics of representation.[9]

In "Laughter of the Medusa," Cixous discusses and deploys *écriture féminine*, a strategic writing practice designed to facilitate the expression of women's subjectivity and desire. For Cixous, *l'écriture féminine* makes it possible to represent what has been most repressed within Western culture: the female body and identity. Incorporating polyvalence, word play, metonymy, and tropes of embodiment, *écriture féminine* rejects binary thought to articulate a sexualized subject position that has heretofore remained overtheorized, underimagined, and radically unspeakable.

In a widely criticized passage of her essay, Cixous claims that authors of *écriture féminine* write in white ink, or mother's milk. Many feminist theorists have rejected this idea for its perceived essentialism or overreliance on biological metaphor. Yet Cixous finds a salient need to affirm the mother's bodily trace in a culture founded on the erasure of the maternal, and on the simultaneous devaluation and appropriation of female labor (especially symbolized by the womb) that gained momentum in the nineteenth century.[10] From Cixous' perspective, a masculinist desire to usurp female creation—accompanied by a privileging of the male-generated "seed," sperm, or idea—has haunted canonical literature ranging from Aristotle, Nietzsche, and Freud to medical pedagogy. As a counterpoint to the patriarchal imagination, Cixous believes that *écriture féminine* will empower women to reclaim their capacity for creation, authorship, and self-invention.

For Cixous, autobiography is as much a writing of the other as a narration of the self; self and other seductively fuse in her work. She abandons a rigid or specular model of identity to emphasize the plasticity and fluidity of subjectivity. Cixous' commitment to thinking about selves in the plural stems in part from her own experience of identity as patchwork—forged in the borderlands between warring cultures, nations, languages, and genders. Given the conflicting allegiances that shape Cixous' identity, she confronts autobiography as an ongoing process of conflict resolution and translation, and as an "infinite conversation"[11] between elements foreign and familiar.

Cixous most explicitly probes her roots in "Albums and Legends," where she crafts a seemingly conventional family album. Her album narrates a "double childhood" (*Rootprints*: 181) that was spent in Oran, Algeria, yet constantly visited by stories of faraway places, especially Europe. With the rise of Nazi Germany, her parents' Jewish family members were scattered across the globe. At the outbreak of WWII, Cixous' paternal relatives fled southwest from Hungary and Czechoslovakia to Spain, Morocco, and, eventually, Algeria. Her maternal relatives hailed from Osnabruck, Hanover, and later moved to Strasbourg in German Alsace. When France reclaimed the territories of Alsace and Lorraine from Germany in 1918, having lost them during the Franco-Prussian war of 1870–1871, Cixous' grandmother was able to obtain dual German-French citizenship. Like a talisman, her newly acquired French passport allowed her to flee Nazi Germany in 1938.

Building on their rich familial legacy of cross-cultural pollination, Cixous' parents spoke German at home during her childhood, despite their disparate geographic roots and permanent residence in Algeria. Growing up in this atmosphere of cultural *métissage*, Cixous identified as neither Algerian nor French. She imagined herself as a transcultural hybrid or outsider who did not easily fit into a particular national family, but rather existed in a space of political disaffiliation. As she explains in "Albums and Legends":

> The logic of nationality was accompanied by behaviors that have always been unbearable for me. The French nation was colonial. How could I be from a France that colonized an Algerian country when I knew that we ourselves, German Czechoslovak Hungarian Jews, were other Arabs? (*Rootprints*: 204)

Cixous' profound sense of unbelonging *vis-à-vis* the French colonial empire mingled with a sense of rootlessness occasioned by her father's early death, and by the anguishing demise of countless relatives in Nazi concentration camps. These childhood experiences of personal and transnational trauma sparked feelings of intense alienation coupled with a sophisticated sense of cosmopolitanism or "worldwide resonance" (*Rootprints*: 189). Cixous belonged nowhere, yet could go anywhere—home became an imaginative rather than a physical territory.

Nationality and nationalism remain highly suspect for the adult Cixous, who—after relocating from Oran to Paris at the age of eighteen—still claims neither French nor Algerian, but "literary nationality" (*Rootprints*: 204). Her suspicion undoubtedly stems from the frequent channeling of nationalist sentiment into xenophobic political and military projects, as in Nazi Germany and Vichy France in Algeria. Perhaps more surprisingly, Cixous also explicitly links her identification as the citizen of an "imagined community"[12] to her experiences of sexism in France. When she first arrived in Paris in 1955, Cixous was shocked to find that femininity was commonly considered a source of shame and social stigma. Although she encountered less anti-Semitism in France than in Algeria,

> I abruptly learned that my unacceptable truth in this world was my being a woman. Right away, it was war. I felt the explosion, the odour of misogyny . . . From 1955 on, I adopted an imaginary nationality which is literary nationality. (*Rootprints*: 204)

After her rude awakening to the "war" of sexual difference, Cixous began to conceive of gender identity as a continuum of shifting impressions and identifications which she refers to as bisexuality ("Sorties": 84–85). Most compellingly, Cixous' immersion in misogynist French culture prompted her to redefine the very concept of nationality. Like Leila Sebbar and Assia Djebar, Cixous understands nationality not in terms of geographic affiliation, but as a state of mind—a vital community of creative sustenance possible only in and through the imagination.[13] In this respect, sexual politics afforded Cixous both the insight and impetus to re-vision home, especially the image and significance of the national family.

In "Albums and Legends," Cixous provocatively interweaves concrete details from her youth with glaring gaps, conjectures, and omissions. On one hand, her family album involves painstaking, almost heroic efforts of excavation. Its pages seem to delight in the monumental task of constructing a family tree—and staging a reunion of sorts—in the face of the traumatic exile and loss wrought by the Holocaust. Indeed, six of the twenty-nine pages of "Albums and Legends" are devoted to the elaboration of a detailed family tree. In this sense, Cixous' album stages a remarkably defiant gesture of gathering, identification, and commemoration in the face of astounding loss and dispersal.

On the other hand, Cixous' album vibrates with gaps, dreams, lost memories, and moments of misrecognition. "Albums and Legends" is most tangibly haunted by scores of lost Jewish relatives, but the text also bears the traces of other forms of loss. On one occasion in her text, for example, Cixous cannot recall whether she actually traveled to her mother's German hometown with her maternal grandmother:

> And I have a memory problem: I do not know if I went to Osnabruck or if I did not go . . . I have the feeling I went to Osnabruck. I seem to see the streets. But I do not know if I dreamed it. Osnabruck, if I went, remains dreamed. I cannot know. (*Rootprints*: 201–2)

Instead of marking this memory lapse as a problematic gap in her genealogical project, Cixous embraces it as evocative of, indeed integral to, her experiences of home, memory, nation, and identity.

Similarly, "Albums and Legends" details two childhood occasions on which Cixous admits that she could not recognize her own father. The first experience occurred shortly after her father's military draft. When he returned home one evening, Cixous was surprised to encounter an unknown soldier at her door:

> Someone foreign, strange . . . I have the feeling of an abduction, a transformation. Nothing tragic. Something fantastic. (*Rootprints*: 199–201)

Upon his return, Cixous quite literally did not recognize her father. Yet her lack of recognition inspired not fear or disturbance, but a magical sense of transformation. A second moment of misrecognition took place while her father was dying of tuberculosis. Shortly before his death, she visited him in the hospital and could not recognize the ailing man as her father. He was no longer able to speak—and given his lifelong love for and fluency with multiple languages, this loss was unfathomable for Cixous. Without words, Cixous' father became unrecognizable to her. Devastated to find her father in this wordless state, Cixous nonetheless pretended that everything was fine in his presence.

Most readers can easily relate to Cixous' sporadic lapses of memory and recognition. Yet her commitment to including these moments in her family album is striking. More remarkably, Cixous makes no attempt to rationalize these errors and omissions, or to supplement memory with hindsight and exhaustive investigation. Imperfect recall, dreams, and misrecognition are not merely tolerated in the pages of Cixous' album; instead, they form the backbone of her narrative. These ellipses resemble uncovered wounds in memory, history, and narration that mark the crucial role of fantasy, loss, and alterity in any effort to compose an identity via the family album.

Given her willingness to acknowledge the primacy of loss and speculation in projects of remembering, Cixous' autobiography emerges as much in the margins of her family album as in its photographs, chronologies, and genealogical notations. In "Albums and Legends," autobiography unfolds not in linear or chronological progression, but rather as a circular passage between self and other, fantasy and recollection, past and present, national history and transnational memory. Although Cixous' diasporic upbringing fosters a deep appreciation for the geopolitical determinants of identity, it also suggests the limits of nationality as either a meaningful category of identification or as a foundation for collective memory.

Cixous' family album dramatically re-visions national and sexual identity. Most explicitly, "Albums and Legends" recalls the arbitrariness of formal citizenship, which is granted and revoked in accordance with the historical vicissitudes of war and colonization. Yet Cixous also comes to understand national (un)belonging partly in terms of sexual difference. Ultimately, her family album documents an ongoing struggle to carve out an imaginary homeland by enlisting traumatic memory, cultural *métissage*, and feminist consciousness in the service of creative disidentification and self-transformation.

III. RETHINKING BLOOD, INTIMACY, AND THE NATIONAL IMAGINARY: THERESA HAK KYUNG CHA'S FAMILY ALBUM

> The first time I glanced at *Dictée*, I was put off by the book. I thought that Theresa Cha was talking not to me but rather to someone so remote from myself that I could not recognize "him."
>
> —Elaine Kim, "Poised on the In-between: A Korean American's Reflections on Theresa Hak Kyung Cha's *Dictée*"

> To other nations who are not subject to the same oppressions, they cannot know. Unfathomable the words: enemy, atrocities, conquest, betrayal, invasion, destruction. . . . Not physical enough. Not to the very flesh and bone, to the core, to the mark, to the point where it is necessary to intervene, even if to invent anew, expressions, for *this* experience, for this *outcome*, that does not cease to continue.
>
> —Theresa Hak Kyung Cha, *Dictée*

Why slip a photograph of Joan of Arc into a Korean-American family album? The shocking displacement enacted by this juxtaposition is, in a sense, the latent goal of Theresa Hak Kyung Cha's work. Like Cixous, Cha is motivated by an ambivalent desire to both specify and resist location. *Dictée* repeatedly unhinges the significance of "pure" national and ethnic origins by "calling attention to the varied locations of its writing, at the boundaries of different cultures and geographies."[14] By conceiving of location not as a singular place but as a network of mobile destinations, fabrications, and confrontations, Cha approaches transnational space as a catalyst for fantasies of identity as well as critical politics of disidentification.

Throughout her work, Cha fashions a distinctly feminist genealogy and imaginary. In her art as well as her autobiographical novel *Dictée*,[15] Cha composes a subversive family album by confounding traditional conceptions of blood, intimacy, and nationality. She approaches genealogy as a vital feminist practice—at once relational, fluid, and politically necessary.[16] Ultimately, she misrecognizes conventional images of the national family in order to map out a transnational feminist "home" that is deliberately disloyal to origins.

Although Cha does not explicitly set out to compose a family album, she creatively explores the potentials of documentary and autobiography in her work. Cha's celebrated novel *Dictée* is an exercise in radical experimentation that nonetheless adopts the autobiographical form by incorporating diary excerpts, handwritten notes, personal correspondence, and family portraits. Interestingly enough, *Dictée* blends these realist elements with a whimsical mix of film stills, medical diagrams, grammar lessons, military photographs, Greek mythology, calligraphy, and official political documentation. Wrested from their customary contexts, the multimedia fragments of *Dictée* ultimately enact a "shattering," or a new kind of arrangement that enlists disjunction as a catalyst for unanticipated relations and (de)compositions.[17] To highlight the political significance of this shattering, Cha is careful to link her efforts of textual fragmentation to minority identity practices.

By strategically misrecognizing the traditional genres of autobiography, documentary, and ethnic memoir, *Dictée* delivers realist technique to the margins, ellipses, and limits of representation. The explosiveness of its words and images derives from their undying commitment to expressing sexual, ethnic, and stylistic difference. By continually insinuating difference into the very fabric of her text, Cha undermines the idea of the essential or sovereign self. Instead, she maps out what feminists of color have alternately described as "identity-in-difference" or "oppositional consciousness."[18]

For Cha, identities are negotiated in the dynamic spaces of collision between sexual, racial, and national fantasies.[19] In this sense, she understands identification not in the binary terms of rejection or assimilation, but as involving "multiple processes of identifying with and against,"[20] particularly for subjects who are hailed by plural and intersecting components of identity. Cha strategically reconfigures identity in order to promote progressive social change for minority subjects. Especially, her work imagines the moment at which women of color "arrive" on the scene of representation to produce a "jolt to the social order . . . that may reverberate in indispensable ways."[21]

Dictée demands a genuine effort of excavation on the part of the reader, who confronts several levels of inscrutability within its pages. Transgressing disciplinary limits or the "law of genre" is just one of the tactics through which Cha involves her audience in the "ruin of representation."[22] *Dictée* also withholds customary hallmarks of narrative form including chronological progression, character development, and dialogue. By sifting through what is, in effect, the wreckage of *Dictée*, readers are able to piece together several strands of Cha's personal history intertwined with Korean national memory. We learn, for example, that Cha's older brother was killed during a student protest in 1960s Korea, and that his death still haunts the family. Yet *Dictée* moves beyond the private despair of familial loss to suggest that national trauma—especially war and colonization—underwrites personal suffering.

Displacement haunts Cha's work. In some ways, Cha embodies Virginia Woolf's metaphoric woman without a country.[23] She spent much of her life in the interstices between—rather than safely within—national borders. Born in Korea in 1951, Cha immigrated to the United States with her family when she was twelve years old to escape the Korean War. After initially settling in Hawai'i, the family later moved to Berkeley, California, where Cha completed her undergraduate and graduate studies.

During graduate school, Cha worked as an usher at UC Berkeley's Pacific Film Archive, where she became acquainted with foreign film genres including the French Nouvelle Vague. Her exposure to New Wave cinema piqued an interest in French film theory, which she pursued at the Centre d'Etudes Americains du Cinéma in Paris in 1976. The following year, Cha was naturalized as a U.S. citizen, and subsequently completed her MFA in 1978. In 1982, shortly after marrying and moving to New York City, Cha fell victim to a random homicide: she was murdered by a security guard as she entered her husband's studio office building in Lower Manhattan. She was only thirty-one years old at the time of her death.

Although her career was tragically cut short, Cha was a prolific artist. She created a dizzying array of publications, videos, performances, sculpture, films, mail art, and works on fabric in addition to the posthumous *Dictée*.[24] Since her death, a growing number of literary critics have reflected on the historical context and stylistic nuances of *Dictée*.[25] Foremost among them, Asian-American studies scholars Lisa Lowe and Elaine Kim have richly contributed to contemporary understandings of *Dictée* as a palimpsest of colonial history and identity. Yet I would agree with Anne Cheng that "what remains unexplored in *Dictée* is the fundamental principle of identification [that structures the categories of nation, gender, and identity, and] whose processes haunt the very formation of Cha's *récit*."[26] Even less explored are the relationships between *Dictée* and Cha's broader portfolio of visual and performance art. With this in mind, I hope to explore the puzzling links between image and identity, or art and identification, in Cha's work. In particular, I will ask how *Dictée*, together with Cha's visual artwork, rethinks the processes of national, sexual, and familial identification. Because images like photo-textual collages are foundational to Cha's oeuvre, I will read *Dictée* along with a few of Cha's conceptual art pieces as a disjointed family album that marks the limits, possibilities, and intersections of transnational identity, belonging, and self-representation. Although I do not mean to suggest that Cha's work is reducible to autobiography by reading it in this way, I do want to think about the acts of memorialization and identification that Cha positions her work to resist. I will peruse Cha's photo album to tease out its enigmatic orchestrations of personal and collective memory, and to explore the relationships between fantasy, nationality, image, and identity that it both establishes and deconstructs. Ultimately, I hope to show how Cha's creative use of misrecognition enables her to effectively resist normative prescriptions for identification within the national family.[27]

IV. DENYING INTIMACY, FISSURING THE FAMILY ALBUM: *DICTÉE* AND "CHRONOLOGY"

> What these images have in common is that they are a space offered but never occupied.
>
> —Marguerite Duras, *Duras by Duras*

> Exile is a series of portraits without names, without context.
>
> —Edward Said, *After the Last Sky*

Since its inception as an art form, the portrait has served to convey one's class and professional status (as doctor, artist, musician, etc.) and to promote wide audience recognition.[28] Family portraits, in particular, employ representational conventions, like "confirming looks," that consolidate group identity and reinforce the conceptual power of the family.[29] When compiled in an album, family portraits insert their members into a compelling story of shared origin, resemblance, hierarchy, and kinship.

Family albums promise their viewers the alluring opportunity to trespass on the intimate space of domestic interiors. From this perspective, it is difficult to imagine a deliberately uninviting family album. Yet Theresa Cha reinvents the family album as a study in dislocation, discomfort, and estrangement. She takes this most personal of genres—family portraiture—and renders it unfamiliar to her audience. Indeed, Cha reworks the very notion of intimacy in order to contest the conventional aesthetic goals of recognition and identification. In both *Dictée* and her visual artwork, she critiques the myth of belonging that sustains the national family as productive of marginality and alienation. Strikingly evident in her work is a view of the nuclear family as overwritten, haunted, and displaced by national trauma. Ultimately, Cha's family album explores the potentials not of integration, but of unbelonging, disidentification, and creative misrecognition.

To disturb her readers, Cha disrupts the narrative flow throughout *Dictée*. She also displaces the omniscient narrator by including multiple sites of authorship within the text, including unattributed print, photography, handwritten notes, film stills, typescript, and calligraphy. Finally, Cha intermittently invokes noisy, inaudible, or incoherent phonemes: "particles bits of sound and noise gathered pick up lint, dust. Speech morsels. Broken chips of stones. The vast ambiant sound hiss" (*Dictée*: 56). Collectively, Cha's aesthetic choices destabilize unitary readings of the text. Because *Dictée* frustrates readers' efforts to identify with its characters or author, it denies the opportunities for intimacy typically afforded by the genres of autobiography and the family album.

Cha's tactics of creative suspension and misrecognition emerge largely in response to the forced identifications of war, colonization, and immigration. Interestingly, the title of her autobiographical novel, *Dictée*, refers to a French grammar exercise designed to aid students' oral comprehension and transcription skills. Most nonnative French speakers initially experience *la dictée*, or dictation, as an arduous journey into the uncomfortable territories of confusion, self-doubt, and alienation. As they listen to the voice that they must subsequently transcribe, students often feel intimidated by its rapidity and fluidity. During the course of *la dictée*, students quickly become aware of the ambiguity of French words and phrases which, as homophones, homonyms, or *faux amis*, can impede their oral comprehension of French.

Especially for the nonnative Francophone reader, Cha's title sparks linguistic memory while also recalling the anxieties and disorienting potentials of foreign language acquisition. Aptly enough, *Dictée* opens to the cacophonous notes of *la dictée*. We first meet the novel's narrator while she is immersed in a historically charged *dictée* that invokes imagery from Roman Catholicism and French national memory. By imperfectly translating the French words that form the subject of her dictation, Cha marks the narrator's status as a foreigner, as well as her refusal to comply with linguistic transmissions of colonial ideology. Instead of fluently repeating her lesson, *Dictée*'s narrator inscribes difference into the very structure of the *dictée*. By so doing, she reveals the mother tongue as always at work in the other tongue,[30] and approaches national identity as inevitably invested in fantasies of sameness and otherness.

By inserting scraps of mistranslation throughout her novel, Cha rewrites difference not as substandard deviation, but as the very condition of possibility for self-invention. Her commitment to recording difference exposes the bewilderment of language, the limits of monolingualism, and the "insolvent debt"[31] of translation. It also suggests the multiple discursive sites through which colonized subjectivity is constituted or dictated. Ultimately, *Dictée* leverages flawed translation as a subversive tactic of "*bi-langue*"[32] with which to resist imperialist alphabets and forced identifications.

Withholding and omission emerge as key aesthetic strategies within *Dictée*. Cha's creative use of omission often centers on photographic imagery, which *Dictée* repeatedly reproduces without captions. By refusing to designate concrete relationships between image and referent, Cha resists photography's promise to supply hard evidence.[33] Instead, she revels in the polyvalent space between signifier and signified.[34] Cha's suspicion of "natural" affinities between image and identity challenges Platonic ideals of essence, origin, and resemblance.

Cha confronts language and religion as two of the primary vehicles for disciplining colonial subjects. The opening scenes of *Dictée* strikingly juxtapose French *dictée* exercises with the holy Catholic rites of communion and confession. By interweaving seemingly incongruent passages of grammatical and religious indoctrination, Cha creates an undercurrent of resistance to their shared objectives of rote repetition, perfect imitation, and assimilation of linguistic or divine origins. As she suggests in *Dictée*, religious and colonial leaders employ a similar rhetoric of correspondence and assimilation to enforce hegemonic identifications among their constituents. To challenge Judeo-Christian and colonialist ideals of divine resemblance, female sacrifice, and masculine creation, *Dictée* explicitly rejects the value of "unidirectional correspondance" (*Dictée*: 33).

Not only does Cha choose a French title and begin her novel with French grammar exercises; she also intersperses French throughout her predominantly English text. By contrast, she includes very few Japanese and Korean characters in *Dictée*, even though Korean is her native language and Japanese was, for a time, the imposed colonial tongue. What explains Cha's predilection for French, which is clearly central to her articulation of Korean-American or "hyphenated" identity?[35] Most strikingly, Cha's use of French—especially the trope of *la dictée*—destabilizes monistic conceptions of nationality, location, and linguistic affiliation. Although Cha insists that geopolitical context is a shaper of identity, she refuses to pledge allegiance to a particular homeland or tongue, preferring instead to dwell in the borderlands of transnational and transcultural signification.

The French language, ripe with alliteration and double entendre, proves a fertile playground and laboratory throughout Cha's oeuvre. From *Dictée* to her museum exhibits and performances in Berkeley and San Francisco, Cha repeatedly delights in the opportunities for ambiguity, creative disjunction, and the free play of desire that she locates in the French language. For example, she begins her video installation "Exilée" (1980) by orally breaking down the title phrase into several constitutive parts, including "exil" and "il." Spoken slowly, these deconstructed syllables function as communicative fragments as well as visual images. In another exhibit entitled "Commentaire" (1980), Cha expands the signifying possibilities of the title by sequentially emphasizing different permutations of the word, including "comment" (with resonance in both the English and French languages—"comment" and "how," respectively); "tear"; and "*taire*" or "*se taire*" (the French expression meaning "to be silent"). By emphasizing these permutations of the title word, Cha subverts the term's original meaning. In effect, she demonstrates how the meaning of *commentaire* (commentary or critique) is constituted in and through differential and ultimately opposing elements (comment; taire; tear). That is, Cha recalls how the apparent unity of signification depends upon the suppression of internal ambivalence. Playing with signification in this way, Cha discovers endless possibilities for experimentation and defamiliarization within the French colonial *langue*.

By limiting her use of Korean in *Dictée*, Cha manages to safeguard the "secret" of her mother tongue. This linguistic strategy recalls the literary tactics of Indian-Guatemalan autobiographer Rigoberta Menchú, who emphasizes the importance, for postcolonial or "native" people, of withholding local secrets from Western audiences in order to maintain a sense of pride, ownership and respect for the integrity of indigenous culture.[36] To heighten outsiders' alienation, Cha deploys the grammatical form of *la dictée* throughout her novel as a metaphor for the impossibility of translation. By selectively borrowing from disparate languages and cultures, Cha resists fixed identifications while simultaneously subverting the ethnic memoir's premise of cultural authenticity.

In a photographic installation entitled "Chronology" (1977), Cha fashions a family album beyond recognition, its pages stained by omission, rupture, and repetition. By withholding the pleasures of intimacy, recognition, and identification customarily enjoyed by viewers of a family album, "Chronology" tests the patience of its audience. Whereas photo albums typically oblige their authors to construct a relationship between image and identity—or a narrative of self—based on recognition, Cha approaches this relationship as fleeting, unrecognizable, and impossible to name or sustain. To intensify viewers' feelings of alienation, "Chronology" strategically thwarts audience identification while constructing an array of seemingly infinite possibilities for fantasy, evasion, and misrecognition. It also subverts the linear progression suggested by its title, and ultimately casts doubt on the redemptive potentials of collective memory, genealogical narration, and the recording of history.

We can trace the origins of "Chronology" to an artist's book created by Cha entitled "presence/absence" (1975). Its first two pages are black with white borders, each imprinted with the word "presence" or "absence." Two of the four remaining pages—white with black borders—are empty. The fourth page reads, "Water fills up all the empty places," and on the sixth page is the family portrait subsequently reproduced on the pages of "Chronology." In its earlier incarnation, however, the portrait is conceived as an enigmatic pencil sketch in which holes, empty spaces, and disconnected lines are more sharply focused than the image itself. In "presence/absence," this family portrait is haunting and elusive. Ghostly and fragile, the image seems to have been traced in the fleeting medium of sand or water. As a result, "presence/absence" compellingly attests to the fragility of life. Cha's work reminds us that although images may help to "fill the empty places" of fantasy, loss, and broken memory, they are nonetheless incomplete bridges that can never lead to solid ground.

Two years after completing "presence/absence," Cha created "Chronology," which reproduces a broken series of Cha's family portraits. Instead of mounting these images within traditional Western frames, Cha displays them on eighteen identical white panels resembling Chinese calligraphy scrolls. Each image is identically positioned on these pressboard panels, amateurishly reproduced with harsh lighting and minute variations of contrast, shadow, and resolution.

"Chronology," which presents an extremely limited repertoire of photographs, denies any relationship between its images by privileging repetition over sequence and context. The first seven images depict Cha's parents either apart or together. Where her parents are individually photographed, Cha creates an illusion of togetherness by superimposing their portraits. The final eleven images of "Chronology" reproduce a single family portrait with subtle variations in processing and development. Repetition with minor variation creates the effect of a haunting echo within this piece. Yet it also undermines the role of sequence in photographic display, and disappoints the viewer's desire to fit Cha's portraits into a linear narrative of genealogical belonging and temporal progression. "Chronology" replaces sequence with seriality, much like the drawings of German-American artist Eva Hesse. As a result, it composes a family album on the basis of fissure rather than filiation. Norman Bryson explains aesthetic fissure in the following terms:

> Once information oversteps the threshold of recognition, a principle of fissure is introduced into the unity of [the visual]. As the viewer moves from one image

> to the next, he confronts each time a new scene—one which has broken free of its sequence, and asks to be viewed in increasing isolation both from its physical neighborhood and from the global *langue*.[37]

Because they exceed viewers' capacity for recognition, Cha's photographs foster alienation. The story that we expect to be told through Cha's family album remains submerged, suggested by ghostly trace rather than explicit presence. In lieu of narrative, "Chronology" offers reassemblage[38]—a jagged composition of cracks and fissures that simulates a state of

> Being broken. Speaking broken. Saying broken. Broken speech. Pidgeon tongue. All chronology lost, indecipherable, the passage of time, until it is forgotten. Forgotten how it stays, how it endures. (*Dictée*: 161)

Traditionally, a chronology—organized as a list or table—clarifies date and sequence, or the "arrangement of events in time."[39] Not so Cha's "Chronology," which does anything but provide a neat timeline of the major events in her life. Indeed, "Chronology" offers no evidence of time or place; unless viewers have prior knowledge of Cha's family history, they will gain little in the way of personal detail from "Chronology." This photographic piece suspends historical meaning, resists the affiliative look,[40] and forces viewers to invent a time before and after the implied tragic break of the repeated family portrait.

Cha's album presents her family members as aliens of inscrutable origin and inestimable destination. Throughout "Chronology," Cha's jarring photographic techniques dispel "the illusion that photographs simply record a pre-existing external reality [and a] mythology of the family as stable and static."[41] Spectators are left to surmise the identities of those pictured in Cha's family album, and to draw their own conclusions about the relationship between trauma, image, and the possibilities of identification.

By dispensing with the photographic conventions of context, sequence, and duration, Cha attempts to "keep pain from translating itself into memory" (*Dictée*: 140), and to mark trauma as a fissure that refuses integration at the levels of self, family, and nation. Traumatic traces are foundational to "Chronology," especially because Cha had experienced the Korean War, exile, and the death of her older brother by the time she created this piece. Her brother's death especially transforms these family portraits into "wishful constructions of what might be,"[42] since his presence is doubly translated into ghostly trace through photographic objectification and untimely death.

At first glance, "Chronology" seems to tell a mundane story, whether viewed in a museum or reproduced in book form. Especially from a distance, the photographic series "reads like a family album, a chronicle made by an insider for domestic use."[43] To encourage viewers to interact more intimately with these images, Cha pastes what appear to be identifying captions on the pictures' white borders, dangling just above or below each image. These captions heighten the effect that one is viewing a family album.

Customarily, captions help to "anchor" and contextualize a photograph.[44] By directing attention toward specific meanings and away from others, they constrain the possibilities of consumption. That is, captions resolve the potentially infinite range of meanings that an image might have by establishing explicit links between image and text to support particular readings of a photograph. Cha's captions, on the other hand, perform no identifying function. Instead, they accentuate the ambiguities of identity, history, and narrative. Composed of varying font styles and sizes, they are hand-stenciled rather than typed. Their lack of uniformity betrays the eccentricity of signature as opposed to the polish of execution. Stripped of any identifying function, Cha's captions resemble shattered remnants of the attempt to represent. As incomplete utterances, Cha's broken phrases seem to have been "caught" in—or perhaps devastated by—the very act of signifying.

Composed thus as a dizzying series of flashbacks and fragments, "Chronology" ultimately emerges as a site of "traumatic memory."[45] The work powerfully attests to the psychic residue and spatio-temporal disorientation that so often follow in the wake of traumatic experience. By juxtaposing incongruous fragments of photo and text, "Chronology" severs the relationship between word and image to map the margins, ruptures, and impossibilities of signification. Stripped of proper referents, Cha's photos deny the traditional family album's promise of coherent narration. Cha's jarring mix of textual and visual cues "breaks the framework" of the traditional family album by evoking national and familial tragedy as crises that cannot be integrated within existing mental schemas. "Chronology" re-visions familial tragedy as something that exceeds our ability to grasp or narrate, and as a form of cognitive dissonance that breaks conventional frames of reference.[46] Ultimately, it suggests that it is impossible to objectively record history, or to narrate lives from the chaotic ruins of personal and collective memory.

Yet "Chronology" also gestures toward a counteraesthetics born of the shattered remnants of memory. By repeating certain words throughout her family album, Cha achieves an ambivalent effect of continuity and irresolution. Most frequently paired with her photographs is the phrase "again, not before." These words reinforce Cha's pictorial emphasis on repetition rather than origination, alluding as well to the psychological stasis of posttraumatic stress disorder. Other phrases cited by Cha include "tell this, tell silence" and "not be named. Knew. Heard." Again, many of these phrases attest to the crippling potentials of silence and memory. The relationship between text and photographs in "Chronology" seems to be governed, if at all, by a dialectics of exile and impossible return. Rather than creating a dynamic of mutual support, "Chronology" conveys "the anxiety and ambivalence of the exile, whose memories and mementos—the tokens of personal and national identity—may seem like encumbrances."[47] These memories are nonetheless expressed in innovative form in "Chronology," which simultaneously manages to evoke, assume, and exceed the "burden" of representation.

Cha's family album proceeds according to a logic of rupture and accumulation, which indefinitely postpones the viewer's ability to apprehend the entirety of its photographic composition. In essence, "Chronology" intercepts the viewer's gaze and affords instead only furtive glances.[48] These glances are temporarily pleasurable as they seem to permit endless desire and to preclude mutual demand or frustration. Yet because the glance can never take in the work of art as a whole, viewers are able to perceive "Chronology" only in terms of fragmentation, marginality, and dispersal.

By denying the gaze, along with other photographic and textual conventions of the family album, Cha exerts outside pressure on the autobiographical genre—forcing it to bend and ultimately break.[49] "Chronology" stages the family album as suggestive "interval" rather than exhaustive citation: "a break without which meaning would be fixed, truth congealed,"[50] and viewer fantasies denied.

Cha's ability to promote the free play of audience desire is crucial to the success of her work. After all,

> To complete the circuit of recording, visibility, and truth set up by the photograph, there has to be someone looking at it. Meaning is produced, finally, in the spectator's look: looking is crucial in reading photographs.[51]

Viewers of "Chronology" initially suspect that the work will yield clarity or resolution if they look long and hard enough. But because spectatorial desire is bound up with the processes of scrutiny and investigation, its maintenance requires that such resolution remain, ironically, just out of reach.[52] In this respect, "Chronology" intensifies audience desire through its unyielding commitment to ellipsis.

For most onlookers, Cha's experimental aesthetic tactics prove deeply disturbing. Given the human desire to perceive the world in terms of relationship and unity, the audience struggles to integrate Cha's disjointed fragments into a coherent whole. Yet, after luring viewers into the comfort zone of the family album, "Chronology" complicates its attraction by misrecognizing the family portrait as a vehicle for facile identification. In this sense, the photo installation creates an effect of "noise" or interference that partially impedes reception of its message.[53] By denying recognition, Cha's work rejects the "belong to me aspect of representation, so reminiscent of property,"[54] and construes the viewer as a nomadic and unsettled voyeur. Or, from another perspective, "Chronology" might be said to "scramble culturally encoded messages . . . to expose their exclusionary interpellations, and to re-circuit their workings to empower minority identities and identifications."[55]

Because it privileges irresolution, uncertainty, and dislocation, Cha's work enacts Donna Haraway's vision of "feminist objectivity."[56] For many viewers, this brand of objectivity is disturbing and radically inassimilable. "Chronology" frustrates both the documentary will to know and the spiritual desire for redemption. Its esoteric blend of repetition and uncanny juxtaposition calls into question the possibility of providing coherent testimony in the face of traumatic experience. Furthermore, by precluding identification, "Chronology" permits its viewers "neither the complacency of spectatorship nor the consolation that bearing witness effects change."[57]

Thus, on further inspection, the serial portraits of "Chronology" do not read at all like a conventional family album. Missing are the neatly labeled, smiling faces centered within photographic frames—and, more crucially, an overarching context or narrative within which to make sense of Cha's images. By pairing unidentified imagery with enigmatic text, "Chronology" creates a disturbing effect of simultaneous presence and absence. Likewise, the form and content of *Dictée* register the necessarily incomplete and flawed aspect of any effort to represent. If looking is a "complicated form of cognition that is not to be trusted,"[58] then Cha compounds our suspicion by crafting a family album premised on fissure and disidentification rather than transparent self-reflection.

What happened on the occasion of Cha's repeated family portrait—or the day before, or the day after? What explains its powerful hold on her memory? These questions are raised but never answered for the viewer, who is effectively denied entry into Cha's family album. Spectators occupy a tense interval of pause and marginality relative to her images, recalling the infinite strangeness and fragmented duration of colonized subjectivity as imagined in *Dictée*, as well as in Marguerite Duras' film *India Song*. Most provocatively, "Chronology" suggests that identity is often experienced as a state of occupation—even colonization—by disturbing images.

"Chronology" dares us to imagine the traumas and ellipses of colonized subjectivity. It composes a family album not on the basis of genealogical resemblance or recognition, but through fantasy, repetition, and withheld identification. As a result, "Chronology" imagines traumatized identity to encompass "incomprehensibility and presence, a past that will neither fade away nor be integrated into the present."[59] By situating its photographs, as *lieux de mémoire*,[60] on the border between memory and forgetting, Cha's family album evokes trauma as a haunting echo rather than a decisive event that would permit explicit disclosure and exhaustive citation. For Cha, the consumption of images takes place not through passive spectatorship, but through deconstructive engagement with malleable cultural fantasies. Never a site of facile identification, Cha's family album forces viewers to reflect on potential disturbances that may jam the circuits between image and identity.

V. BLOODSTAINS, MEMORY, AND FILIATION

Blood: (n.) 1. The fluid circulated by the heart in a vertebrate, carrying oxygen, nutrients, hormones, etc., throughout the body and waste materials to excretory organs. 2. A fluid resembling blood, such as the juice of certain plants. 3. Life; lifeblood. 4. Bloodshed; murder. 5. Kinship: *related by blood*. 6. Racial or national ancestry.

Stain: (v.) 1. To discolor, soil, or spot. 2. To corrupt; taint. 3. To color with a penetrating liquid dye or tint. 4. To deprive of color. (n.) 1. A spot or smudge of foreign matter. 2. A blemish on one's name; stigma. 3. A liquid substance, as a dye, used to stain.

From *Dracula* to contemporary AIDS policy and literature, blood exerts a powerful hold on the popular imagination. Female blood, in particular, has been especially associated with contamination throughout Western philosophic, religious, and psychoanalytic traditions. As Elizabeth Grosz points out, "In the West, the female body has been constructed not only as lack or absence but with more complexity, as a leaking, uncontrollable, seeping liquid; as formless flow—a disorder that threatens all order."[61] Most fearful is the fluid's uncontainability. Bodily fluids are reminders of the body's permeability, and of the indefensible boundaries between self and other.

Female bodily fluids, especially blood, continue to provoke unique fear and repression in contemporary society, as evidenced by the dizzying array of commercial products available to control the flow of menstrual blood and vaginal discharge. Women's blood is considered a pollutant in most orthodox religious traditions, which forbid menstruating women to enter temples, mosques, and synagogues, or to walk before a church's altar. These contemporary cultural and religious contexts situate female blood as a uniquely impure and potent source of contamination.

In a more universal or asexual sense, however, blood has historically symbolized kinship, intimacy, and spiritual union. First and foremost, the blood flowing through our veins signifies familial belonging. Where biological relationship does not exist, people often try to simulate the power of blood ties.

From the earliest days of human civilization, lovers, childhood friends, and secret societies have practiced bloodletting to profess intimacy and loyalty. Group members have interpreted their exchange of blood as the expression of a profound, unspeakable, and everlasting oath. Today, the sharing of blood persists as a secret solidarity ritual and badge of group identity.

In Christian religious tradition, blood is similarly construed as a symbol of sacred union and redemption. Parishioners routinely participate in the holy rite of communion, during which they drink wine designated by the priest or pastor as "the blood of Christ, shed for you." Blood is the organizing metaphor of this ritual, which invites worshippers to drink of Christ's "blood" as a vital and unifying agent of redemption.

Theresa Cha misrecognizes blood as conceived in these diverse historical and religious contexts. Instead, she considers it to mark the limits of familial intimacy, redemption, and assimilation. In *Dictée*, blood signifies, above all, civil unrest and national unbelonging. Cha's association of blood with national politics reflects her broader project to understand how difference is variously absorbed or rejected by, and resistant to assimilation within, the national imaginary. Throughout *Dictée*, she evokes blood as a metaphor for national trauma, as well as sexual and racial alienation.

Dictée first refers to blood in a chapter entitled "Melpomene . . . Tragedy," in which Cha describes a return to her native land of Korea. Amidst this homecoming, Cha is suddenly caught up in the chaos of a street protest. The circumstances remind her of a similar student uprising eighteen years earlier, during which her older brother had died.

As Cha relives the turbulent moments leading up to his death, she unhinges chronological time in her novel: "It is 1962 eighteen years ago same month same day all over again. I am eleven years old. Mother, you are holding my older brother pleading with him not to go to the demonstration" (*Dictée*: 83). Lost in a suspended sense of time characteristic of posttraumatic stress disorder, Cha narrates this trauma as if no time had elapsed since its occurrence, and as if—like the fabled storyteller Sheherazade—she might escape its fate through the powers of narration. Refusing to offer details, she instead evokes the tragedy elliptically, with a repetitive voice and stagnant tempo.

As the memory of her brother's death transports Cha through time and space, *Dictée*'s narrator employs an increasingly frenzied pace and syntax. She describes the chaotic street scene in terms of "cries resisting cries to move forward. Orders, permission to use force against the students have been dispatched. They fall they bleed they die" (*Dictée*: 83). What slowly drops out of Cha's account is any clear identification of the agents and victims of this event. Who cries? Who issues orders? Who dies? Are there any overlapping interests between the students and police in this incident? Withholding details, Cha prefers to linger in the polyvalent space of omission. Readers of *Dictée* are at once alienated by—and entrusted with the task of filling in—the blanks, holes, or lacunae of its narrative.

After sifting through dissonant memories, *Dictée*'s narrator eventually reaches the unspeakable moment of her brother's death. Again, rather than evoking this trauma in precise detail, Cha portrays it as a radical rupture that precludes the possibility of narrative closure, familial intimacy, or political redemption. Instead of rendering an intimate sketch of her fallen brother, Cha symbolizes his presence and absence as an indelible bloodstain:

> My brother. You fell you died you gave your life. That day. It rained. It rained for several days. I heard that the rain does not erase the blood fallen on the ground. The blood stains still. Year after year it rained. The stone pavement stained where you fell still remains dark. Except for the blood. Because. Remain dark the stains not wash away. (*Dictée*: 82–85)

Rather than indulge in the personal pleasures and restorative powers of memory, Cha surrenders her text to a death that is rendered impersonal, inassimilable, and beyond representation. By so doing, she denies readers the details that would allow them to recognize or identify with her brother, and rejects the intimate voice usually associated with autobiography. Instead, Cha uses her family album to acknowledge the failures of representation, the impossibility of redemption, and the bewildering alienation occasioned by familial loss.

Throughout this passage, Cha evokes a bloodstain that won't wash away in order to critique the nationalist ideal of self-sacrifice for community benefit. In particular, Cha rejects the rhetoric of martyrdom, which would sanctify her brother's death for the sake of democratic progress. Cha problematizes martyrdom, especially female sacrifice, throughout *Dictée.* However, her text provokes tension between a Buddhist critique of individuality, on one hand, and a postcolonial feminist critique of community-sanctioned sacrifice, on the other. This tension is especially apparent in Cha's word choice surrounding her brother's death, which elevates impersonal landscape imagery (rain, stone, pavement) over sentimental detail even as it abandons a discourse of national heroics.

For Cha, the indelible bloodstain symbolizes how national trauma can never be fully integrated within, or absorbed by, the nuclear family. *Dictée* similarly characterizes traumatic memory as an ineradicable and all-consuming stain on the fabric of personal identity:

> The memory stain attaches itself and darkens on the pale formless sheet, a hole increasing its size larger and larger until it assimilates the boundaries and becomes itself formless. All memory. Occupies the entire. (*Dictée*: 131)

By reformulating blood and memory in these ways, Cha invents a unique symbolic economy with which to represent trauma. For Cha, traumatic memory, like the bloodstain, is at once a marker of absence and overflow: not a liquid to be absorbed, but an aberrant trace that at first threatens to consume, but eventually conforms to its surroundings. Drawing on Lacanian formulations of the stain and mimicry, Cha evokes the bloodstain as the trace of a subject "fixed" in the attempt to become part of—or to offer oneself to the gaze already in the guise of—a particular "picture" or fate.[62] Central to Cha's text, the stain metaphor collapses the distance between body and image and recasts identification in Barthesian terms as the transformation of flesh into fantasy, or the "cunning advent of myself as other." Ultimately, the stain in *Dictée* signifies the impossibility of integrating the inhumanity of death within personal and national narratives of identity; the chasm between political ideal and reality; and the inevitable inarticulacy of any attempt to represent traumatic experience. As a territory of irreparable loss, trauma necessitates a whole new aesthetic vocabulary for Cha—one that elevates absence over presence, inhuman stain over flesh and blood. *Dictée* provocatively imagines blood as capable of both staining and vampirically absorbing or obfuscating the boundaries between self and other.

The death of Cha's brother translates to missing pictures in the family album—haunted gaps that beget fantasy, ellipsis, and alienation. On one hand, his lingering bloodstain—the product of civil unrest—recalls a tragic history of minority efforts to identify with the nation, and reminds us that the relation between bodies and representation often demands compliance or corporeal assimilation. Yet the vampiric qualities of his stain also suggest the strategic potentials of offering oneself to the culture at large as a particular fantasy, spectacle, or image of "otherness"—a "body double" with which one identifies only from a critical distance.[63] In the following discussion, I will trace the contours of these ambivalent histories and possibilities of (dis)identification.

VI. STAINING THE NATION: BIOLOGY, RACE, AND DISSIMILATION

> What is home? The place I was born? Where I grew up? Where my parents live? Where I live and work as an adult? Where I locate my community, my people? Who are "my people"? Is home a geographical space, a historical space, an emotional, sensory space? What interests me is the meaning of home for immigrants and migrants. I am convinced

> that this question—how one understands and defines home—is a profoundly political one.
>
> —Chandra Talpade Mohanty, "Crafting Feminist Genealogies"

> Race is a fracturing trauma in the body politic of the nation—and in the mortal bodies of its people . . . What's not collected in a reproductive family story does not finally count as human. For all a photo album's emphasis on difference, this is the grammar of indifference, the multiplication of sameness.
>
> —Donna Haraway, "Universal Donors in a Vampire Culture"

Dictée evokes blood imagery to explore the ambivalent meanings of race and belonging within the national family. In particular, Cha reworks the bloodstain to subvert dominant symbolic economies of racial difference, assimilation, and identification *vis-à-vis* the nation. By reconceiving of blood as something that might both absorb and stain, Cha challenges nationalist and racialized discourses that posit the relations between self and other in terms of deviance and assimilation. Her critical perspective recalls a troubling history of scientific thought regarding genealogical purity and racial degeneration.

Degeneracy was a popular obsession within nineteenth-century British biological science. Scientific research of the late 1800s conceived of "race" as synonymous with species, nation, ethnicity, or culture. Gradually, Victorian scientists came to regard biological—especially racial and sexual—difference as a blueprint for human progress, evolution, and social hierarchy. Several prominent biologists and eugenicists of the era deployed concepts such as "bad blood" and "degeneration" to explain the dangers of interracial (hence "cross-species") mixing or miscegenation, and to suggest the degrading impact of non-Western people and places on white, Western subjects.

Based on these budding scientific desires to correlate biology with social hierarchy, scientists increasingly labored to trace evolutionary "family trees" of the human race. In the nineteenth century, Herbert Spencer and his partners mapped out the influential "Tree of Man," which visually portrayed the various human races as successive rungs on a vertical ladder toward "progress." White European males occupy the apex of this evolutionary ladder, whereas African men inhabit the penultimate rung, which is intended to designate their status as direct descendants of apes and savages. Women—conspicuously missing from these family trees or "genealogies of power"[64]—are altogether denied the status of historical agent or legitimate member of the coveted "Family of Man."[65] In this sense, while the discourse of race formalizes distinctions between social classes within the human family tree, the erasure of gender identity or sexual difference underwrites the entire endeavor of human classification. Ultimately, as Anne McClintock points out, these influential tropes of blood and family in nineteenth-century science successfully upheld social hierarchy, especially the subordination of women and minorities, and authorized state and imperial intervention into domestic affairs.[66]

Public anxieties about purity and contagion tended to reinforce degeneracy theory, which explicitly linked biological difference, geography, and personal conduct to survival of the race or species. The offspring of interracial couplings, portrayed in social Darwinian thought as the horribly disfigured products of unnatural unions, drew particularly intense scrutiny. By the late 1800s, biological metaphors of disease and contagion—tied to the mixing of blood, race, and place—sanctioned a complex weave of social fears and legal prohibitions.

Polygenesis, or tropical degeneration theory, predicted the dangers of white exposure to the tropical climates of Asia and Africa, which were believed to stunt European moral and intellectual growth. Proponents of tropical degeneration theory discouraged geographical mixing, insisting that the races should remain in their "proper" places to avoid migration-induced degeneracy. For example, the biologist Van Evrie maintained that "the Negro is as much a product of the tropics as the orange or banana."[67] Along these lines, many biologists regarded Algeria as the most dangerous place in the world for white Westerners—a hotbed for the transmission of homosexuality, venereal disease, and moral decrepitude.[68]

Although degeneracy discourse began as a biological perspective on cross-species fertilization, experts in other fields evoked the presumed objectivity and authority of science to sketch the implications of racial and sexual mixing for all forms of human thought and endeavor. Sexologists and psychoanalysts regarded sexual and racial degeneration as an impediment to "normal" human development and reproduction, and characterized women and minority "degenerates" as "the essence of pathology."[69] In their view, women possessed dangerous sexual tendencies that, if not closely regulated, threatened to contaminate the bodies of white men. As McClintock explains:

> Body boundaries were felt to be dangerously permeable and demanding continual purification, so that sexuality, particularly women's sexuality, was cordoned off as the central transmitter of racial and hence cultural contagion.[70]

Especially suspect were the bodies of African and lower class women, which quickly became targets of relentless quasiscientific observation. Beginning in 1810, British and French medical experts publicly exhibited a native African indentured servant named Saartje Baartman, whom they regarded as a pathological specimen of clitoral malformation and "deviant" or lesbian sexuality. Deemed the "Hottentot Venus," Baartman was renowned for what scientists deemed her unusually large buttocks and genitalia. For five years, she was displayed for profit as a spectacle of "excessive" femininity. Her body caged and "regarded by the disciplinary gaze of male medical science and the voyeuristic public [as a] grotesque icon of deviant womanhood,"[71] she was exhibited at natural history museums in London and Paris. Classified as a "Hottentot"—an exotic label for an apelike human, or a being located on the very edge of humanity—Baartman was regarded by evolutionary biologists as the most primitive of human species, or the nadir of degeneration.[72] When she died of smallpox and complications of alcoholism in 1815, Georges Cuvier, a prominent French zoologist, dissected Baartman's body and presented her skeleton, corpse, and excised genitals for display at the Musée de l'Homme in Paris. Remarkably, Baartman's preserved genitals remained on display until the late 1990s, when her remains were finally returned to her native land of South Africa. Her extraordinary "success" as a museum object and scientific specimen powerfully demonstrates how the discourses of gender, race, sexuality, and colonization mutually inform cultural constructions of the "pathological" and the "human."

Degeneration theory attests not only to the discursive ambivalence of race, class, sexuality, and empire, but also to the fragility of the colonial social order. By the late 1800s, degeneration theory authorized regulatory practices in Europe and its overseas colonies that defined specific parameters of belonging *vis-à-vis* the national family. As evident in contemporary debates about immigration throughout Western Europe, Scandinavia, and the United States, anxieties about national belonging as well as racial and sexual "contamination" persist today, and map individual and national Western bodies as permeable surfaces rife with cracks, limits, and orifices that render them infinitely susceptible to infiltration by the "other."

Throughout her work, Cha exposes these anxieties and fantasies about racial, national, and sexual belonging as foundational to "stories about the origins and purposes of the nation."[73] By contesting traditional definitions of lineage, she indirectly challenges national legal and political concepts of purity, authenticity, and legitimacy. In particular, Cha explores how contemporary immigration policies deploy racialized images of the national family, many of which date back to nineteenth century degeneration theory. For example, *Dictée* evokes Edward Steichen's photographic exhibit, "The Family of Man," by critiquing the image of sameness revered in its sexually and racially charged family album.

Opposed to assimilation in its philosophical, artistic, and political senses, Cha regards difference as a catalyst for productive transcultural exchange, rather than as a disabling force that must be absorbed by the nation. For Cha, the racist politics of assimilation stains a nation; throughout her work, she confronts national assimilation policy as an effort to enforce a fictive sense of cultural purity and national belonging.[74] To challenge this ideal of assimilation, especially its alienating potentials for immigrant populations, *Dictée* reformulates the bloodstain as not only the dark remnant of violence, but also as a productively contaminating force with the potential to profoundly change its environment:

> Should it happen to appear all of a sudden, suddenly, begin to flow to collect begin to spill over flow flood should it happen to . . . It takes her seconds less to break the needle off its body in attempt to collect the loss directly from the wound. *Stain begins to absorb the material spilled on*. Something of the ink that resembles the stain from the interior emptied onto into upon this boundary this surface. Whenever possible to puncture to scratch to imprint. (*Dictée*: 64–65)

Throughout *Dictée*, blood symbolizes ethnic and sexual difference and their perceived threat to national order. Yet Cha's re-visioning of the bloodstain in personal and national memory also recalls how creative practices of rupture and disidentification may "scratch," "puncture," or otherwise "imprint" cultural memory.

Dictée metaphorically extends Cha's reformulation of the bloodstain to a personal and political commentary on citizenship, exile, and the myth of return. In one passage, *Dictée*'s narrator describes a return to Korea after eighteen years of self-imposed exile. Instead of experiencing this visit as a joyous homecoming, Cha likens her return to a risky act of border crossing that entails rigorous identity checks and physical inspections. Rather than enlisting customary fantasies of return, *Dictée* catalogs the numbing bureaucratic rituals that punctuate an emigrant's homecoming, and construct the exile as a subject-in-question:

> You return and you are not one of them. All the time you understand what they are saying. But the papers give you away. They ask you [*sic*] identity. They comment on your inability or ability to speak. Whether you are telling the truth or not about your nationality. They say you look other than you say. As if you didn't know who you were. You say who you are but you begin to doubt. They search you. Every ten feet they demand to know who and what you are, who is represented. The eyes gather toward the appropriate proof. Towards the face then again to the papers, when did you leave the country why did you leave this country why are you returning to the country. You open your mouth half way. Near tears, nearly saying, I know you I know you, I have waited to see you for long this long. They check each article, question you on foreign articles, then dismiss you. (*Dictée*: 56–58)

Cha envisions the return to national origins as a traumatic break in her attempt to weave a coherent narrative of identity. Although she is a native Korean, her dissimilar speech and mannerisms nonetheless brand foreignness onto the very surface of her skin and construct her as an inscrutable alien. As Cha wanders the streets of Seoul, she is disoriented by a tyranny of ethnic and national sameness that renders her inalterably "other." Throughout her urban explorations, Cha remains intelligible to resident Koreans only on the basis of her perceived difference and unrecognizability.

Dictée chronicles Cha's official entry into U.S. citizenship in 1977 as a similarly traumatic episode of national familial disintegration. Throughout her naturalization ceremony, Cha feels abducted by, rather than inducted into, the discourse of American citizenship. At a moment typically described by new immigrants as the pinnacle of national belonging and civic pride, Cha expresses instead a profound sense of alienation. In fact, she compares the naturalization ceremony to an experience of identity theft and coercive indoctrination:

> I have the documents. Documents, proof, evidence, photograph, signature. One day you raise the right hand and you are American. They give you an American Pass port. Somewhere someone has taken my identity and replaced it with their photograph. The other one. Their signature their seals. Their own image. (*Dictée*: 56)

Ultimately, the naturalization ceremony is an attempt to foster complete and unquestioning identification with one's new nation—a posture which Cha finds impossible to adopt. By describing her experience in terms of estrangement rather than interpellation, Cha effectively "denaturalizes" discourses of citizenship that expect an immigrant to compliantly absorb or submit to "unidirectional correspondence"(*Dictée*: 33). She conceives of citizenship along the lines of colonial and religious indoctrination, as a mode of dictation that seeks to remake its subjects in the image of the One, the same, or the *propre*. By overlaying the naturalization ceremony with an aesthetic tone of disjunction, Cha misrecognizes the nation's ideological bids for perfect assimilation and identification. Throughout her work, she specifies sex and race as particularly threatening forms of difference that are not easily incorporated within the American body politic.[75] Especially in *Dictée*, she imagines the possibility of forging a community that would embrace—rather than absorb or violate—sexual, racial, and ethnic difference.

By narrating her naturalization experience as an exhausting series of "documents, proof, evidence, photograph, signature," Cha minimizes the sentimental appeal of an immigrant's entry into U.S. citizenship. She emphasizes instead the rote, mechanistic aspects of the naturalization ceremony, especially the alienating potentials of civic ritual. By so doing, Cha reminds us that national identity is inevitably an exercise in unbelonging:

> One can be either a resident or illegal immigrant, but one is always an alien. There is no confusion here, no melting pot ideology or narratives of assimilation: one's status as an "alien" is primary.[76]

Despite Cha's desire to register the forced identifications of nationalist discourse, *Dictée* nonetheless resists these interpellations, especially by employing a fragmented narrative style. At a moment designed to inspire fantasies of personal fulfillment and obligation through seamless incorporation with the American nation, *Dictée* emphasizes disidentification as a catalyst for mapping the margins of nation and identity.

Cha's traumatic experiences of national return and naturalization are constantly mediated by the other's gaze, which directly impacts her creative efforts to navigate the space in between image and identity. If Cha is "coerced by the image of American ideal citizenship, she is equally divorced from a 'native' image of herself."[77] Perceived as a foreigner in both her native and adopted homelands, Cha explores how foreignness is produced by the external gaze, especially in relation to aesthetic and political ideals of sameness and recognition.

Cha further navigates the ambivalence of national belonging in a conceptual work entitled "Amer" (1976). This installation presents a modified American flag draped vertically on the wall. Stamped on one of its white stripes are the letters "amer." Similarly, one of the letters "a," "m," "e," or "r" occupies each of the flag's stars. In light of Cha's preoccupation with issues of homeland and national identity, her use of fragmented text might initially resemble an unfinished attempt to spell out the word "America," especially if one reads the flag as a cohesive weave of national identity.

Yet on closer examination, the benign surface of "Amer" yields a mordant critique of the ways in which certain identities are either enabled or effaced by national symbolic politics. Because French is central to Cha's work, her ironic deployment of the French word for bitter (*amer*) in the title and content of this piece should not be overlooked. Taken separately, the letters "amer" also suggest the French expression *à mer*, "to the sea" or "at sea," thus evoking the Pacific passage of Asian immigrants bound for the United States. Playing in the ambiguous space between French and English signification, Cha creatively reweaves the American flag to encompass the difference, discord, and ambivalence central to diasporic experience, yet so often displaced by the nationalist rhetoric of assimilation.

By working both with and against the traditional symbolism of the American flag, "Amer" provokes an uneasy confrontation with the complicated meanings of home and national identity. Its message is especially *à propos* in the post-9/11 United States, where political manipulations of patriotic sentiment have sparked intense debate about the perceived conflicts between freedom and security. Ultimately, Cha's re-visioning of the American flag challenges her audience to imagine a homeland *not* founded on the erasure or violation of racial, sexual, and ethnic difference.

VII. BEYOND THE NATIONAL FAMILY

> Multicultural feminism that is radical, anti-racist, and non-heterosexist needs to conceive of itself as also crossing national and regional borders. Questions of home, belonging, nation, and community thus become profoundly complicated . . . Women are not only mobilized in the "service" of the Nation, but they also become the ground on which discourses of morality and nationalism are written.
>
> —Chandra Talpade Mohanty, "Crafting Feminist Genealogies"

Most revolutionary about *Dictée* is its struggle to articulate a feminist politics of home that abandons traditional categories of identity and nationality. Wary of boundary and assimilation rhetoric, Cha rejects the logic of nationality to craft a transnational feminist imaginary. To do so, she sifts through a troubling legacy of nationalist portrayals of women, misrecognizes masculinist ideals of female sacrifice for the sake of the nation, and critiques historical oppositions between nationalism and feminism. Although she troubles our notions of home, intimacy, and genealogical origin, Cha nonetheless stages her own feminist lineage or family tree by uniting an eclectic group of women in the pages of *Dictée.*

If *Dictée* were an "official" family album of the Korean nation, it would not be a flattering one. Missing are the glorified images intended to inspire collective pride, and to enforce particular versions of national fantasy, remembrance, and identity. *Dictée* replaces pictures of decorated war veterans, victorious battle scenes, and solidarity marches with unidentified portraits of female leaders and martyrs largely forgotten or unknown within collective memory. In effect, *Dictée* composes a striking countermemory of the Korean nation by fashioning a gynocentric pantheon to contest the historical erasure, sacrifice, and invisibility of women relative to the nation. Cha also "disturbs the spectator's ideological positioning" by making women of color visible in a cultural and aesthetic tradition that has historically excluded them.[78] Not only does Cha construct a genealogy of "partial citizenship" *vis-à-vis* the Korean nation; she also foregrounds moments of resistance to that partiality.[79]

Rather than conventional chapters, *Dictée* is divided into nine sections named for the classical Greek muses.[80] In this sense, the novel is both haunted by, and structured on, the simultaneous presence and absence of female sources of creative inspiration. *Dictée* engages the muse as a point of departure to rethink the relationship between nationality, sexual difference, and female creation.

As Elaine Kim notes, the state often "treats female devotion to the nation with ambivalence."[81] Likewise, nationalist movements usually incorporate a gendered hierarchy of national duty. Within the national family, women are typically expected to tend to children, domestic affairs, and matters of the heart. To challenge the nationalist association between femininity, reproduction, and domesticity, *Dictée* highlights the courageous stories of female nationalist rebels, heroines, and religious martyrs including Joan of Arc, Saint Thérèse, Yu Guan Soon, and Cha's mother. By celebrating their unconventional legacies, *Dictée* misrecognizes nationalist rhetoric that identifies strong female leaders as "traitors" to the nation,[82] and that assesses women's value to the state only on the basis of domesticity and reproduction. *Dictée* particularly laments a legacy of male-dominated politics in Korea, where masculinist Korean nationalism replaced patriarchal Japanese colonialism.[83]

By recovering the stories of several iconoclastic women formerly repressed within national memory, *Dictée* sketches the outlines of what Luce Irigaray has called a "female imaginary"—or a symbolic economy grounded in sexual difference rather than masculinist solipsism.[84] Despite Cha's attentiveness to the historical and geopolitical shapers of women's traumatic experience, she gestures beyond the boundaries of the nation to construct a transnational feminist family album that incorporates both image and text. *Dictée* reproduces eleven photographs altogether, most of which document archaeological relics; episodes of Korean suffering and forced labor under Japanese colonization; Korean civil unrest; and (the majority) female nationalist and/or religious icons. Here, I will explore the images of women resurrected by Cha's family album.

In a chapter entitled "Melpomene . . . Tragedy," Cha pieces together her mother's life story as recounted in diary excerpts. Forced to speak Japanese during occupation, Cha's mother furtively indulged in her native tongue wherever possible. By so doing, she eked out a small space of resistance to colonial culture. She spoke "in the dark, in secret, very softly, in a whisper. Mother tongue is your refuge. It is being home. Being who you are. Truly" (*Dictée*: 45). Cha interprets her mother's subversive use of language as a courageous means of claiming her identity and heritage, and as a strategic refusal to internalize the colonial mandate of perfect resemblance or assimilation. Highlighting this linguistic rebellion, Cha regards her mother as a passionate nonconformist and unsung national hero.

Another chapter entitled "Clio . . . History" describes the life of Yu Guan Soon, a Korean heroine and martyr who died shortly after leading the historic anticolonial protest of 1 March 1919. Yu Guan Soon was initially ostracized by the Korean nationalist party, which refused to acknowledge "her seriousness, her place [in the movement] as a young woman" (*Dictée*: 30). Unwilling to pander to the masculinist sensibilities of this organization, she eventually formed her own revolutionary group to advocate Korean autonomy.

Cha parallels Guan Soon's story to that of Joan of Arc, the posthumously celebrated French heroine who was burned at the stake in Rouen in 1431, and later beatified and canonized in the early twentieth century. Evoked throughout *Dictée* (28, 119), Joan of Arc reappears in Cha's video installation entitled "Other Things Seen, Other Things Heard" (*Ailleurs*: 1978). Within *Dictée*, Joan of Arc joins a legion of female heroines—including Sappho, Saint Thérèse de Lisieux, and Yu Guan Soon—"whose response to a higher calling enabled them to become forces of history."[85] Because they managed to transcend or subvert the masculinist dictates of the nation-state, these heroines are critical constituents of Cha's transnational family tree. Memorialized within her genealogical project, their stories expose the national family as dependent upon sexualized fantasies of civic duty and belonging.

Joan of Arc's presence in Cha's family album recalls the contradictory symbolism with which women are represented in the national imaginary—as both heroines and martyrs, or scapegoats to be sacrificed for the sake of collective redemption. These complicated symbolic investments in "woman" and femininity reveal the stakes of state efforts to regulate gender and sexuality. As Leslie Bow maintains, "female specificity is not merely excluded in the projection of abstract, disembodied citizenship but is fundamental to its construction."[86] In other words, sexual difference is never negligible to nation-building efforts; instead, its erasure is crucial to the myth of abstract citizenship. Female specificity is often obliterated in religious tradition as well. For example, the theological revolution that devastated sixteenth-century European churches "primarily consisted in the destruction of feminine iconography [accompanied by] an increased masculinization of piety."[87]

By including Joan of Arc in her text, Cha strategically recalls how women's ideas are often ridiculed or compromised in the name of religious propriety and national progress. To counter this tradition, she invokes Joan of Arc as a figurehead of sorts in her effort to trace a lineage of forgotten women. Although Joan of Arc can be seen as an ambivalent figure in Korean memory given her status as a product of French missionary exportation, Cha recasts her as an inspiring model of feminist disidentification, a woman who dared to break with dominant ideology to pursue her own visions of duty, citizenship, and religiosity. By so doing, Cha populates history, and the national imaginary, with unruly or "troubling" women.

By relaying the stories of female nationalists and martyrs in a chapter named for the muse of tragedy, Melpomene, Cha creatively undermines a political repression of the "feminine" that women have experienced as traumatic in diverse national and colonial contexts. To rescue women from oblivion is crucial to Cha's genealogical project and articulation of a feminist imaginary. She repeatedly cites a need to move beyond violation toward feminist recuperation and activism:

> Nation against nation, nations against themselves. Repels her rejects her expels her from *her* own. Violation of *her* by giving name to the betrayal, to remedy, to justify the violation. Of *her* . . . Arrest the machine that purports to employ democracy but rather causes the successive refraction of *her*. Suffice Melpomene, to exorcise from this mouth the name the words the memory of severance through this act to utter *Her* once, *She* without the separate act of uttering. (*Dictée*: 88–89)

Melpomene's presence in *Dictée* strategically counters nationalist erasures of female creation, and infuses national memory with sexual difference.

Throughout her text, Cha tries to imagine how national utterance might be appropriated or "stained" by the feminine. The muse-identified chapters of *Dictée* suggestively coalesce around the question of how sexual difference, especially women's experiences of trauma, might figure differently within national memory. In this respect, *Dictée* strives to tell feminist stories that would undermine the perceived unity and coherence of identity and "make difference visible again."[88]

Central to Cha's efforts of feminist genealogy and linguistic disidentification is the figure of the *diseuse.* Her name ambiguously evokes the French word for female speaker *(diseuse)*, as well as the English words "disease" and "disuse." For Cha, *la diseuse* embodies a feminist spirit of linguistic and political appropriation. Rejecting the religious, political, and aesthetic ideals of correspondence and recognition, the *diseuse* instead delights in subversive repetition. Like Irigaray, the *diseuse* identifies mimicry as an interim strategy for unfounding the masculinist and racist inflections of dominant discourse.[89] Strategic mimicry allows her to insinuate difference into the very marrow of language and representation, and while so doing to take "pleasure in the image pleasure in the copy pleasure in the repetition" (*Dictée*: 17). This playful strategy of "repetition with a difference" is evident in the works of Sebbar, Cixous, and Djebar as well, all of whom forsake masculinist ideals of sameness and repetition to pursue feminist aesthetic tactics of echo and misrecognition.[90]

The *diseuse* creates new forms of seeing and being in an effort to misrecognize the mandates of nationalist and colonialist representation. Using an "improper" syntax that marks her difference within the masculinist imaginary, Cha's *diseuse* relentlessly pursues symbolic innovation. Her commitment to innovation is at times exhausting for *la diseuse*, who finds that the "essential words must be pretended invented she try on different images essential invisible" (*Dictée*: 15). Nonetheless, *la diseuse* continually challenges existing representations of sexual and ethnic difference in order to foster transnational feminist awareness. Ultimately, she constructs an imaginative homeland from the ruins and *ratures* of nationalist consciousness, which she insists is "always in the process of break-down."[91] Thanks to the *diseuse*'s adroit tongue, *Dictée*

> finds itself positively charged with the role of collective, even revolutionary, enunciation. It is literature that produces an active solidarity—and if the writer is in the margins or completely outside her fragile community, this allows her all the more ability to express another possible community, and to forge the means for another consciousness and sensibility.[92]

Cha's *diseuse* enacts a space of misrecognition in which to revolutionize enunciation for the purpose of promoting feminist consciousness and community. In a novel centered on modes of dictation and domination, the *diseuse* emerges as a potent counterpoint to the *dictée*. Whereas colonial efforts of linguistic and ideological transmission seek to "transform subjects into subjected others,"[93] Cha metaphorically rewrites dictation as an imperfect and uneven process—one in which deviation might enable self-invention rather than submission.

By putting language to "strange and minor uses," *Dictée* functions as Deleuzian minor literature to "bring language slowly and progressively to the desert. To use syntax in order to cry, to give syntax to the cry."[94] But if the novel essentially destroys conventional forms of representation, it also creates feminist "intervals" of alliance and community in response to transnational trauma. Although Cha's *diseuse* rejoices in the ambiguities of fantasy and misrecognition, for example, she also registers the pain of silence to conceive of language as an economy of wound and potential transformation for the traumatized female subject. Leveraging both the fearful and creative potentials of contamination, Cha's *diseuse* locates *jouissance* in the disjunctive experience of national, sexual, and racial unbelonging.[95]

By uniting feminist national rebels including the *diseuse*, Joan of Arc, Cha's mother, and Yu Guan Soon on a virtual family tree, *Dictée* explicitly challenges the perceived conflict of interest that opposes nationalism and feminism. Cha's effort to stage a transnational family reunion of feminist leaders inspires a flurry of questions. What does it mean to represent women relative to the nation? How are women's interests represented, effaced, or sacrificed within the national family? How are female heroines honored in national memory? Why is female martyrdom so often "required" for the benefit of community or nation? How do race, class, and sexuality impact these formulations? And "if women have been for the most part misrepresented or unrepresented in history as subordinate to men, how might women break through these images that are based primarily on masculine self-idealization?"[96] Cha attempts to think through these questions and their implications, especially as they pertain to women's status *vis-à-vis* Korean national memory. By disruptively transmitting the repressed tales and images of ostracized women, *Dictée* mourns the nation's failure to productively integrate and represent sexual difference.

At the same time, Cha's novel constantly imagines alternative openings, fissures, and cracks for the feminine within transnational memory. As readers work through these negative spaces of silence, flaw, and omission in Cha's work, they encounter:

> not only the whites of erasure and departure, but also the whites of beginnings and climaxes. As the red of gender absorbs/leaves its imprint on the page, the white of virginity [or new beginnings] slowly gives off words.[97]

While *Dictée* records the virtual impossibilities of representing women relative to the nation, it also actively unmaps a "trajectory of masculine creation that displaces the female, and that is premised on self-reflection."[98] Cha's family album unites disparate women within a vital transnational community—at once essential to, yet productively outside of, the national family. By persistently derailing racist and sexist modes of interpellation, Cha envisions not only the limits inherent in any act of identification, but also the potentials for pleasure in women's resistant practices of creative misrecognition.

For Cha, the historical breaks, pauses, and bruises of traumatized identity give birth to artistic experimentation. Throughout her work, Cha establishes an innovative vocabulary with which to represent trauma, difference, and assimilation. She misrecognizes the national family by reconceiving of blood, intimacy, and nationality. Ultimately, her family album inscribes racial, sexual, and ethnic difference into the very foundations of the nation.

Cha especially tries to imagine the impact of symbolic violence for women, who are most often represented in nationalist discourse as agents of contamination and sexual provocation. To this end, she recalls women's experiences of trauma relative to the projects of assimilation and collective forgetting that belie national identity. In this sense, Cha takes up the work of mourning in order to speak the nation otherwise. Yet she ultimately rejects national boundaries to promote transnational feminist alliances that might be grounded in critical inquiries into the politics of "home."

Cha stains national memory with difference by suspending, rather than granting, recognition in her work. Her family album constructs a "feminist figure of humanity" that "both resists representation and still erupts in powerful new tropes, new turns of historical possibility."[99] By simultaneously engaging in and resisting the act of representation, Cha stages a dynamic interface between trauma, image, and identity.

Readers are often estranged by the experimental format of *Dictée*, which, like Cha's visual artwork, privileges repetition, interference, and omission. Critical reviews of *Dictée* should take this estrangement seriously, since Cha's aesthetic tactics are clearly orchestrated to frustrate, rather than inspire, audience identification. Why does Cha strive to create effects of distance, alienation, and misrecognition in her work? This line of inquiry is critical to pursue if we hope to acknowledge the unresolved ambivalence of Cha's work.

I want to suggest that audience alienation is a symptom of Cha's successful artistic rendering of the complex passages between image and identity. By provoking unease rather than facile identification, Cha's oeuvre powerfully grasps the "complex and indeterminate relations by which subjectivity is constituted in the spaces *between* race, gender, ethnicity, and sexuality."[100] In both form and content, Cha's family album mobilizes the disturbing potentials of misrecognition to challenge political projects of identification, assimilation, and domination. It forges explosive spaces of parallax between image and identity.

Cha dramatically rewrites blood, intimacy, and nationality to reveal the other's gaze as foundational to self-portraiture. Asking what it means to represent the traumatized self to others, she re-visions identity as both the nexus of external projects of fantasy and domination, and as a site of resistance that permits varying degrees of affiliation, disidentification, and creative misrecognition. In this sense, Cha—like Cixous—approaches autobiography as an endless exchange between self and other. She also problematizes nostalgia for lost origins by foregrounding the violence and repression that make "home" possible.

Although Cha highlights the limits of nationalist discourse for a nation's "others," she simultaneously stages stunning interventions into the nationalist imaginary to consider "how political community might be reconceptualized within [transnational] feminist practice."[101] Mining the gaps and margins of national memory, Cha maps out a lineage of feminist activism *vis-à-vis* the nation. She does not propose a plan of action per se; instead, she draws attention to an overlooked history of women speaking up and acting out against national injustice. Challenging her audience to experience the violence of alienation and split subjectivity—which all too often define the terms of engagement for women and minorities relative to the nation—Cha performs an act of "diva citizenship" to map out "unrealized potentials for subaltern political activity."[102]

Inspired by a rich tradition of critical inquiry in feminist and ethnic studies, Cha's portfolio betrays an overwhelming suspicion of origins. Biology, religion, psychology, linguistics, political theory, philosophy—no origin story or creation myth is left unchallenged by her work. Eager to invent new avenues for female expression and appropriation, Cha has brokered a certain peace with the ambivalence of origins—which exists in her work not to be resolved, but to be fully imagined and strategically deployed.

Cha's work reflects the concerns of feminist inquiry more broadly, which has evolved on the basis of a profound suspicion of origins. Especially since the 1980s, feminists have struggled with the exclusionary beginnings of feminist organizing. Still today, feminist scholars seek to balance the political imperative to assert group identity as "women," on one hand, with the need to reject essentialist definitions of "woman" that elide key differences among women such as race, class, and sexuality. This tension, rather than its resolution, perpetually invigorates feminist scholarship, and ensures that it will become both answerable and relevant to a more diverse constituency. Theresa Cha's work reinforces the notion of identity as intersectional and fluid, yet as distinctly "situated" in relation to critical social parameters including race, language, ethnicity, nation, and religion.

At their best, feminist art and scholarship stimulate fundamental shifts in political and historical consciousness—shifts that are profoundly unsettling because they involve

> A displacement and a self-displacement: leaving or giving up a place that is "home" for another place that is unknown and risky, a place from which speaking and thinking are at best tentative and uncertain. *But the leaving is not a choice: one could not live there in the first place*.[103]

It is precisely this type of displacement that Cha provokes throughout her work. Disturbing as it may be, Cha's work initiates an "unsettling" process to spark transnational feminist consciousness.[104] Her artwork especially underscores the feminist need to envision new symbolic politics, new ways of seeing and engaging with existing representation, so as "not to repeat history in oblivion" (*Dictée*: 33). Although Cha's family album is indeed a space of doubt, misrecognition, and alienation, these are perhaps the hallmarks of feminist representation—forever ripe with potentials for mobility, displacement, and denaturalization. Ultimately, the unsettling quality of Cha's work underscores its commitment to engineering new visions. For originality is almost always disturbing—monstrous even—in its desire to conceive of difference or "otherness" as simultaneously a threat, a promise, an ethical imperative, and an opening onto a new aesthetics.[105]

NOTES

1. Hélène Cixous, *First Days of the Year*, trans. Catherine MacGillivray (Minneapolis: University of Minnesota Press, 1998); originally published as *Jours de l'an* (Paris: Les editions des femmes, 1990), 101.

2. Hélène Cixous, "Writing Blind," Northwestern University, Evanston, IL (1997).

3. Whereas Cixous is best described as a Francophone writer, Cha is, instead, a French-speaking writer. She uses French selectively throughout her written and visual work in order to both capitalize on its phonetic ambiguity, and to evoke the uncomfortable mandates of an imposed colonial tongue.

4. Chandra Talpade Mohanty, "Crafting Feminist Genealogies: On the Geography and Politics of Home, Nation, and Community," in Ella Shohat, ed., *Talking Visions: Multicultural Feminism in a Transnational Age* (Cambridge: The MIT Press, 1998), 491.

5. Marianne Hirsch, *Family Frames: Photography, Narrative, and Postmemory* (Cambridge: Harvard University Press, 1997), 53.

6. Kaja Silverman, *The Threshold of the Visible World* (New York: Routledge, 1996), 199.

7. Pierre Bourdieu, "The Cult of Unity and Cultivated Differences," in *Photography: A Middle-brow Art*, trans. Shaun Whiteside (Stanford: Stanford University Press, 1990), 19.

8. Hélène Cixous, *Rootprints: Memory and Life Writing*, trans. Eric Prenowitz (New York: Routledge, 1997).

9. Hélène Cixous, "Sorties," in Hélène Cixous and Catherine Clement, *The Newly Born Woman*, trans. Betsy Wing (Minneapolis: University of Minnesota Press, 1986), 65.

10. For more on this see Marie-Hélène Huet, *Monstrous Imagination* (Cambridge: Harvard University Press, 1993).

11. Maurice Blanchot, *The Infinite Conversation*, trans. Susan Hanson (Minneapolis: University of Minnesota Press, 1993).

12. Reference is made to Benedict Anderson, *Imagined Communities: Reflections on the Origin and Spread of Nationalism* (London: Verso, 1991).

13. Of course, Cixous is not the first to conceive of nationality in this way; many other scholars—prominent among them Ernest Renan and Benedict Anderson—have also conceptualized the nation as an imaginative artifact or community rather than a strictly geographical or political entity.

14. Lisa Lowe, "Unfaithful to the Original: The Subject of *Dictée* " in Elaine Kim and Norma Alarcón, eds., *Writing Self, Writing Nation: Essays on Theresa Hak Kyung Cha's Dictée* (Berkeley: Third Woman Press, 1994), 36.

15. Theresa Hak Kyung Cha, *Dictée* (Tanam Press, 1982. Berkeley: Third Woman Press, 1995). My page citations refer to the reprint edition.

16. For more on this see Chandra Talpade Mohanty, "Crafting Feminist Genealogies: On the Geography and Politics of Home, Nation, and Community," in Ella Shohat, ed., *Talking Visions: Multicultural Feminism in a Transnational Age* (Cambridge: The MIT Press, 1998), esp. 500.

17. See Maurice Blanchot, *L'Entretien infini* (Paris: Editions Gallimard, 1969); reprinted as *The Infinite Conversation*, trans. Susan Hanson (Minneapolis: University of Minnesota Press, 1993), 308.

18. For more on these terms, see Gloria Anzaldúa and Cherríe Moraga, eds., *This Bridge Called My Back: Writings by Radical Women of Color* (New York: Kitchen Table/Women of Color Press, 1981), and Chela Sandoval, *Methodology of the Oppressed* (Minnesota: University of Minnesota Press, 2000).

19. For more on identity as a process of collision, and on the notion of disidentification, see Jose Muñoz, *Disidentifications: Queers of Color and the Performance of Politics* (Minneapolis: University of Minnesota Press, 1999), 1–34.

20. Eve Kosofsky Sedgwick, *The Epistemology of the Closet* (Berkeley: University of California Press, 1990), 61.

21. Muñoz 1999: 6.

22. Michele Montrelay, "Recherches sur la fémininité," *Critique* 278 (July 1970), cited in Craig Owens, *Beyond Recognition: Representation, Power, and Culture* (Berkeley: University of California Press, 1992), 168.

23. As evoked in Virginia Woolf, *Three Guineas* (New York: Harcourt Brace and Company, 1938), 109.

24. For a comprehensive list of Cha's artwork and exhibitions, please refer to the appendices in Constance Lewallen, ed., *The Dream of the Audience: Theresa Hak Kyung Cha (1951–1982)* (Berkeley: University of California Press, 2001).

25. See for example Elaine Kim and Norma Alarcón, eds., *Writing Self, Writing Nation: Essays on Theresa Hak Kyung Cha's Dictée* (Berkeley: Third Woman Press, 1994); and Constance M. Lewallen, ed., *The Dream of the Audience: Theresa Hak Kyung Cha (1951–1982)* (Berkeley: University of California Press, 2001).

26. Cheng 2001: 141.

27. See Muñoz 1999: esp. 4–5.

28. See John Berger, "The Changing View of Man in the Portrait," *Selected Essays and Articles: The Look of Things* (Harmondsworth, England: Penguin, 1958), 37–38.

29. Hirsch 1997: 47.

30. For more on the creative possibilities of translation, see Abdelkebir Khatibi, *Maghreb pluriel* (Paris: Denoel, 1983), esp. 179.

31. Jacques Derrida, "Des Tours de Babel," in J. F. Graham, ed. and trans., *Difference in Translation* (Ithaca: Cornell University Press, 1985), 174.

32. Again, see Khatibi 1983 for more on the creative deployment of "*bi-langue*," or the forked tongue.

33. Cheng 2001: 144.

34. As famously illustrated by René Magritte's painting entitled *La Trahison des Images*.

35. Trinh T. Minh-ha, "Outside In Inside Out," *When the Moon Waxes Red: Representation, Gender, and Cultural Politics* (New York: Routledge, 1991), 73.

36. See Rigoberta Menchú, *I, Rigoberta Menchu: An Indian Woman in Guatemala*, ed. E. Burgos-Debray, trans. A. Wright (London: Verso, 1984), esp. 68–69.

37. Norman Bryson, *Vision and Painting: The Logic of the Gaze* (New Haven: Yale University Press, 1983), 98.

38. Reference to Trinh T. Minh-ha's film *Reassemblage*.

39. *The American Heritage Dictionary*, 2nd edition (New York: Dell Publishing Corporation, 1983).

40. See Hirsch 1997: 108.

41. Ibid. 51.

42. Ibid. 57.

43. Leah Ollman, "Pictures that Develop With Layers of Time," *The Los Angeles Times*, July 5, 2002, F26.

44. Roland Barthes, *Image-Music-Text*, trans. Stephen Heath (New York: Hill and Wang, 1977), 25–26.

45. See Leigh Gilmore, *The Limits of Autobiography: Trauma and Testimony* (Ithaca: Cornell University Press, 2001), esp. 28–33.

46. For more on this concept of breaking the framework, see Shoshana Felman and Dori Laub, *Testimony: Crises of Witnessing in Literature, Psychoanalysis and History* (New York: Routledge, 1992).

47. Edward Said and Jean Mohr, *After the Last Sky* (London: Pantheon, 1986), 14.

48. See Bryson's distinction between the gaze and the glance in Bryson 1983.

49. See Bryson 1983: 122.

50. Trinh T. Minh-ha, *When the Moon Waxes Red: Representation, Gender, and Cultural Politics* (New York: Routledge, 1991), 30.

51. Annette Kuhn, *The Power of the Image: Essays on Representation and Sexuality* (London: Routledge, 1985), 27.

52. Kuhn 1985: 30.

53. For more on noise and interference, especially in relation to biological parasitism, see Michel Serres, *Le Parasite* (Paris: Grasset, 1980).

54. Jacques Lacan, *The Four Fundamental Concepts of Psychoanalysis: The Seminar of Jacques Lacan Book XI*, trans. Alan Sheridan (New York: W. W. Norton & Co., 1981), 81.

55. Muñoz 1999: 31.

56. Donna Haraway, "Situated Knowledges: The Science Question in Feminism and the Privilege of Partial Perspective," in *Simians, Cyborgs, and Women: The Reinvention of Nature* (New York: Routledge, 1991), 198–99.

57. Cheng 2001: 150.

58. Hirsch 1997: 101.

59. Ibid. 40.

60. See Pierre Nora, "Between Memory and History: *Les Lieux de Mémoire*," in *Representations* 26 (Spring 1989): 19.

61. Elizabeth Grosz, *Volatile Bodies* (Bloomington: Indiana University Press, 1994), 194.

62. Jacques Lacan, *The Four Fundamental Concepts of Psychoanalysis*, trans. Alan Sheridan (New York: Norton, 1981), 99.

63. Silverman 1996: 202.

64. Anne McClintock, *Imperial Leather: Race, Gender, and Sexuality in the Colonial Contest* (New York: Routledge, 1995), 37.

65. I allude here to Edward Steichen's photographic exhibit entitled "The Family of Man" (first displayed in the United States in 1955), which provides an anthropological family album of sorts, intended to trace human resemblance, lineage, and kinship.

66. McClintock 1995: 45.

67. Cited in Nancy Stepan, "Biological Degeneration: Races and Proper Places," in J. Chamberlin and S. Gilman, eds., *Degeneration: The Dark Side of Progress* (New York: Columbia University Press, 1985), 100. See also the essays by Boon and Gilman in this anthology.

68. See Dana Fuss, *Identification Papers* (New York: Routledge, 1995), 160.

69. Sander Gilman, "Sexology, Psychoanalysis, and Degeneration: From a Theory of Race to a Race to Theory," in Gilman, ed., *Degeneration: The Dark Side of Progress* (New York: Columbia University Press, 1985), 83.

70. McClintock 1995: 47.

71. Rosemarie Garland Thomas, *Extraordinary Bodies* (New York: Routledge, 1996), 71.

72. See McClintock 1995: 42.

73. Donna Haraway, "Universal Donors in a Vampire Culture: It's All in the Family: Biological Kinship Categories in the Twentieth-Century United States," in W. Cronon, ed., *Uncommon Ground: Toward Reinventing Nature* (New York: W. W. Norton & Company, 1995), 321.

74. For a more detailed discussion of assimilation and the attempt to impose fictive purity, see Françoise Lionnet, *Postcolonial Representations: Women, Literature, Identity* (Ithaca: Cornell University Press, 1995), esp. 14.

75. Bow 2001: 44.

76. Mohanty 1995: 492.

77. Cheng 2001: 148.

78. See Kobena Mercer, "Reading Racial Fetishism: The Photographs of Robert Mapplethorpe," in E. Apter, ed., *Fetishism as Cultural Discourse* (Ithaca: Cornell University Press, 1993), 324.

79. See Lauren Berlant, *The Queen of America Goes to Washington City: Essays on Sex and Citizenship* (Durham, NC: Duke University Press, 1997). Berlant imagines the "partial citizen" as a "marked" minority who cannot easily identify with the "universal" (white, male, heterosexual) citizen-subject position.

80. For more on this see Wong's essay in Kim 1994: 113–16. As Wong notes, Cha substitutes a name of her own invention, Elitere, in place of the ninth muse called Euterpe. Cha begins her novel with a quote attributed to Sappho, who was acknowledged in antiquity as the tenth muse.

81. See Kim 1994: 15. As Kim points out, the state accepts female devotion to the nation only when it is "expressed through the filter of the family." In the Korean context, she states that "public displays of female patriotism have not been greeted with unequivocal approval in traditional Korean society, where the most patriotic thing a woman can do is to give birth to or be the wife of a great [male] patriot" (16).

82. For more on this see, for example, Norma Alarcón, "Traddutora, Traditora: A Paradigmatic Figure of Chicana Feminism," in Anne McClintock, Aamir Mufti, and Ella Shohat, eds., *Dangerous Liaisons: Gender, Nation, and Postcolonial Perspectives* (Minneapolis: University of Minnesota Press, 1997).

83. See Kim 1994: 20.

84. See Irigaray 1985.

85. Emily Apter, *Continental Drift: From National Characters to Virtual Subjects* (Chicago: University of Chicago Press, 1999), 41.

86. Leslie Bow, *Betrayal and Other Acts of Subversion: Feminism, Sexual Politics, Asian American Women's Literature* (Princeton: Princeton University Press, 2001), 40.

87. Huet 1993: 28.

88. Shelly Sunn Wong, "Unnaming the Same: Theresa Hak Kyung Cha's *Dictée*," in Kim and Alarcón, eds. 1994: 113.

89. See Luce Irigaray, *This Sex Which Is Not One*, trans. Catherine Porter (Ithaca: Cornell University Press, 1985), esp. 68–85 and 220.

90. For an analysis of mimicry in the works of Assia Debar and Leila Sebbar, see Anne Donadey, *Recasting Postcolonialism: Women Writing Between Worlds* (Portsmouth, NH: Heinemann, 2001), esp. chapters 4, 5, and 6.

91. Gilles Deleuze and Felix Guattari, "What Is a Minor Literature?" in *Kafka: Toward a Minor Literature*, trans. Dana Polan (Minneapolis: University of Minnesota Press, 1986), 17.

92. Ibid.

93. Fuss 1995: 14. Lowe provocatively explores Cha's resistance to discourses of likeness in terms of the Althusserian "bad subject" that resists absolute interpellation. See Lowe in Alarcón and Kim, eds. 1994: 55.

94. Deleuze and Guattari 1986: 17 and 26.

95. I mean to evoke the French word *jouissance* in both of its senses, to refer to both pleasure (esp. sexual pleasure) and ownership, property, or appropriation.

96. Cynthia Pon, "'Passages' in Mary Shelley's *Frankenstein*: Toward a Feminist Figure of Humanity?" *Modern Language Studies* 30, no. 2 (Fall 2000): 43.

97. Trinh T. Minh-ha, "White Spring," in Constance Lewallen, ed., *The Dream of the Audience* (Berkeley: University of California Press, 2001), 41.

98. Pon 2000: 37.

99. Donna Haraway, "Ecce Homo, Ain't (Ar'n't) I a Woman, and Inappropriate/d Others: The Human in a Post-Humanist Landscape," in Judith Butler and Joan Scott, eds., *Feminists Theorize the Political* (New York: Routledge, 1992), 86.

100. Mercer 1993: 324.

101. Biddy Martin and Chandra Talpade Mohanty, "Feminist Politics: What's Home Got to Do With It?" in Teresa de Lauretis, ed., *Feminist Studies/Critical Studies* (Bloomington: Indiana University Press, 1986), 210.

102. Lauren Berlant, "Notes on Diva Citizenship," in *The Queen of America Goes to Washington City: Essays on Sex and Citizenship* (Durham, NC: Duke University Press, 1997).

103. Teresa de Lauretis, "Displacing Hegemonic Discourses: Reflections on Feminist Theory in the 1980s," *Inscriptions* ¾ (1988): 138–39.

104. For more on feminist consciousness as an ongoing process of unsettling see Trinh T. Minh-ha, *Woman, Native, Other* (Bloomington: Indiana University Press, 1989), 40.

105. For more on the etymology of "monster" and the ambivalent connotations of monstrosity, see Huet 1993.

Chapter Four

Dismembering the Gaze

Speleology and Vivisection in Assia Djebar's L'amour, la fantasia

> Images of Algerian women are not displayed in homes, they are kept to themselves. We cannot be feminist except by circulating things among ourselves.
>
> —Assia Djebar, Lecture at UCLA, May 2001

I. INTRODUCTION: BURNING IN

How to explain the power of an image, or why certain images wield power over us? Representation always involves fragmentation and omission: one story instead of another, an artist's decision about what to leave in and what to leave out. From this perspective, the image seems innocent—we might be tempted to read it in purely aesthetic terms. Yet it is crucial to attend to the political force of imagery, as well as the links between representation and violence.

As Nietzsche reminds us in *On the Genealogy of Morals*, seeing is always an exercise of power; that is, ways of seeing are inevitably invested in quests for epistemological and ideological mastery.[1] From this perspective, it is crucial to understand images as powerful shapers of identity and political possibility. When particular visions are imbued with the will to power and articulated from sites of authority, they attain the status of truth and foundation. In this sense it is impossible to speak of an existence apart from representation; seeing creates being, just as language formalizes experience.

Although Assia Djebar, an Algerian novelist and filmmaker with Berber roots, does not explicitly cite Nietzsche in her work, her autobiographical fiction shares his conception of knowledge as perspective in order to imagine not only how certain visions achieve truth status, but also how those visions impact interpersonal and international power relations. Born to an Arabo-Berber family in Cherchell, Algeria, in 1936, Djebar actively participated in student protests and anticolonial resistance efforts throughout the early years of the Algerian revolution. She also contributed to *El-Moujahid*, the official newspaper of the anticolonial FLN (Front de Liberation National), by interviewing Algerian refugees in Morocco.

Djebar's exposure to Western philosophy was facilitated by her "modernist" father, a French teacher who enrolled her in French boarding schools from an early age to supplement her Qur'anic education. She was the first Algerian woman to be accepted at the Ecole Normale Superieur in Sèvres, France, which she attended during the Algerian revolution in order to train as an historian. After teaching history, theater, and film for several years at the University of Rabat in Morocco and the University of Algiers, Djebar moved to Paris in 1966, shortly after the war's end and the subsequent rise of Arab nationalism in Algeria. She returned to Algeria in 1974 to teach at the University of Algiers, but moved back to Paris in 1980 after a new Algerian Charter (1976) declared Islam the official state religion. In 1995, in the wake of a brutal civil war that initiated a wave of fundamentalist killings of artists and intellectuals in Algeria, Djebar moved to the United States, where she became the director of the Center for French and Francophone Studies at LSU. Since 2001, Djebar has served as professor and Silver Chair of French and Francophone Studies at NYU. Already one of North Africa's most acclaimed writers, Djebar earned the additional distinction of becoming the fifth woman and first Muslim to be elected to the Academie Française, France's most esteemed cultural institution, in 2005.

Djebar has spent over twenty years composing a projected quartet of works that she describes as an attempt, trace, or aspect of autobiography ("*apparence d'autobiographie*").[2] Her bursts of literary production have been punctuated with gaps, most notably when Djebar has fled from or returned to her Algerian homeland in times of political crisis. "*J'ai eu plusieurs parentheses*," explains Djebar ("I've had several parentheses.") These "parentheses," including her relative absence from the literary scene in the 1970s, affirm Djebar's commitment to the indivisibility of personal, political, and artistic life.

I will focus here on Djebar's *L'amour, la fantasia* (*Fantasia*),[3] the first and most celebrated volume of her autobiographical quartet. Composed of three distinct parts, *Fantasia* more closely resembles a series of orchestral movements than a conventionally structured narrative. The first two sections of *Fantasia* interweave Djebar's childhood memories with historical and political accounts of the French colonization of Algeria in 1830. Part III of the novel recalls the Algerian Revolution of 1954–1962 by incorporating archival materials with oral testimony from Algerian women participants in the revolution.

A plethora of gazes circulates in the first two sections of *Fantasia*. To craft a history of the Oriental look, Djebar persistently marks the colonial rush to represent, and considers how subjective visions are enlisted to support political projects of domination. Djebar draws the first battle lines in her novel by observing the presence of war correspondents enlisted by the French government to represent the colonial conquest of Algeria. By foregrounding the Orientalist visions designed to increase French public support for military conquest, Djebar frames fantasy as a crucial component of national and sexual politics, and highlights the material and epistemic violence of colonization. Ultimately, she understands images as foundational to subjectivity, and insists on their power to haunt personal and collective memory.

Djebar is especially interested in the power of the colonial gaze to fabricate exotic "otherness." In this sense, her work engages with contemporary theoretical insights regarding Orientalist representation. Like Edward Said, Djebar explores the role of Orientalist imagery in projects of colonial conquest. Said conceives of Orientalism as a culturally hegemonic discourse or, more specifically, a "Western style for dominating, restructuring, and having authority over the Orient."[4] In this sense, he regards Orientalist imagery not as a reflection of reality, but as a "man-made" vision of political domination. In order to interrupt hegemonic claims to truth at play within the Orientalist image, Said identifies a need to renounce the enabling fantasies of Oriental representation. Without renunciation, he sees no hope for ethical exchange as a basis for cross-cultural representation.

Djebar is equally committed to figuring out what to make of the horror of photographs that have been handed down throughout history, particularly Orientalist and nationalist portrayals of women. Especially interested in the sexual politics of truth, Djebar is not content to disavow colonial fantasies of sexual and racial otherness. Instead, she orchestrates a narrative economy that challenges binary conceptions of truth and fantasy, and disturbs our faith in singularity and equivalence as necessary foundations for identity. If the Orientalist imagination is premised on a "sovereign Western consciousness,"[5] then Djebar problematizes the sovereign subject, especially its primacy within autobiographical projects. By so doing, she seeks not to return the colonial gaze, but to dismember[6] its very conditions of possibility. In this sense, *Fantasia* frames colonial imagery as a catalyst for traumatized yet creative visions of memory and identity among colonized people.

In order to reimagine Algerian experiences of colonization, domesticity, and revolution, *Fantasia* engages in a painful odyssey of re-membering, or "a putting together of the dismembered past to make sense of the trauma of the present."[7] Djebar pays particular attention to the fantasies of women that circulate within the Orientalist and nationalist imaginaries. Her efforts to radically reconfigure images of Algerian women compel her to "go under" in a Nietzschean sense in order to excavate the "minor" (unseen and untold) details of national memory, historiography, and colonized subjectivity.

While guided by this spirit of genealogical inquiry, *Fantasia* is simultaneously haunted by a profound suspicion of origins. The narrator of *Fantasia* continually reflects on the impossibility of claiming an authentic or stable identity within the context of colonization, especially by alternately referring to herself in the first and third person. In this sense, Djebar's project

> will never confuse itself with a quest for "origins." On the contrary, it will cultivate the details and accidents that accompany every beginning. Where the self fabricates a coherent identity, the genealogist sets out to study numberless beginnings. To follow the complex course of descent is to discover that truth or being does not lie at the root of what we know and what we are.[8]

In essence, *Fantasia* stages an "unfounding" of nationalist and Orientalist historiography. Djebar confronts a long history of imagery in order to express the complex interface between female sexuality and national political identity.

As Djebar traces the descent of colonial and nationalist symbolism, her genealogical project constantly spills over or contaminates the *topos* of the body. Like Foucault, Djebar regards bodies as the primary sites of inscription for regulatory discourses that seek to establish particular effects of "truth." Throughout her work, the wounding or empowering potentials of representation linger in bodily surfaces, contours, and cavities. Djebar probes the female body as a terrain especially ravaged by competing projects of representation and descent. She explores the innermost cavities of the female body, including the larynx and vagina, in order to advance her critique of historical foundations. Not a fully colonized territory, however, the female body in *Fantasia* also houses the subversive potentials of the voice, particularly the cry.

Fantasia takes as its point of departure the work of French writers and artists employed by the state to draft impressionistic accounts of the French conquest of Algeria. Because they so often present Algerian women as exotic objects for colonial contemplation, these images have fracturing implications for female subjectivity and embodiment. In response to war correspondents' phantasmic visions of Algerian women, Djebar tries to imagine the female body apart from—although indelibly marked by—the Oriental look.

Djebar also challenges the symbolic economy that underlies masculinist nationalist portrayals of women. In *This Sex Which Is Not One*, Luce Irigaray theorizes the "specular economy" as a complex network of images, symbols, discourses, and institutions that erases sexual difference by reflecting the masculine subject, or the "One," back to himself ad infinitum.[9] Privileging masculinity as the "standard" or universal trait, the specular economy promotes indifference to, or devaluation of, sexual difference by assigning greatest value to correspondence, similitude, and self-reference. Women's bodies serve as a medium of exchange within this economy, wherein what remains most forbidden to and impossible for women is to speak about sexual difference and to "express something of [their] own sexual pleasure."[10] Ultimately, Irigaray contends that within the specular economy,

> The feminine cannot signify itself in any proper meaning, proper name, or concept, not even that of woman . . . "She" must only be the shutter set up to allow the eye to frame its view; the path, the *mirror*, which leads back, by a process of repetition, to the recognition of (his) origin for the "subject."[11]

The material effects of this symbolic economy become both "graspable" and chilling when we trace historical representations of the female body and sexuality. Especially in the West, femininity and the female body have been routinely ignored, erased, or devalued in the founding discourses of a broad range of academic disciplines ranging from philosophy, religion, medicine, and psychoanalysis to aesthetics and political theory. Disdain for the feminine as an object of study has proven remarkably tenacious, and has repeatedly motivated characterizations of female sexuality as monstrosity, deviation, disease, contamination, madness, perversion, passivity, and abyss throughout the history of Western thought and popular culture.

The concrete effects of this symbolic economy were clear during the Algerian revolution, when women's bodies became a battleground for French colonial and Algerian nationalist male aggression. Algerian women's bodies were simultaneously idealized, exchanged, and violated throughout the revolution. On a symbolic level, the nationalist movement idealized women as repositories of Algerian custom and tradition. Yet this symbolism had socially retrograde effects, especially by aligning women with "national" traditions that French colonizers then sought to violate or undermine. Furthermore, despite women's symbolic value within the nationalist imaginary, nationalist leaders devalued women and femininity in practice by denying women full participation in the revolution, and by disavowing women's claims of physical and sexual abuse by Algerian male nationalists. These daily practices ultimately silenced women's experiences, and upheld an ideal of national solidarity as dependent upon the "abstract" or "universal" citizen, whose value was established on the basis of masculinity. Within this ambivalent context of symbolic valorization and material exclusion, sexual difference was simultaneously affirmed and disavowed by the Algerian nationalist movement.

Women who wanted to assume substantive roles to support nationalist military objectives were prevented from doing so on the grounds of their intractable "difference." Denied entry to the nationalist movement often had fracturing effects for Algerian women who wanted to mobilize as both women and nationalists. Their experiences testify to the real political effects of an economy premised on sameness, or intolerance for difference.

In response to the violent effects of the specular economy for women, *Fantasia* proposes a subaltern feminist symbolic economy founded on a heightened sensitivity to all forms of difference. Djebar formulates a new way of "seeing" by launching a series of clandestine missions to unexplored depths and hidden interiors. Her "missions," that resemble the exploratory efforts of speleology and vivisection, shed new light on the cave (as historic and philosophical symbol); the female body and sexuality; and the entire project of representation. The enunciated "I" of Djebar's text—which incorporates the witnessing eyes, hands, and tongues of female revolutionaries—explores caves and (as) female bodies to envision novel modes of being and becoming.

Although the cave motif throughout *Fantasia* is most often analyzed in relation to colonialist burning campaigns in Algeria, it is also essential to understand the cave in *Fantasia* as a space of epistemological unfounding. The cave, with its cascading or serial openings and its echoes of colonial massacre and memory, provides an apt site for Djebar's ambivalent genealogical project of unfounding. Because it renders futile the pursuit of origins as well as the distinction between copy and original, the cave offers Djebar a tantalizing, subterranean *topos* from which to subvert the world of representation.

Throughout *Fantasia,* caves serve as privileged sites of feminist vivisection. From these sites, Djebar dissects Algerian masculinist nationalist rhetoric by challenging the social and spatial confinement of women's bodies within the harem and beneath the veil, as well as the nationalist alignment of women with motherhood and cultural transmission. Most significantly, Djebar's vivisection positions female desire and its censure as constitutive elements of traumatized female identity. In this sense, Djebar's spelunking mission implies an excavation not only of national memory and historiography, but also of the female body, genitals, and sexuality. I will discuss these parallel excavations later in more detail, especially as they relate to Irigaray's reflections on the resonance of the cave as a metaphor for the female body and genitalia.

Djebar's effort to conceive of an alternative symbolic economy that questions the ideals of similitude, correspondence, and reflection constitutes a significant feminist intervention into philosophy, colonial politics, national history, and autobiography. Emphasizing the need to create a new language to express female desire, Djebar's work uniquely integrates the gaze (vision), the cry (voice), and the hand (touch). By launching a series of missions to unexplored depths and hidden interiors throughout *Fantasia*, Djebar engages in a novel project of re-visioning that can be read as both an effort to see the revolution from a fresh perspective and as a feminist act of survival. Djebar hopes to reclaim historical vision by "seeing difference differently," focusing not on particular images of women but on the ways of seeing that produce those images.[12] Through this project of re-visioning, *Fantasia* identifies the female body, desire, and identity as the stakes not only of foundational projects to establish truth and history, but also of destructively creative acts of "unfounding"[13] (*effondement/effondrement*) and misrecognition. By so doing, the novel understands postcolonial feminist subjectivity as the site of ambivalent negotiations between image and identity.

In her travels through "memory's subterranean store-house" (*Fantasia*: 109), Djebar foregrounds the intersections between sexuality and war, and defaces the borders of the personal and political. As a result, her voyage into the female body is best understood as a revolutionary attempt to express female sexuality and desire within a philosophical and linguistic tradition in which it has forcibly remained underground, unthinkable, and inarticulable. For Djebar, this revolution of the female body is tantamount to the Algerian revolution. Both are profoundly political, personal, and sexualized efforts of decolonization.

Like Irigaray's feminist speculum or concave mirror, the symbolic economy set in motion throughout *Fantasia* aims to distort, to preclude simple reflection, and *to burn*.[14] Yet Djebar's text is not the product of a generically feminist speculum, or "speculum of the 'other' woman."[15] Instead, her radical vision emerges from a dichotomy of location that complicates her relationship to language, culture, and politics.

Djebar recasts Irigaray's speculum as *sistrum*: a "jingling instrument or rattle used by ancient Egyptians esp. in rites of Isis" (*Fantasia*: 109). The *sistrum* permits Djebar to create a subversive representational economy that signifies through the ambivalence of the gaze and, especially, the culturally forked tongue. It registers the dissonant echoes of sound, music, and *les cris*: "coils curling in the throat, streams of abyssal sounds, interlacing echoes, cataracts of murmurs, hushed hisses, cacophony, shards of shipwrecked sighs, molten words, scattered laughter, staccatoed notes, splintered firestones" (Ibid.). By highlighting cacophonous fragments of sound throughout *Fantasia*, Djebar deterritorializes language and adapts it for "strange and minor uses."[16]

Within the narrative economy of *Fantasia*, bodies, voices, and gazes circulate on the basis of fragmentation and misrecognition rather than equivalence, substitution, reflection, or identification. Yet the physicality, musicality, and split subjectivity expressed in Djebar's work cannot be read in purely aesthetic terms; they also need to be understood in the context of postcolonial feminist praxis. Djebar enlists the *sistrum* to delineate the cultural and colonial space of the Maghreb, and to imagine the specificity of women's positions therein. By "re-membering" the symbolic politics of colonization and revolution, Djebar constructs a national past that includes Algerian women's voices as well as their sexual experiences of desire and violation.

II. GOING UNDER: KNOWLEDGE AND CAVE EXPLORATION

> In order for woman to reach the place where she takes pleasure as woman, a long detour by way of the analysis of the various systems of oppression brought to bear upon her is assuredly necessary.
>
> —Luce Irigaray, *This Sex Which Is Not One*

In *The Gay Science*, Nietzsche invites his readers to accompany Zarathustra, the ancient Persian prophet, in a search for the foundations of knowledge, truth, and existence. Zarathustra's quest culminates with the gesture of *untergehen*, or "going under."[17] The Nietzschean project of "going under" involves a cycle of degeneration and demise; hence, it is introduced in *The Gay Science* with the words "*Incipit tragoedia*."[18] Yet morbidity occasions a startling sense of possibility chez Nietzsche—an ardent philosopher of bodily illness and decrepitude, which he refers to as "the great health." Especially through his conception of eternal return, Nietzsche identifies pain, disease, and suffering as sources of profound wisdom and as opportunities to affirm the will to live. Enamored of metamorphosis, Nietzsche draws inspiration from alchemy or the art-science of transforming filth to gold. In a parallel gesture, he translates personal torment into a body of philosophy lined with flesh and blood. Nietzsche likewise understands destruction as a catalyst for creation, and poetically finds "all events profitable, all days holy."[19]

Traumatic suffering and proximity to death transform life into an urgent question for Nietzsche, and spur his commitment to critical reflection or "self-overcoming" as a means of formulating knowledge:

> From pain one emerges as a different person, with a few more question marks—above all with the *will* henceforth to question further, more deeply, severely than one had questioned heretofore. The trust in life is gone: life itself has become a problem.[20]

Surprisingly, life lived as a "problem" does not engender resignation, despair, or defeat for Nietzsche. On the contrary, it awakens delight and the will to overcome:

> The attraction of everything problematic is so great . . . that this delight flares up again and again like a bright blaze over all the distress of what is problematic, over all the danger of uncertainty. We know a new happiness.[21]

Living life as a problem entails *jouissance* and empowerment for Nietzsche. From the abyss of questioning, he emerges newborn—"with a second dangerous innocence" (*Gay Science*: 37). Newborn status is precisely what Zarathustra tries to recover by "descending to the depths" (*Gay Science*: 275) or going under.

The Nietzschean ideal of "living dangerously" (*Gay Science*: 228), or questioning everything, is premised on a spirit of epistemological resistance. In this sense, going under involves a genealogical inquiry into descent that is informed by profound suspicion of origins. In Foucauldian terms, such a genealogy of knowledge or analysis of *Herkunft* (descent)

> will never confuse itself with a quest for "origins." On the contrary, it will cultivate the details and accidents that accompany every beginning; it will not be reticent in "excavating the depths." Where the self fabricates a coherent identity, the genealogist sets out to study the beginning—numberless beginnings. To follow the complex course of descent is to discover that truth or being does not lie at the root of what we know and what we are.[22]

Practiced as this type of excavation, genealogy yields misrecognition, and enacts displacement rather than ossification of self and history. It is precisely this practice of genealogical "descent" or going under that Djebar initiates in *L'amour, la fantasia*. Although concerned with traumatic memory rather than free-spirited "gay science," Djebar shares a Nietzschean delight in living the self and history as questions. In Part I of *Fantasia*, she stages an "unfounding" of Orientalist historiography that recalls Zarathustra's downward-spiraling epistemological journey. Djebar treks to the historical underworld or cave of representation to dissect and disarm the images that inform Algerian national memory and sexual politics. Her cave exploration resembles Rimbaud's slow and deliberate *dérèglement de tous les sens*.[23] Within this speleological mission, Djebar positions herself as a "warrior of knowledge" who understands that "knowledge is made for cutting."[24] Just as Irigaray chooses to "have a fling with the philosophers" (*This Sex*: 150) to arrive at her own perspectives on female desire and identity, Djebar, too, engages the history of representation in order to reconceive female sexuality and subjectivity.

Djebar evaluates Algerian women's oppression from the point of intersect between French colonization and Algerian nationalism. She especially hopes to show how the founding images of both discourses violently brand women's bodies with inflexible truths that limit their possibilities for identification and political mobilization. Highlighting complex negotiations between image and identity, Djebar confronts the "I" as a *topos* of division, aphasia, aporia, and mutilation.

Remarkably evident in *Fantasia* is a series of difficult choices that Djebar has made in the conception of her work. Foremost among these is Djebar's decision to write in the semiautobiographical mode, since autobiography is often understood as an exercise in self-mastery and reflection. Yet Djebar confounds the autobiographical voice by repeatedly decentering the Cartesian or sovereign subject presumed to be at the heart of autobiographical projects. *Fantasia* strategically positions the "I" in the interstices between first and third person, subtly interweaving the voices of self and other. In addition, Djebar names one of her primary narrators Isma, the Arabic word for "she is called_____" (akin to the French "*elle s'appelle . . .*").[25] By figuring this unnamed and inassimilable woman as a central voice in her text, Djebar challenges both the stability of identity and the proper name—two of the foundations of traditional Western autobiography. By so doing, she implicitly rejects the "autobiographical pact," or contract of equivalence between self and narrator that has been identified as a hallmark of autobiography.[26]

Yet Djebar also refuses to express herself "appropriately" *vis-à-vis* traditional Algerian oral culture, i.e., through orality alone. By this refusal, she violates a national law of genre that would seem to govern her decolonizing project, and launches her narrative into the realm of the impure, improper, and inauthentic. Given the primacy of oral culture and collective expression within traditional Algerian society, Djebar's decision to write an autobiographical text reminds readers of the contingency of her project, and the radicality of her attempt to promote cross-cultural *chocs* or collisions.

Djebar also chooses to write predominantly in French rather than Arabic. This choice has debilitating implications for her articulation of the "I" as a coherent identity. Djebar's choice of language in *Fantasia* plunges readers into a dizzying abyss in which the issues of culture, authenticity, and complicity assume agonizing proportions. She scatters fragments of Arabic throughout her text, noting that French alone is insufficient: it often lacks the words, the musicality, and the gestures to accompany her story. By experimentally navigating between the languages of oppressor and oppressed, *Fantasia* undermines the presumed singularity of cultural identity, i.e., "Frenchness" or "Algerianness."

Language is an especially fraught issue for Djebar: in adolescence, her father transferred her from a traditional Qur'anic school to a French school in Algeria. Later, during the Algerian revolution, Arabic was declared the official language of the nascent Algerian nation. In response to competing discourses regarding the superiority of the French or Arabic tongue, Djebar centers bilingualism not only as a crucial component of her identity, but also as an intractable problem that circumscribes the very project of subaltern autobiography. Throughout her work, Djebar strategically deploys French as a playful "*bi-langue*" in order to contaminate the French language, rendering the "true French" strangers in their own tongue.[27]

To challenge the symbolic alignment of women with cultural purity and sexual violability, Djebar's autobiography restores the complexities of female embodiment to national memory. *Fantasia* foregrounds the problem of representation not only to debunk specular models of identity and autobiography, but also—and more crucially—to commemorate the untenable subject positions of Algerian women within the national imaginary.

Djebar's novel asks what it means to represent history: who decides what counts as historical truth? Who counts as an authentic knower of Algerian society? By so doing, *Fantasia* attempts to do battle with history, especially with the ways of seeing that severely limited the options available to women both during and after colonization and revolution. I want to take seriously the constitutive power of images that Djebar attempts to navigate, and to explore the alternative lines of vision and (dis)identification that she enacts in *Fantasia*.

III. WRITING THE VEIL: PERSONAL UNFOUNDING

Djebar envisions the "caves" of the female body and national history as interlocking—endless openings onto each other and into space. As she ventures into the recesses of subjectivity, Djebar disinters the masculinist, Orientalist imagery that informs her sense of self. By so doing, she realizes that she is doubly penetrated by the eyes of the French colonizer and her Algerian brother.[28] Djebar experiences her body as if it were physically ensnared; she is at pains to imagine an "I" unmarked by the tattoo of this double gaze.

While spending a childhood summer with three cloistered sisters in a tiny Sahel village, Djebar and her friends excavate some disturbing images from their brother's bookcase. Toward the rear of the dusty shelves, they discover an album of erotic photography and an envelope stuffed with postcards depicting "bare-breasted Ouled-Nail girls, loaded with jewels" (*Fantasia*: 11). After making this discovery, Djebar and the other girls reevaluate the brother's oppressive prohibitions and volatile temper. Whereas the girls had previously regarded their brother as an authority figure, they are now disturbed by his secret life—"suddenly aware of his uncomfortable presence in those dim siesta hours" (*Fantasia*: 11). They comprehend their Algerian brother as a voyeur who has silently observed their daily movements from the shadowy recesses of the harem. Rather than a stern, paternalistic figure, the brother now looms large in their imaginations as a patriarchal voyeur who is furtively nourished by French Orientalist images of Algerian dancers and prostitutes.

With this realization, the girls feel violated and sad. Yet they also feel that their newfound knowledge has somehow catapulted them to the edge of transgression. In particular, they perceive themselves as more strategically positioned *vis-à-vis* their oppressive brother: "We feel we have trespassed into some forbidden territory; we feel we have aged" (*Fantasia*: 11). In effect, they have opened their eyes to the sexual politics of truth, a politics that becomes visible only in relation to a complex web of complicity and resistance.

Djebar suggests that although encounters with the male voyeuristic gaze can be shocking, wounding, and even stultifying, they might also provide a starting point for feminist critiques of representation and of women's double colonization by foreign occupiers and nationalist "brothers." Throughout *Fantasia*, Djebar strives to portray Algerian women not as immobile victims trapped in the silent world of the harem, but as instigators of "unprecedented women's battles" (*Fantasia*: 13) that yield new forms of knowledge and identity.

One such battle is a love-letter campaign instigated by the narrator's three cloistered girlfriends. Day after day, the girls write florid love letters to pen pals in distant lands. Unbeknownst to their parents, they daily escape the confines of the harem to post their letters in a mailbox. Covertly dispatched to the outside world, these letters openly circulate before countless male eyes. The girls' "clandestine operation" informs Djebar's imaginary no less profoundly than their brother's pornographic photography. She regards both interactions with images as opposing sides in a battle to constitute the sexual politics of truth. As complex emblems of oppression and resistance, these contradictory images spark a representational crisis or unfounding of sorts:

> Everything is a jumble in my memories: the forbidden pictures in the bookcase and the mysterious letters that arrived by the dozen. In the periods when sleep crept over me I imagined written words whirling furtively around, about to entwine invisible snares around our adolescent bodies, lying side by side across the antique family bed. (*Fantasia*: 13)

Within the love-letter operation, Djebar's narrator figures her girlfriends as political agents or emissaries, and recasts the male gaze as a failed attempt at voyeurism. She imagines the postman's feverish wonder and jealousy as he delivers an endless flurry of love letters to the girls—replies from their foreign pen pals. Of the postman, Djebar muses that "the continual arrival of these letters, from every corner of the world, must have weighed upon his mind, feeding some secret frustration!" (*Fantasia*: 12).

Djebar marvels at the audacity of the clandestine love-letter operation. Pen in hand, the cloistered girls commit their first offense or act of aggression within Algerian society. By launching their letters beyond the closed doors and blackened windows of the harem to the outside world, they stage illicit passages between private and public space. At the same time, their love letter campaign represents an explicit attempt to forsake the native custom of arranged marriage in favor of romance and love-based partnerships. Reading their love letters as multilayered texts of resistance, Djebar views the cloistered girls as trespassers, agitators, and cultural mediators par excellence. For Djebar, these girls provocatively recast the trope of the foreign correspondent who wields the pen as political weapon to report from a war zone.

Equally formative for Djebar's sense of self is a postcard sent by her father to her mother. Mailed during an out-of-town business trip, this postcard is especially meaningful in light of her mother's increasing fluency in French. Studying French empowers Djebar's mother to wage several revolutions at the level of personal identity. Most strikingly, it allows her to express love in the spoken word, and to address her husband with the personal possessive pronoun ("my husband") instead of the impersonal *lui*.[29] As she gains proficiency in the French language, Djebar's mother begins to call her husband by his proper name, Tahar.

These gradual changes, which seem to be of purely linguistic consequence, facilitate a form of self-expression that would be virtually impossible—or, at best, shameful—within Arabic alone. In this sense, expanding her linguistic frontiers allows Djebar's mother to transgress cultural and sexual boundaries. Consequently, Djebar approaches the French language—especially when used in conjunction with Arabic—as a tool of empowerment that allows women to transcend the spatial and social borders of the harem. Without the "weapon" of bilingualism, Djebar suggests that Algerian women would be "trapped in a web of impossible revolt," confined to an immobile world in which "the 'I' of the first person is never used" (*Fantasia*: 154). Djebar is acutely aware of the pitfalls of state-mandated monolingualism, which often works to censor women's expression in the name of cultural tradition and national interest.[30] For, as Djebar asks:

> How could a woman speak aloud in Arabic? How could she say "I," since that would scorn the blanket-formulae ensuring that [women] journey through life in collective resignation? (*Fantasia*: 156)

By learning French, Djebar's mother radically reformulates her relation to herself, her husband, and the outside world. From this perspective, she might be understood as the *ghostly* writer[31] of her husband's postcard. His postcard is brief since, as Djebar notes, he would not have dared to couple his signature with professions of intimacy. Yet in a move that dramatically rewrites the traditional relations between Algerian husband and wife, he spells out the addressee: "Madame" followed by his surname. In this act of address, Djebar's father names his wife, and denotes their status as a couple by pronouncing their shared surname.

This simple gesture constitutes a profound symbolic upset. Customarily within Algerian society, men refer to their wives only with the vague designation of "the household." Boldly defying this practice, Djebar's father not only names his wife, but also dares to identify her in Western fashion. Furthermore, by registering his wife's name and status on a document that will circulate in the outside world en route to the harem, Djebar's father confides his audacious act to an audience of countless men. By violating seemingly impenetrable cultural and spatial thresholds, his postcard ultimately disorients the male gaze. It wrests "so many masculine eyes" (*Fantasia*: 37) from their voyeuristic hold, and invites them instead into a position of feeble spectatorship *vis-à-vis* an outrageously feminist act of authorship.

By reading women's manipulation of image and text as potentially destabilizing strategies of social and political engagement, Djebar dramatically reimagines the space of the Oriental postcard as envisioned by Malek Alloula in *The Colonial Harem*. Not content to represent Algerian women as passive victims of the male gaze, Djebar highlights the ambivalence of colonial imagery by recording a series of radical yet "imperceptible revolutions" (*Fantasia*: 36) authored by women. Ultimately, she transforms the colonial postcard into a palimpsest of feminist creativity and resistance.

Djebar locates Algerian women at the sullied intersection of colonialist and nationalist oppression, subject to a "double gaze." This position has splintering effects for female subjectivity and citizenship. As Djebar notes, the ambivalent image of the warrior woman "prefigures many a future Muslim *mater dolorosa*" (*Fantasia*: 19). Her words allude to political history: during the Algerian revolution, for example, female nationalists were raped by both French and Algerian men. In addition, their revolutionary roles consisted primarily of domestic tasks such as cooking, sewing, nursing, and cleaning. After the revolution, Algeria's new leaders quashed feminist rallies and sent women back to the harem. As Djebar acknowledges, feminist liberation is not easily located within this history. Yet neither is absolute oppression; instead, she highlights nuanced performances of creative misrecognition and recuperation.

IV. HAUNTED: CAVE REFLECTIONS

> "No one," Pascal once said, "dies so poor that he does not leave something behind." Surely it is the same with memories too—although these do not always find an heir.
>
> —Walter Benjamin, *Illuminations*

> A picture held us captive. And we could not get outside it, for it lay in our language and language seemed to repeat itself to us inexorably.
>
> —Ludwig Wittgenstein, *Philosophical Investigations*

By highlighting the risky circulation of eyes and words, Djebar centers symbolic politics as a problem throughout her work. She understands words and images as constitutive of subjectivity, and continually reflects on their traumatic effects for both individual and national identity. Yet Djebar also locates possibilities for recomposing identity by resisting and destabilizing popular iconography. She situates her efforts of reorchestration in the cave, which has also figured prominently in the works of Plato, Nietzsche, and Irigaray as a metaphor for impossible origin, eternal return, and the womb or symbol of female creation.

In *The Gay Science*, Nietzsche pronounces the death of God—and, by extension, of the customary moorings of truth, essence, knowledge, morality, and origin—in the cave:

> After Buddha was dead, his shadow was still shown for centuries in a cave—a tremendous, gruesome shadow. God is dead; but given the way of men, there may still be caves for thousands of years in which his shadow will be shown.—And we—we still have to vanquish his shadow, too. (*Gay Science*: 167)

For Nietzsche, this cave shadow reflects the tenacity of humanity's founding mythologies. Even when the "horizon" of moral and religious thought has been blotted out, God continues to dominate human life through his lingering representation or shadow. Humans are unwilling to part with this profoundly embedded religious icon; for if God is dead, who will take his place? What will become of the familiar anchors that have forever defined the very parameters of human thought and action?

At several points within her text, Djebar similarly refers to shadows projected on caves. As she describes in "Deletion," the closing passage of Part I:

> The flickering flames of successive fires form letters of French words, curiously elongated or expanded, against cave walls. And for a fleeting moment I glimpse the mirror-image of the foreign inscription, reflected in Arabic letters, writ from right to left in the mirror of suffering; then the letters fade . . . To read this writing, I must lean over backwards, plunge myself into the shadows, lend an ear to the whispers that rise up from time out of mind, study this geology stained red with blood. What magma of sounds lies rotting there? (*Fantasia*: 46)

Significantly, the Arabic characters cited here are only temporal or fleeting. As opposed to their elongated French counterparts—colonial conquest writ large—the Arabic words inscribe a suffering that requires a whole new way of seeing, or a contortion of the body and concentration of the senses, to become legible.

Fantasia attempts to dissect the epistemic violence of representation, especially the wounding potential of the symbolic economy that underwrites war and all other forms of brutality toward difference. In this sense, cave reflections carry a profusion of meanings throughout *Fantasia*. First, as in the above passage, they can be understood as visions that attain the status of "truth," or founding images. Cave inscriptions are the vestiges of a specular economy that subsumes all difference under a uniform standard, thereby authorizing hierarchical relations between self and other. Because the specular economy assimilates difference, the One emerges as the implied referent of all representation. In Nietzschean terms, shadows projected on caves linger in the collective unconscious long after an ideology is unfounded, and constitute a site of archaic memory.

Djebar's cave-shadows also symbolize the inevitable death that accompanies any attempt to represent. With reference to the colonial practice of cave-burning used to drive Algerian rebels from their cave hideaways, Djebar evokes the dead as "empty shadows" that linger in the countryside and "find their inverted mirror images in the funeral caves"(*Fantasia*: 78–79). Words objectify rather than animate life; hence Sartre's injunction to "live or tell."[32] Like Sartre, Djebar regards the written word as the burial of something in silence, and especially as a denial of the "secret, polygamous pleasures" of voice (*Fantasia*: 180). Shadows projected onto caves are fingerprints of human becoming and sites of national memory; like the cave paintings at Lascaux, they are elusive traces effaced by the very attempt to represent. (For as I write I deny my body that hungers, my body that aches after days spent in various states of contortion before my computer, my body that yearns to dance and stops suddenly, tenses at the acute pain of some memory. The body's material needs are concealed to perfect this illusion of continuity, *to write*.) Although writing holds out the promise of memorialization and resurrection, it often erases and intensifies hunger, desire, absence, death, and longing: "to speak, *and above all to write*, is to fast."[33]

Fantasia's cave shadows can also be understood as a metaphor for the power of images to shape identity. Throughout her work, Djebar approaches imagery as a catalyst for traumatized forms of subjectivity. The breaking points, afflictions and losses of faculty that haunt Djebar's narrator—aphasia,[34] autism,[35] paroxysm, schizophrenia—point to the structuring absence of her authorial position. Aphasia, in particular, traces the rupture between language and identity experienced so often in the wake of colonialism. Ultimately, the cave shadows featured in *Fantasia* attest to the haunting power of images to shape personal and collective memory.

V. ENVISIONING THE FEMALE BODY: GENEALOGY AND VIVISECTION

> The fourth language, for all women, is that of the body: the body which male neighbours' and cousins' eyes require to be deaf and blind, since they

> cannot completely incarcerate it; the body which, in fits of hope and despair, rebels, and unable to read or write, seeks some unknown shore as destination for its message of love . . .
>
> —Assia Djebar, *Fantasia*

In many respects, our bodies provide the ultimate limit, target, and end-point of representation.[36] The female body, in particular, bears the marks of a history of intense struggle over its representation. With this in mind, I will view Djebar's mission into the innermost cavities of her body as both a genealogical act of recovery and a vivisection that probes female voice, sexuality, and desire.

As Foucault reminds us, the task of genealogy is "to expose a body totally imprinted by history and the process of history's destruction of the body."[37] Djebar's descent into the "dark continent"[38] of the female body is similarly motivated by a desire to understand how female identity and sexuality are marked, haunted, and often violated by conventional historiography. Within the pages of *Fantasia*, Djebar enters her body as she would a cave, and performs something akin to a feminist speleology or vivisection in order to burn her own images of female subjectivity and sexuality.

As Djebar recalls episodes from her childhood, she realizes that she has often lived her body as a snare. Her body emerges as the "dream's navel" that she cannot surpass, a knot of uninterpretability to which she must always return.[39] On one hand, because her "modernist" father sent her to a French school during adolescence, Djebar was able to escape "traditional" Algerian practices that daily subjected female bodies to unique forms of social and spatial confinement, such as veiling and seclusion.[40] Although her position as a cultural intermediary afforded Djebar an unusual degree of physical mobility, it also exposed her to conceptions of the female body as a vulnerable object to be protected within the private space of "domestic interiors, always interiors" (*Fantasia*: 21). Djebar's limited experiences of seclusion, gained during the summers that she spent in a country house full of cloistered girls, prompted her to imagine her body as a target for the male gaze, perpetually at risk of rape and violation. Yet her discussions of the veil, seclusion, and her eventual escape from these practices through education and writing suggest that she also considers the female body as a powerful "fourth language"—a site of power, knowledge, and resistance with the capacity to disrupt the masculinist status quo.

Djebar's autobiography attests to the formative effects of these ambivalent images of female embodiment for her identity. *Fantasia* is littered with voiceless, wounded, or imprisoned bodies "bereft of voices" (*Fantasia*: 156). In many ways, Djebar's "attempt at autobiography" resembles a vivisection; its undertaking in the enemy tongue involves a careful probing of live tissue and membrane, and enlists Djebar on a voyage to the deepest cavities of her body. As Djebar herself notes:

> To attempt an autobiography using French words alone is to lend oneself to the vivisector's scalpel, revealing what lies beneath the skin. Wounds are reopened, veins weep, one's own blood flows and that of others, which has never dried. (*Fantasia*: 156)

For Djebar, the body's voicelessness often results from imposed tongues. Although she writes in French, Djebar continually explores the silenced cries and split affinities that inform her identity as a French-Algerian woman. Frozen cries often immobilize her and leave indelible traces of complicity on her body and psyche. The incisions of the writer's scalpel unite her body so intimately with the pain of other Algerian women that their blood streams in unison, intermingling in a copulative gesture of intersubjectivity.

VI. DOWN UNDER: THE FEMALE BODY AS CAVE

Throughout *Fantasia*, the cave emerges as a metaphor for the feminine. This symbolism is not without precedent; in *Speculum of the Other Woman*, Luce Irigaray investigates the cave of Platonic philosophy as the site of a foundational "project of representation" that inaugurates the specular economy, or economy of sexual indifference.[41] Irigaray describes how this Platonic cave symbolizes the transposed womb or *hystera*, turned upside-down and back-to-front. At the cave's entrance is a long passage leading upward, toward the light of the day; the entire cave is oriented relative to this opening. Within the cave, male prisoners are chained together facing forward—which in this inverted space is really toward the back wall of the cave. Unable to walk around, they simply gaze straight ahead. Directly behind the prisoners, another group of men appears to roam freely about the cave. Yet an interior wall or curtain (for Irigaray, a symbol of the hymen) prevents them from advancing further into the recesses of the cave/womb. Another passageway, similar to the entry, marks the front end of the cave. Neither inside nor outside the cave, this passageway mirrors the space of the vagina.

As the prisoners gaze at the cave wall opposite them, it is transformed into a theatrical stage or filmic screen. Lights suspended above and behind the prisoners project a simulacrum of the scene unfolding behind them onto the cave wall ahead. Behind the screen, the roaming men create shadows and reflections through their bodily movements and contortions. In this sense, the cave wall doubles as a funhouse mirror in a representational project that holds everyone spellbound. Within the cave, "all is but the image of an image [since] the cave is already an attempt to represent another cave, the womb" (*Speculum*: 246). Cave dwellers inhabit a distorted space of illusion, watching multiple iterations of the same scene that confound their ability to discern between original and copy.

Founded on infinite repetition of a single scene, Plato's symbolic economy lays the foundations for the erasure of difference in Western philosophy. If the cave is understood as a womb, then its loop of infinite repetition erases female specificity, or sexual difference, by construing the vagina as an inverted penis (or fully external conduit). In a sense, the flickering simulacrum projected on the cave wall inaugurates the specular economy, in which sexual difference is taken for distorted sameness. The source of this difference (the female body and genitalia) is both assimilated and repressed by male cave dwellers. For Irigaray, the specular economy encourages blindness to female creation and origin, or sexual difference and the maternal womb.

Because she locates the cave as the *topos* of the foundational specular economy, Irigaray finds it imperative to embark on projects of speleological unfounding in order to see otherwise. Her work continually engages with influential representations of the female body and sexuality. In this sense, Irigaray's project is without precedent, for the material details of the female body—especially the clitoris—are precisely what the founding fathers of Western philosophy, anatomy, and psychoanalysis variably construed as inferior, excessive, marginal, or "nothing to see."[42] Irigaray resists the specular economy by lingering in the space of difference: "No mirror offers itself to be seen and read in this speleology. And the truth of what we see depends on this" (*Speculum*: 255).

Djebar engages in a similar spelunking mission into the cave of the female body and sexuality to decode their symbolic role within nationalist and Orientalist representative projects. While writing her autobiography, she realizes that her body overflows with silence, spatial constraint, and prohibition due to the images that she has internalized. To loosen the powerful grip of masculinist imagery on her body and identity, Djebar seeks to dismember its conditions of possibility. To this end, she navigates the inner cracks and crevasses of her body to find traces of resistance alongside the postures of inferiority, silence, and conformity to which her body has become accustomed. She dissects colonial and nationalist symbolism to orchestrate an alternative self-portrait—"an untouchable, unkissable, forbidden photo that can only take pleasure (*jouir*) in its *own* sight."[43]

Throughout *Fantasia*, Djebar expresses her body in terms of silence, song, cry, and speech; it is not fully apprehensible within the scopic economy. Poised between the confinement of the harem and the freedom of Parisian streets, her body registers the ambivalence of these borderlands as blips of sound:

> I have been moving freely outside the harem since my adolescence, but every place I travel through is nothing but a wilderness [of] faceless voices, murmuring strangers, snatches of dialogue, an impenetrable mumble of sounds detached from the magma of faces, preserved from probing eyes. (*Fantasia*: 218)

Her vivisection especially exposes the wounding effects of imagery for the female body and cry. Like Irigaray, she identifies the ecstatic cry of *jouissance* as that which is most forbidden for women to express within the specular economy.

Djebar considers rape a particularly troubling intersection of body, voice, and symbolic politics for Algerian women. As discussed earlier, both French and Algerian men raped Algerian women during the anticolonial revolution. By "exchanging" women's bodies in this way, they effectively silenced women's voices and undermined their power of consent. Throughout the revolution, women remained fearful of voicing rape accusations. If an Algerian woman acknowledged rape by French soldiers, her words would bring social stigma and, ultimately, ostracism from the Algerian community. If, on the other hand, she accused an Algerian man of rape, she would be perceived as a traitor to the national liberation movement. In light of this dilemma, women's voices were forced underground. Female bodies often bore evidence of the weight of this silence in posture, gaze, or traumatic symptom.[44]

Women who hoped to break their silence on the eve of national liberation were sorely disappointed. The new leaders of Algeria quashed feminist rallies and relegated women once again to the social, political, and spatial confinement of sex segregation. By opposing the male exchange of women during revolution to the nationalist image of the "heroic" Algerian woman-patriot, Djebar locates the female body as a contentious meeting ground for the related discourses of patriotism, state regulation, and masculinist domination. In particular, she situates the female body at the crossroads of political projects to establish national legitimacy.

On her missions to apprehend the role of the female body in the Algerian imaginary, Djebar highlights the intersections between colonial and nationalist oppression. She traces collusion especially in the symbolic figuration of women as actual or potential, yet virginal, mothers. The virgin mother is a founding figure of both religious and nationalist rhetoric. Witness the prevalence of the *mater dolorosa,* or Virgin Mary, as an icon of motherhood-minus-sexuality.[45] The Virgin Mary is an especially ambivalent figure, for, as Julia Kristeva points out:

Si d'une femme il ne peut être dit ce qu'elle est (au risque d'abolir sa différence), peut-être en serait-il autrement de la mère puisque c'est la seule fonction de 'l'autre sexe' à laquelle nous pouvons attribuer, à coup sur, de l'existence? Pourtant, là aussi, nous sommes pris dans un paradoxe. (Histoires: 295)

The crucial paradox of the "virgin mother" is, of course, that birth is a product—however distant—of sexual union.[46] That is to say, intersubjective "contamination," rather than purity, is the enabling condition for motherhood. Djebar examines this paradox as it informs the masculinist national imaginary. On one hand, nationalist discourse invokes women as mothers of the nation, guarantors of pure origin, and transmitters of native culture. In this sense, women occupy nationalist discourse not as women per se, but as melancholic referents to a lost or imagined community. Women represent the nation as agents of cultural purity rather than as embodiments of material difference.

Yet war and sexuality form an incestuous couple; nations at war typically enlist sexualized vocabularies of conquest and penetration. In *Fantasia*, war maneuvers are routinely described in sexual terms, just as military instruments (guns, missiles) are lovingly christened with sexual metaphors (projectile, erection, penetration). Rape routinely surfaces as a war tactic, even when nationalist movements rally around the image of the pure mother. Within nationalist movements as in broader society, motherhood—as a marker of female sexuality and material difference—constitutes the "most solid knot in the almost complete incommunicability between the sexes."[47]

Fantasia underscores the dynamic interface between sexual politics and representation. The novel repeatedly troubles oppositional models of the "personal" and "political," and highlights the effects of representation for the female body and subjectivity. For Djebar, the Algerian war and the struggle to unfound cultural constructions of the female body are equally significant revolutions aimed at decolonization. In particular, she contests the simultaneous appropriation of female creation and erasure of sexual difference that converge in masculinist nationalist iconography of the pure or virgin mother.

In an exemplary passage within *Fantasia*, Djebar describes two encounters with the opposite sex in the nocturnal streets of Paris. She describes her experiences in the alternating registers of the first and third person. Although her body delights in its illicit mobility on these peregrinations, it also emits an uncontrollable cry of unfathomable origin:

> I feel quite alone, I see myself as whole, intact, how can I express it? "At the beginning," but of what? At least of this new journey. The space is blank, the long empty road is mine alone, I walk at ease, letting my footsteps beat out my own

> rhythmic accompaniment . . . Suddenly the voice bursts forth. It drains off all the scoriae of the past. What voice? *Is it my own voice, scarcely recognizable?* I am only a wandering exile, in flight from other shores where women are shrouded figures buried upright, precisely to prevent what I am doing now, to prevent them uttering such a constant howl: such a wild, *barbaric cry* . . . (*Fantasia*: 115)

Djebar's travels are especially subversive since the street is considered a "male" or public space in Algeria, as in most Arab countries. Unchaperoned and uncovered women have no right to freely wander the streets; only madwomen and prostitutes are expected there. By trespassing on male territory, Djebar asserts a distinctly feminist presence since, as Fatima Mernissi points out, "[Arab] women in male spaces are considered both provocative and offensive."[48] Djebar's joyous placement of the female body in male space is an act of aggression that subverts the trope of "sexual availability" attributed to wandering women in traditional cultural-religious interpretation. Significantly, female nationalists experienced the complications of this perspective throughout the Algerian revolution. Mistaken for prostitutes, they were often accosted by their fellow men as they performed nationalist tasks in the streets of Algeria.[49]

By searching for new ways to represent women's "barbaric cries," Djebar reminds us that we might *think* these cries not only as melancholic traces of bodily violation, but also as unauthorized and ineffable expressions of female *jouissance*. In this sense, she creatively misrecognizes the restrictive images of female sexuality and space valorized within nationalist, cultural, and religious discourse. Ultimately, Djebar's reflections on the pleasures of the cry and street work the female body into a forbidden narrative of sexual agency and desire.

Within the specular economy, woman functions as "what is at stake in a transaction, usually rivalrous, between men. She has functioned as merchandise, a commodity passing from one owner to another, a possible currency of exchange."[50] Djebar enacts, instead, a postcolonial feminist symbolic economy—one that explicitly aligns female voice and sexuality with the political imperative of decolonization. *Fantasia* sets in motion a new symbolic economy—a circulation of eyes, words, and cries with endless potential for travel and resistance. Although Djebar cites oppressive imagery in her work, she continually traces lines of flight from the specular economy—moments at which female voices and visions betray the indifference of language, culture, and nation. These moments are recuperated in creative symphonies of misrecognition, or "*revolutions imperceptibles*."

In her study of imperceptible movement or revolution, Djebar pays particular attention to women's exchange of domestic miniatures, like jam jars and children's spoons. *Fantasia* takes an "inventory of tiny objects passed on thus, from febrile hand to fugitive hand" (*Fantasia*: 177). By so doing, it traces women's history to an economy of tiny, loving objects transmitted across generations. Djebar's invocation of tiny objects recalls the "daydream of the miniature," which is to reveal a secret history or unexplored interior outside the given field of perception.[51] Within the illusory world of representation, the miniature fosters dialogue between inside and outside, visible and unknown—in other words, it insists on articulating that which is typically construed as "different" or invisible. Likewise, in the interstices between French and Arabic words, bodies, and gestures, Djebar fashions a tongue that restores the "interior" world of female desire to the palimpsest of national political memory.

VII. GOING UNDER: THE WEDDING NIGHT

The most dramatic leg of Djebar's journey to the hidden depths of her body is prompted by a recollection of her wedding night or "night of blood."[52] In *Women of Algiers in Their Apartment* (1980), Djebar contextualizes the ambivalence of this night by pointing out that a woman's "yes" is, if not unspeakable, irrelevant within Arabic society. During the wedding ceremony, an Algerian woman must affirm her vows ("yes" or "I do") through a male intermediary who speaks on her behalf. If she fails to do so, the wedding officiator will attribute her hesitation to feminine modesty. In this case, a woman's silence or tears may be construed as legitimate expressions of acquiescence.[53] This interpretive leap renders woman's formal, verbal consent meaningless; it is "deflowered, violated, before the *other* deflowering, the *other* violation intervenes."[54] Against the backdrop of this cultural and religious tendency to trivialize female consent, Djebar tries to imagine whether or how her body consented to "the other deflowering"[55] that took place on her wedding night.

As she narrates her wedding preparations, Djebar intersperses their intimacy and banality—"an arcane play in which she felt like a minor character" (*Women*: 104)—with fervent political debates about whether she and her fiancé should return home to Algeria to join in the anticolonial revolution. By interweaving her reflections on the intimate rite of marriage with political concerns, Djebar rejects any presumed opposition between the "personal" and "political," and acknowledges both as inextricable strands of identity. Although Djebar is eager to join the FLN (nationalist movement), her fiancé suspects that fellow male revolutionaries will not treat her as an equal. Fractured by this push and pull between personal rites and political rights, Djebar's nuptial preparations emerge, above all, as "permeated with nostalgia for her native soil" (*Women*: 106). They are profoundly complicated by the ceremony's location in Paris, her father's absence, and her own status as a female nationalist torn between French and Algerian culture.

On the morning after an Arab bride's wedding night, she is expected to provide physical evidence of prior virginity. To fulfill this obligation, she must present a bloodstained sheet to her male relatives. The stained sheet is construed as proof of female virginity, evidence of the rupture of a previously intact hymen. Yet, as Nawal El Saadawi notes, obtaining a stained sheet often requires desperate measures. She points out that a bride's hymen "must be capable of bleeding profusely, of letting out red blood that can be seen as a visible stain on a white bed sheet" stolen from the wedding night.[56] Furthermore, although the hymen often breaks during physical exertion unrelated to sex, this reality is not acknowledged within traditional Islamic practice. Instead, the soiled sheet as evidence of chastity reigns supreme as a cultural-religious symbol and nuptial imperative.[57] As a result, "no girl can be more unfortunate than she who is born with an elastic hymen . . . or whom nature has forgotten to provide a hymen, or whose hymen is so delicate that it is torn away by childhood exercise or accident."[58]

Framed by mandatory bloodstains, passive voice, and silent acquiescence, Djebar's first sexual experience is, above all, an attempt to navigate a complicated web of social and sexual symbols. Sex, defined according to masculinist cultural and religious imperatives, enlists Djebar in a feminist vivisection of sorts. As she struggles to distinguish between her feelings of sexual violation and pleasure, Djebar mobilizes the creative powers of vision to decode the meanings of female embodiment within masculinist discourse and—ultimately—to reimagine the female body as means of sexual and social empowerment

As she recalls her wedding night—performing this vivisection, traveling back in time through bodily memory—Djebar labors to find her own voice. She dissects every timbre of her cry during intercourse, a cry that reveals the profoundest grief and the most intense liberation that her body has ever known. On one hand, Djebar's cry narrates a journey to unprecedented pain. For Djebar, sex is excruciating not only because of the blood that flows, but also because of the unspoken "No!" that trembles on her lips. Her cry also signifies the ache of silence—silence that seems to drain all color from the scene as she recalls its intensity.

Because of its painful reverberations, Djebar partly understands her wedding night as an experience of rape; or rather, she imagines a fine line between consensual sex and rape. What can consent mean when it emerges from a body mired in silence and seclusion, when it is uttered by a voice inessential to the formal exchange of wedding vows? How can a woman imagine the sound or value of her consent when that consent is officially construed as irrelevant to the personal undertaking of marriage?

By weaving these questions into her narrative, Djebar implicitly situates conjugal sex on a continuum with wartime rape. As she notes elsewhere in *Fantasia*, the word "rape" was unspeakable during the Algerian revolution. Even if its euphemism, "damage," was presented to a rape victim as a question or concern, this question was almost always answered in silence: "swallowed" (*Fantasia*: 202). Djebar's reflections on the meaning of consent shake the very foundations of her being, and seem to put her in touch with a universality of female suffering. As she describes her wedding night, she increasingly adopts the interrogative form:

> The cry rises in the air; falling, at its nadir, in multi-layered sediment, lurks an unspoken "No!" Did I feel this refusal tremble on my lips? Travelling on the Metro during the next few days, I stare closely at all the women I see around me. I am devoured with curiosity as if I were some primitive creature: "Why do they not say, why will not one of them say, why does each one hide this fact: love is the cry, the persistent pain, which feeds upon itself, while only a glimpse is vouchsafed of the horizon of happiness?" (*Fantasia*: 107)

Djebar experiences sexual initiation as an unfounding of both the Imaginary and the Symbolic orders. So acute is this trauma that on the day after her wedding night, she is unable to look in the mirror. Sex triggers a crisis of representation (or an undoing of the accomplishments of the Lacanian mirror stage), and a disorientation of the self characterized by autistic withdrawal and alienation. Although Djebar is shattered by this self-implosion, *Fantasia* effectively integrates traumatic rupture within its narrative of identity by moving beyond a facile understanding of sex as entailing women's absolute oppression or liberation. Instead Djebar asks, "How can this blood be transformed into a ray of hope?" (*Fantasia*: 106). While formulating this question, Djebar begins to imagine feminist potentials for creative misrecognition.

Djebar powerfully transforms "blood to hope" by registering the ambivalence of her cry and the amplitude of its desire. Her cry induces vertigo: "a voice of infinite range in aerial flight, opening onto a vertiginous void and only gradually growing aware" (*Fantasia*: 106). Most importantly, it propels her into a space without boundaries or physical restrictions. Sex allows Djebar to establish a new relationship with her body, and gives her license to explore the invisible details of its pleasurable caverns. Resplendent with sounds for female desire and *jouissance*, Djebar's cry enacts a new symbolic economy with which to represent the female body, sexuality, and identity. Ultimately, her cry gives birth:

> The sharp cry of relief and sudden liberation, then abruptly checked. Long, infinite, first cry of the live body. (*Fantasia*: 106)

As she writes about her ambivalent cry and rebirth, Djebar stages a painful undoing of the self. Yet she also reinvents her conditions of possibility as a subject. If Djebar's spelunking mission to the inner depths of the female body initially required a scalpel, she now wields forceps and, as obstetrician, facilitates her own delivery. After exploring the cave of her body by way of a grueling vivisection, Djebar manages to emerge alive. Yet the "I" of her identity is decentered, for her cry does not mark a moment of self-presence. Instead, it issues from "the brief absence of a woman and a little girl" (*Fantasia*: 107), or the transitional space of becoming. In this space that denies closure, autonomy, and specular reflection, Djebar confronts the untenability of the mirror image.

Djebar's story of her wedding night hovers between autobiography, genealogy, and obstetrics. Djebar strategically employs the speculum or *sistrum* in order to trace her body's descent; to record its minute "details," such as the clitoris and sexual ambivalence; and to articulate embodied identity within the parameters of a feminist symbolic economy. Misrecognizing the cry as a pure expression of pain, she takes it elsewhere, restaging it as an orchestral movement rich with expressions for female desire and *jouissance*:

> The plaintive moan escapes, then the prolonged song, the drawn-out song of the rich female voice closes round the copulation, follows its tempo and its figures, is exhaled as oxygen, a tumescent twisted coil of *forte* notes hanging in the air. (*Fantasia*: 109)

Djebar's expression of female *jouissance* discounts the Freudian model of female sexual development, whereby a young girl must renounce clitoral pleasure to achieve "normal" (i.e., vaginocentric, heterosexual) femininity.[59] With this passage, Djebar fulfills her mission through the female body in order to create a representational economy that "sings and sizzles" female desire.[60]

By apprehending the tiny details of the female body and genitals—especially the clitoris—Djebar's *sistrum* reframes the feminine within contemporary fields of vision. Interestingly, the Arabic slang for "eye" doubles as a contemptuous word for the female genitals in Algeria. In a parallel and deliberate conflation of female sexuality and vision, Djebar's autobiographical work persistently refers to the female genitals as "the eye-that-is-sex." By so doing, it recalls the perilous links between sexual politics and visual culture.

As she traces the physicality of her cry on its virtual journey from genitals to eyes to larynx to lips, Djebar displaces the privileged male gaze of the specular economy. At the same time, she gives to representation precisely what it has historically forbidden: the female voice, body, sexuality, and *jouissance*. Ultimately, *Fantasia* recuperates the severed hand (or "floating metonym")[61] of a mutilated female body that Fromentin was unable to represent in his paintings of Algerian battlefields. By reframing national loss in terms of sexual difference, Djebar insinuates women into "the project of representation." With her cry, she exceeds the moment of radical inassimilability and completes a journey through the live female body in order to

> *parler près de, et si possible, TOUT CONTRE: première des solidarités à assumer pour les quelques femmes arabes qui obtiennent ou acquièrent la liberté de mouvement du corps et de l'esprit.*[62]

Djebar locates creative potentials for liberation precisely in the moment when the fiction of a unified "I" becomes unsustainable. In this sense, she understands her first sexual experience as a drama of political and sexual awakening as well as subjective undoing. She concludes the narration of her wedding night with a series of negative affirmations that induces a destructively creative "spiral of refusal":

> There were no peeping women . . . Normally the bride neither cries out nor weeps: she lies an open-eyed victim on the couch, and the closed thighs prevent any cry from escaping. There was no bloodstained sheet on display the following days. (*Fantasia*: 108)

Yet Djebar's refusal should not be confused with simple reversal. Instead, Djebar analyzes the descent of intersectional experiences of oppression, and takes her gaze and cry to an "elsewhere" in which female desire may be(come) articulable. She conceives of a signifying economy that does not privilege the visual, but instead mobilizes the musical potentials of fugue, *fuga*, cadence, and cacophony to trace lines of flight from masculinist and Orientalist fields of vision. Within this economy, the creative possibility for misrecognition emerges in the moment of critical distance—when a woman "closes her eyes to herself."[63] By searching for new ways to represent women's "barbaric cries," Djebar reminds us that we might think these cries not only as melancholic traces of bodily violation, but also as unauthorized expressions of female *jouissance*. Djebar's rich evocation of her wedding night cry indulges subversive musicality in order to sing female subjectivity, embodiment, and *jouissance* as the "traces of some ruptures that have reached their term."[64] Djebar's rupturing, rapturous coda is this cry (magma, fingerprint, ululation) which is not exactly a bloodstain, but rather a powerful blood-memory.[65]

VIII. PICASSO AND RESISTANCE

> Subjectivity cannot be reduced to a mere expression of the self. The identity question and the personal/political relationship is a way of rewriting culture.
>
> —Trinh T. Minh-ha, *When the Moon Waxes Red*

> We are living in an age where the conceptual foundation of an ancient culture is being undermined by millions of a species of mole (Topoi, ground mines) never known before.
>
> —Hélène Cixous, "Sorties"

Throughout *Fantasia*, recurrent allusions to magma (subsoil, loose soil beneath the earth's crust) recall a "certain species of mole"[66] that furtively slips into secret cavities underground. These figures of the mole and magma symbolize Djebar's creative project of "going under," or examining the symbolic foundations of nationalism, Orientalism, revolution, and the female body in order to rewrite cultural memory and national historiography. If foundations are the necessary fictions by which we live, then the mole, digging around in magma, precipitates their collapse—and undermines the truth effects of the symbolic economy.

Djebar's autobiographical project takes up the speculum, or *sistrum*, to venture into the hidden *topos* of the cave and the female body. She undertakes a variety of genealogical explorations to examine the constitutive and wounding effects of representation, and to burn like Irigaray's speculum. By means of speleology and vivisection, Djebar asks why historical projects of representation so often depend on female dismemberment and aphasia. Yet she also emphasizes how female voice and desire often emerge in a spirit of resistance to epistemological foundations. In this sense, her project can be placed in relation to a long history of creative efforts to articulate a distinctly female or feminist imaginary.

Images are formative for Djebar; as she has confessed in an interview, visual culture allowed her to "settle her accounts" with the French language.[67] In *Women of Algiers in Their Apartments*, she especially acknowledges Picasso as the creator of a radical perspective, or an unhinged gaze, with which to re-vision Algerian women's relationships to corporeality, space, history, and desire. For Picasso, as for Djebar, the fiction of a "sovereign subject" is untenable. He evokes subjectivity instead as a mosaic of conflicting perspectives in time and space. In this sense, Picasso might be imagined as Nietzsche's painterly heir: for him, all knowledge is perspective, all truths shattered, and all foundations sublimely misrecognized. In effect, Picasso is the painter of the overfull yet aphasiac and schizophrenic "I" that stutters, cries, and dances; yet for whom it is only representation per se that is impossible.

Just as Picasso evokes identity as decentered pastiche, *Fantasia* highlights the necessarily fragmented, traumatized, and kaleidoscopic eye/I that inhabits the interstices between warring nations, cultures, languages, histories, and identities. As Djebar reminds us in *Women of Algiers in Their Apartment*, Picasso spent the first year of the anticolonial revolution in Algeria. During that time, he sketched his own renditions of Delacroix's fabled Orientalist tableau, *Women of Algiers*. His efforts proved fruitful; Picasso left Algeria with fifteen original canvases and two lithographs. Most importantly, Picasso's images of Algerian women marked a radical break with existing representation. In signature cubist style, his canvases depict Algerian women as dissonant compositions of color, light, and conflicting perspective.

For Djebar, Picasso's portrayals of Algerian women reject the Orientalist and colonialist motives of voyeurism and "emancipation." Instead, they dare to imagine Algerian women's "rebirth to their own bodies,"[68] bathing their nude heroines in the light that traverses a "door open to the full sun."[69] Inspired by Picasso's innovative work, Djebar concludes that feminist liberation can only be achieved through similar projects of rupture and radical revisioning. Finding the seeds of such a project in Picasso's Algerian oeuvre, she pursues this commitment to radical re-visioning throughout her work.

In light of Picasso's disdain for art historical foundations, Djebar views his Algerian tableaux as subversive appropriations of the Orientalist odalisque. For Djebar, the female subjects of Picasso's paintings seem to interact not in the cloistered space of the harem, but at the gravesite of Pauline Rolland, a French schoolteacher, leftist agitator, and eventual political prisoner. A particularly potent symbol in *Fantasia*, Rolland's grave evokes more than the resting place of a brave woman. More significantly, it marks the presence of a "woman pregnant with the future"—one who embodies the potentials for creating a "convulsive sisterhood" of women engaged in cross-cultural dialogue, commemoration, and political mobilization.[70]

Like Picasso, Djebar sets the stage for "female trouble" within the harem-turned-gynaeceum.[71] She traces the impotency of colonial and nationalist men to "penetrate" Algerian women who are already elsewhere, who defy recognition in favor of phantasmic *fuga* or *fantasia*-stic becoming. Djebar invents a new way of seeing whereby cognitive dissonance, musical flight, and rupture—rather than specularity—permit subversive reworkings of identity. She uses the space of parallax to map selves, in the first and third person, as dispossessed mosaics that intertwine the familiar with fantasies of the exotic other. Djebar sculpts passages between silence and voice, omission and representation. Ultimately, she envisions the Orient as an imagined geography of flesh and fantasy, one in which fictions of identity provocatively collide with sexual, symbolic, and international politics.

Fantasia closes on the notes of memory, mutilation, and impossible integration. Djebar describes the severed hand of an Algerian woman—a hand that Eugene Fromentin discovered on a deserted battlefield, yet was unable to paint. Djebar notes that "later, I seize on this living hand, hand of mutilation and of memory" (*Fantasia*: 226). She tries to pick up where Fromentin left off; to express the brutality of a war that left women particularly exposed and dismembered. What to do with this hand? How to make of it a bridge between past suffering, present narration, and future political mobilization? How to work the specifics of its grotesque violence into a new story of the Algerian revolution informed by sexual politics? How can Djebar rewrite the revolution as a feminist looking "toward the past,"[72] writing in the colonial tongue, and seeing only potentials for continued violence against women on Algeria's political horizon?

Boldly, Djebar seizes on the severed hand that Fromentin was unable to represent. By re-membering national identity as dependent upon masculine fantasies of sexual difference, Djebar insinuates women into the cracks, gaps, and fissures of official projects of national representation. Yet the ghostly hand resurrected at *Fantasia*'s conclusion also symbolizes the ambivalence of Djebar's "attempt at autobiography." Her narrative cannot deliver memory from the anonymous Algerian woman's severed hand, for that hand—like Djebar's sense of self—is fragmented, unspeakable, and radically unassimilable. Thus, the "I" of *Fantasia* coalesces around "a self that cannot accede to an *ego sum*, to the *iste ego sum* of writing."[73] For Djebar, self-representation is necessarily a record of undoing, as well as an opening onto the possibilities for imagining different histories, images, and identities.

NOTES

1. Friedrich Nietzsche, *On the Genealogy of Morals*, trans. Walter Kaufmann (New York: Random House, 1967; reprint, New York: Vintage Books, 1989).

2. Remarks at a public address at UCLA, 2003.

3. Assia Djebar, *L'amour, la fantasia* (Paris: Albin Michel, 1985). Also Assia Djebar, *Fantasia: An Algerian Cavalcade*, trans. Dorothy Blair (Portsmouth, NH: Heinemann, 1993).

4. Edward Said, *Orientalism* (New York: Vintage Books, 1979), 3.

5. Said 1979: 8.

6. With this term I mean to evoke a sense of both physical or bodily tearing apart (dismemberment), and a critical engagement at the level of representation that acts as an interruption, interference, or "disservice" to national memory and/or "official" history.

7. Homi Bhabha, "Foreword: Remembering Fanon: Self, Psyche, and the Colonial Condition," in Frantz Fanon, *Black Skin, White Masks*, trans. Charles Markmann (London: Pluto Press, 1986), xxiii.

8. Michel Foucault, "Nietzsche, Genealogy, History," in Paul Rabinow, ed., *The Foucault Reader*, trans. Donald Bouchard (New York: Pantheon Books, 1984), 80–81.

9. Luce Irigaray, *This Sex Which Is Not One*, trans. Catharine Porter (Ithaca, NY: Cornell University Press, 1985). Within this system of exchange, masculinity is presumed standard, and femininity can be understood only in terms of sameness, difference, or deviation.

10. Irigaray: 1985: 157. See also Irigaray, *Speculum of the Other Woman*, trans. Gillian Gill (Ithaca: Cornell University Press, 1985).

11. Irigaray 1985: 156; Irigaray, *Speculum*: 239–40

12. I borrow this notion of re-visioning from Adrienne Rich, as discussed in Teresa de Lauretis, "Aesthetic and Feminist Theory: Rethinking Women's Cinema," in Sandra Kemp and Judith Squires, eds., *Feminisms* (Oxford: Oxford University Press, 1997), 34.

13. By "unfounding" (*effondement*) I refer to the joyfully destructive and creative process of challenging the metaphysical foundations of knowledge, truth, and identity; Nietzschean philosophy best exemplifies this art. But I also want to evoke the American legal definition of "unfounding," which refers to the ways in which law enforcement officials routinely discredit or delegitimize women's charges of rape or sexual assault. (See Catharine MacKinnon, *Sex Equality*: unpublished manuscript, 2001.) I think this second, legal meaning foregrounds a central issue with which this paper will be concerned; namely, the devaluation and silencing of female voice, cry, and *jouissance* within the specular economy. My paper will argue that both of these senses of "unfounding" spur Djebar's project to create a feminist symbolic economy in *L'amour, la fantasia*.

14. With the metaphor of burning, I hope to evoke the creative darkroom technique of "burning" an image; the contemporary digital technology of burning one's own musical compilation or CD; and Irigaray's elaboration of a speculum that would burn rather than reflect female identity.

15. Reference is made to Irigaray's book of the same name.

16. Deleuze and Guattari 1986: 17.

17. Friedrich Nietzsche, *The Gay Science*, trans. Walter Kaufmann (New York: Vintage Books, 1974), 275.

18. Nietzsche 1974: 274. This is the title of section 342, which concluded the original edition of *The Gay Science*, and is repeated in the introduction of Nietzsche's next book, *Thus Spoke Zarathustra*.

19. Nietzsche here refers to Emerson: "to the poet, to the philosopher, to the saint, all things are friendly and sacred, all events profitable, all days holy, all men divine." *Gay Science*: 8.

20. Nietzsche 1974: 36.

21. Ibid. 37.

22. Paul Rabinow, ed., and Donald Bouchard, trans., "Nietzsche, Genealogy, History," in *The Foucault Reader* (New York: Pantheon Books, 1984), 80–81.

23. Arthur Rimbaud, "Lettre à Paul Démeny," in *Poésies; Une saison en enfer; Illuminations* (Paris: Gallimard, 1965), 202. Both Djebar and Nietzsche share a certain affinity with Rimbaud, who wants to rid history of its revered corpses.

24. Reference to Foucault: "knowledge is not made for understanding; it is made for cutting" in "Nietzsche, Genealogy, and History," *The Foucault Reader* (88) and Nietzsche: "and if you cannot be the saints of knowledge, at least be its warriors" in Friedrich Nietzsche, *Thus Spoke Zarathustra*, trans. R. J. Hollingdale (New York: Penguin Books, 1961), 74.

25. Gayatri Spivak, "Echo," in D. Landry, ed., *The Spivak Reader*, ed. D. Landry (New York: Routledge, 1996), 187.

26. Philippe Lejeune, "The Autobiographical Pact," in *On Autobiography* (Minneapolis: University of Minnesota Press, 1989).

27. In addition to Abdelkebir Khatibi's formulations of the "*bi-lingue*" in his collection of essays entitled *Maghreb pluriel* (Paris: Denoel, 1983), see his novel *Amour bilingue* (Paris: Editions Fata Morgana, 1983).

28. Note that this is precisely the "double gaze" that Alloula does not fully acknowledge or theorize.

29. "*Lui*" in this context is a generic, universal term (he) that defies relationality, and a quasireligious designation that evokes omnipotence ("He," "God"). I mean to evoke both senses of the term here in order to suggest the important power dynamics that underwrite the prescribed usage in Arabic.

30. By "state-mandated monolingualism," I refer to the nationalist and colonialist practice of imposing an official language on a nation's citizens. In the colonial era, French was imposed on Algeria as its official language. During the anticolonial revolution, the FLN declared Arabic, instead, as the official language of the Algerian people. In both cases, the official language became the only language used in schools, government, and other major state institutions.

31. I mean to oppose this to the "ghostwriter," or someone who acts as a scribe for—and gives credit of authorship to—the "true" author.

32. Jean-Paul Sartre, *Nausea*, trans. Lloyd Alexander (New York: New Directions, 1964), 39.

33. Gilles Deleuze and Felix Guattari, *Kafka: Toward a Minor Literature*, trans. Dana Polan (Minneapolis: University of Minnesota Press, 1986), 20.

34. *Fantasia*: see esp. 125–29.

35. In *Fantasia*, Djebar refers to harem life as a form of autism. For a lengthier discussion of Algerian women's autistic existence within society, see Assia Djebar, "Forbidden Gaze, Severed Sound," in *Women of Algiers in Their Apartment*, trans. Marjolijn de Jager (Charlottesville: University Press of Virginia, 1992).

36. By this I mean the following: (1) that the body, as flesh/material, is the diametric opposite or "limit" of representation; but that, nonetheless, (2) the body, as the seat of subjectivity and identity, is always molded by discourse, and (3) that representation's ability to impact or engrave the body is enforced by disciplinary regimes of power and regulations of space, which literally force the body into various states of conformity with the "law" of the Symbolic.

37. Michel Foucault, *The Foucault Reader*, ed. Paul Rabinow (New York: Pantheon Books, 1984), 82–83.

38. See Sigmund Freud, "Femininity," in James Strachey, ed. *The Standard Edition of the Complete Psychological Works of Sigmund Freud*, vol. 22 (London: Hogarth and the Institute of Psychoanalysis, 1964).

39. For a lucid formulation of Freud's concept of the dream's navel, see Michael Sprinker, "The End of Autobiography," in James Olney, ed., *Autobiography: Essays Theoretical and Critical* (Princeton: Princeton University Press, 1980), 339–42. Freud's own articulation is in Sigmund Freud, *The Standard Edition of the Complete Psychological Works of Sigmund Freud*, 24 vols., trans. James Strachey (London: Hogarth, 1963).

40. Yet her guilt at escaping these cultural traditions also sparked a crisis of language and national allegiance.

41. Luce Irigaray, *Speculum of the Other Woman*, trans. Gillian Gill (Ithaca: Cornell University Press, 1985). Originally published as *Speculum de l'autre femme* (Paris: Les Editions de Minuit, 1974).

42. Irigaray 1985: 47.

43. Deleuze and Guattari 1986: 4.

44. Djebar discusses her own body's posture as a function of cultural in-betweenness and language education, as well. When studying Arabic, her body assumes a different posture than it does when she speaks French. *Fantasia*: 184–85.

45. Julia Kristeva, "Stabat Mater," in *Histoires d'amour* (Paris: Denoel, 1983), 295. Also Julia Kristeva, *Tales of Love*, trans. Leon Roudiez (New York: Columbia University Press, 1987), 235.

46. By this I mean to acknowledge "disembodied" or assisted technologies of birth, such as in vitro fertilization (IVF).

47. Assia Djebar, "Forbidden Gaze, Severed Sound," in *Women of Algiers in Their Apartments*, trans. Marjolign de Jager (Charlottesville: University Press of Virginia, 1992), 147.

48. Fatima Mernissi, *Beyond the Veil: Male-Female Dynamics in Modern Muslim Society* (Bloomington: Indiana University Press, 1987), 143.

49. Frantz Fanon, *A Dying Colonialism* (New York: Grove Press, 1967), 53.

50. Irigaray 1985: 157

51. See Susan Stewart, *On Longing: Narratives of the Miniature, the Gigantic, the Souvenir, the Collection* (Baltimore: Johns Hopkins University Press, 1984), 54.

52. Djebar 1992: 141.

53. Ibid. 145.

54. Ibid.

55. Ibid.

56. Nawal El Saadawi, *The Hidden Face of Eve*, trans. Sherif Hetata (London: Zed Press, 1980), 25.

57. Of course, this imperative often leads women to devise creative and unofficial "ways around" it. Also, "traditional" Islam, as Leila Ahmed points out, is by no means "inherently" sexist. Instead, Ahmed distinguishes tradition from phallocentrism by arguing that the Qur'an is actively *interpreted* in misogynist ways by a male elite. See Leila Ahmed, "Feminism and Cross-Cultural Inquiry: The Terms of the Discourse in Islam," in Elizabeth Weed, ed., *Coming to Terms: Feminism, Theory, Politics* (New York: Routledge, 1989).

58. El Saadawi 1980: 25.

59. Freud lays out three possible avenues for the development of femininity: neurosis, the masculinity complex, or "normal" femininity. Sigmund Freud, "Lecture XXXIII: Femininity," in *The Standard Edition of the Complete Psychological Works of Sigmund Freud, Vol. XXII*, trans. James Strachey (London: Hogarth Press, 1963), 126.

60. This is a feminist appropriation of Nietzsche's gay science, a philosophy that "sings and sizzles."

61. Clarisse Zimra, Disorienting the Subject in Assia Djebar's "L'amour, la fantasia," in Lynne Huffer, ed., *Yale French Studies* 87 (1995), 162.

62. Ibid.

63. Nietzsche, *Gay Science*: 128.

64. Djebar 1992: 2.

65. Whereas the bloodstain is a trace of blood, I conceive of a "blood-memory" as a conscious attempt to *remember* that blood of the female body in its specific circulations and connotations.

66. Hélène Cixous and Catharine Clement, *The Newly Born Woman*, trans. Betsy Wing (Minneapolis: University of Minnesota Press, 1986), 65.

67. Zimra 1995: 151.

68. Assia Djebar, "Forbidden Gaze, Severed Sound," in *Women of Algiers in Their Apartment*, trans. Marjolijn de Jager (Charlottesville: University Press of Virginia, 1992), 150.

69. Djebar 1992: 151.

70. Of course, this gravesite represents a polar opposite to Djebar's fateful (and pessimistic) prediction for the possibilities of postcolonial "liberation" for Algerian women.

71. Term elaborated by Emily Apter in "Female Trouble in the Colonial Harem," in *differences* (1992).

72. Reference is made to Walter Benjamin's notion of the "angel of history" facing the past, wanting to stay and repair "wreckage upon wreckage," yet being propelled into the future by the "storm of progress." See Walter Benjamin, *Illuminations: Essays and Reflections* (New York: Schocken Books, 1968), 257–58.

73. Spivak 1996: 191.

Final Overture

Of Mutilation and Re-Membering

> It is part of morality not to be at home in one's home.
>
> —Theodor Adorno, *Reflections from a Mutilated Life*

> In order to constitute the space of a habitable house and a home, you also need an opening, a door and windows, you have to give up a passage to the outside world (*l'étranger*). There is no house . . . without a door or windows.
>
> —Jacques Derrida, *Of Hospitality*

In *Of Hospitality*, Jacques Derrida addresses the problem of hospitality as an ethical imperative to account for one's home, identity, space, and limits. Reflecting on the xenophobic sentiment that increasingly characterizes our global political milieu, Derrida suggests that the laws of citizenship and hospitality need to be rethought from an(other) perspective, one that interrogates and ultimately confounds the borders between self and other ("stranger" or "foreigner") that provide the very basis for contemporary personal and international relations. Derrida concludes his meditation on the necessity of "opening" one's home to the outside with two Biblical parables about the disastrous ethical consequences that arise when a polity observes "phallic" laws of hospitality at the expense of ethical obligations to its female community members.

The first of these parables, relayed in Genesis, conveys the "great founding scene of Abrahamesque hospitality."[1] After inviting two angels to stay in his house in Sodom, Lot is confronted by his townsmen. Infuriated by his act of hospitality toward strangers, they ask to see the angels "so that we may abuse them." Rather than allow his fellow men to take liberties with his houseguests, Lot offers to them his daughters instead:

> Listen, I have two daughters who are virgins. I am ready to send them out to you, to treat as it pleases you. But as for the men, do nothing to them, for they have come under the shadow of my roof.[2]

In a rush to accommodate his male guests and townspeople, Lot proves all too willing to sacrifice the women of his family by offering their bodies for any desired violation or pleasure. Derrida notes that this same "law of hospitality" governs the famous Biblical scene on Mount Ephraim in Judges. After welcoming foreigners into his home, their host is approached by male members of the community who ask to sexually "penetrate" the foreigners. In the name of hospitality, the host offers his virginal daughter instead:

> No my brothers; this man has become my guest; do not commit this crime. Here is my daughter; she is a virgin; I will give her to you. Possess her; do what you please with her, but do not commit such an infamy against this man.[3]

When the townsmen are not satisfied with this offer, the host provides them with his concubine. The men have intercourse with her until dawn, perpetrating all forms of outrage against her. When they finally release the concubine, she returns to the host's home and collapses at its threshold. Her fate, suggests Derrida, is well-known: limb by limb, she is cut into twelve pieces by the houseguest, who has become her "master." The guest then sends her dismembered body throughout Israel, accompanied by the following message:

> "Has any man seen such a thing from the day the Israelites came out of the land of Egypt, until this very day? Ponder on this, discuss it; then give your verdict." And all who saw it declared, "Never has such a thing been done or been seen since the Israelites came out of the land of Egypt."[4]

The violence of these encounters would, perhaps, be more shocking if we did not have before us the specter of a woman's mutilated hand resurrected by *Fantasia*. Yet after being exposed to the mournfully creative acts of remembering initiated by Djebar, Cha, Cixous, Sebbar, and Kim-Gibson, we might note instead the striking similarity of the abuses to which women are subjected in the name of national solidarity and brotherhood. A persistent failure to represent sexual difference within the national imaginary, or an unwillingness to extend the basic "laws of hospitality" to women, is the catalyst for the diverse tactics of creative misrecognition that I have discussed in this book. Postcolonial feminist efforts to reimagine sexual, ethnic, and national difference are all the more remarkable because they emerge from this "tradition" of hospitality to which we are heirs: a brutal history of sexual and symbolic trauma that "testifies without end in our memory."[5]

The transnational feminist aesthetic projects that I have studied in this book share two crucial goals: to disturb existing representational paradigms; and to invent visual, oral, and linguistic economies that can account for the ways in which sexual, ethnic, and cultural difference haunt the national imaginary. Especially, these artists challenge us to re-vision the subjects of intercultural exchange, to shift the terms of engagement from "this representation disempowers me because it is false" to "I laugh, disrupt, misrecognize, disown." An emphasis on misrecognition can locate the powers of the false and the bastard to force a productive break and critical passages between image and identity. Although a focus on parallax or disjuncture does not suppose that the subject can somehow find an "outside" of power, it does allow one to study the ambivalent traces of the lens, and to leverage the self as a decentered eye/I of becoming. By acknowledging the fantasies at play in images of the self, practices of creative misrecognition force a kind of "stammer" within dominant discourse.[6] We might learn to *think* this stammer in a triple sense: first, and most problematically, as a fissure actualized in the postcolonial body and identity[7]; second, in a more generous sense, as an ethical imperative for new modes of exchange between self and other; and finally, as a stimulant for alternative stories and "joyful discoveries, poetic as well as warlike."[8]

NOTES

1. Jacques Derrida with Anne Dufourmantelle, *Of Hospitality*, trans. Rachel Bowlby (Stanford: Stanford University Press, 2000), 153.

2. Genesis 19:1–9, *The Jerusalem Bible* (London: Darton, Longman, and Todd, 1966).

3. Judges 19:23–30.

4. Ibid.

5. Derrida 2000: 155.

6. For more on this stammer, see Abdelkebir Khatibi, *Love in Two Languages*, trans. Richard Howard (Minneapolis: University of Minnesota Press, 1990).

7. I do not want to underestimate this schism. Fanon powerfully attests to the crippling potential of the image in *Black Skin, White Masks*: "I took myself off from my own presence, far indeed, and made myself an object. What else could it be for me but an amputation, an excision, a hemorrhage that spattered my whole body with black blood?" (112). Bhabha similarly refers to colonialism's attempt to "split the soul." Especially *vis-à-vis* Algerian women's split subjectivity and double oppression, I have looked for answers to Fanon's cry, "*what else could it be for me?*" Throughout this work I (have tried to) think about this.

8. Michel de Certeau, *The Practice of Everyday Life,* trans. Steven Rendall (Berkeley: University of California Press, 1984), xix.

Bibliography

Ahmed, Leila. "Feminism and Cross-Cultural Inquiry: The Terms of the Discourse in Islam." In *Coming to Terms: Feminism, Theory, Politics*, ed. Elizabeth Weed. New York: Routledge, 1989.

Alarcón, Norma. "The Theoretical Subject(s) of *This Bridge Called My Back* and Anglo-American Feminism." In *Making Face, Making Soul: Creative and Critical Perspectives by Feminists of Color*, ed. Gloria Anzaldúa. San Francisco: Aunt Lute Books, 1990.

———. "Traddutora, Traditora: A Paradigmatic Figure of Chicana Feminism." In *Dangerous Liaisons: Gender, Nation, and Postcolonial Perspectives*, eds. Anne McClintock, Aamir Mufti, and Ella Shohat. Minneapolis: University of Minnesota Press, 1997.

Alloula, Malek. *The Colonial Harem.* Trans. Myrna and Wlad Godzich. Minneapolis: University of Minnesota Press, 1986.

Althusser, Louis. *Lenin and Philosophy*. Trans. Ben Brewster. New York: Monthly Review Press, 1971.

Amrane-Minne, Daniele Djamila. *Des femmes dans la guerre d'Algerie*. Paris: Karthala, 1994.

Anderson, Benedict. *Imagined Communities: Reflections on the Origin and Spread of Nationalism*. London: Verso, 1991.

Anthias, Floya, and Nira Yuval-Davis. *Woman-Nation-State*. London: Macmillan, 1989.

Anzaldúa, Gloria. *Borderlands/La Frontera*. San Francisco: Aunt Lute Books, 1987.

———, and Cherríe Moraga, eds. *This Bridge Called My Back: Writings by Radical Women of Color*. New York: Kitchen Table: Women of Color Press, 1981.

Apter, Emily. "Female Trouble in the Colonial Harem." *differences* 4 (1992).

———. *Continental Drift: From National Characters to Virtual Subjects*. Chicago: University of Chicago Press, 1999.

Arbus, Diane. *Diane Arbus*. New Jersey: Aperture, 1972.

Bal, Mieke. "The Politics of Citation." *Diacritics* (Spring 1991).

——. *Double Exposures: The Subject of Cultural Analysis*. New York: Routledge, 1996.

Barrett, Terry. *Criticizing Photographs: An Introduction to Understanding Images.* California: Mayfield Publishing Company, 2000.

Barthes, Roland. *Image-Music-Text*. Trans. Stephen Heath. New York: Hill and Wang, 1978.

——. *Camera Lucida*. Trans. Richard Howard. New York: Hill and Wang, 1981.

Begag, Azouz and Abdellatif Chaouite. *Ecarts d'identité*. Paris: Seuil, 1990.

Belau, Linda. "Introduction: Remembering, Repeating, and Working-Through: Trauma and the Limit of Knowledge." In *Topologies of Trauma: Essays on the Limit of Knowledge and Memory*, eds. Belau and Ramadanovic. New York: Other Press, 2002.

Benjamin, Walter. *Illuminations: Essays and Reflections*. Trans. Harry Zohn. New York: Schocken Books, 1968.

Berger, John. *Selected Essays and Articles: The Look of Things*. Harmondsworth, England: Penguin, 1958.

——. *Ways of Seeing*. London: Penguin Books, 1972.

Berlant, Lauren. *The Queen of America Goes to Washington City: Essays on Sex and Citizenship*. Durham: Duke University Press, 1997.

Bhabha, Homi. "Foreword: Remembering Fanon." In *Black Skin, White Masks, 2nd ed.*, Frantz Fanon. Trans. Charles Lam Markmann. London: Pluto Press, 1986.

——. *The Location of Culture*. New York: Routledge, 1994.

Blanchot, Maurice. *The Infinite Conversation*. Trans. Susan Hanson. Minneapolis: University of Minnesota Press, 1993.

Bonnefoy, Yves. "Igitur and the Photographer." *PMLA* 114:3 (May 1999).

Bourdieu, Pierre. "The Cult of Unity and Cultivated Differences." Trans. Shaun Whiteside. In *Photography: A Middle-brow Art*. Stanford: Stanford University Press, 1990.

Bow, Leslie. *Betrayal and Other Acts of Subversion: Feminism, Sexual Politics, Asian American Women's Literature*. Princeton: Princeton University Press, 2001.

Brahimi, Denise. "Orientalisme et conscience de soi." *Litterature maghrébine d'expression française de l'écrit à l'image* ed. Guy Dugas. Meknes, Morroco: Faculté des Lettres et des Sciences Humaines de Meknes (Morocco), Universite Sidi Mohamed Ben Abdellah, 1987, 29–36.

Brown, Sarah Graham. *Images of Women: The Portrayal of Women in Photography of the Middle East 1860–1950.* New York: Columbia University Press, 1988.

Bryson, Norman. *Vision and Painting: The Logic of the Gaze*. New Haven: Yale University Press, 1983.

Butler, Judith. *Bodies That Matter*. New York: Routledge, 1993.

——. "The End of Sexual Difference?" In *Feminist Consequences*, eds. Elisabeth Bronfen and Misha Kavka. New York: Columbia University Press, 2001.

de Certeau, Michel. *The Practice of Everyday Life*. Trans. Steven Rendall. Berkeley: University of California Press, 1984.

Cha, Theresa Hak Kyung. *Dictée.* Berkeley: Third Woman Press, 1995; reprint, New York: Tanam Press, 1982.

Cheng, Anne Anlin. *The Melancholy of Race: Psychoanalysis, Assimilation, and Hidden Grief*. Oxford: Oxford University Press, 2001.

Cherry, Deborah. *Beyond the Frame: Feminism and Visual Culture, Britain 1850–1900*. London: Routledge, 2000.

Chow, Rey. *Writing Diaspora: Tactics of Intervention in Contemporary Cultural Studies*. Bloomington: Indiana University Press, 1993.

——. "The Dream of a Butterfly." In *Human, All Too Human*, ed. Diana Fuss. NewYork: Routledge, 1996.

Cixous, Hélène. *First Days of the Year*. Trans. Catherine MacGillivray. Minneapolis: University of Minnesota Press, 1998. Originally published as *Jours de l'an*. Paris: Les editions des femmes, 1990.

——. *Rootprints: Memory and Life Writing*. Trans. Eric Prenowitz. New York: Routledge, 1997.

Cixous, Hélène, and Catherine Clement. *The Newly Born Woman*. Trans. Betsy Wing. Minneapolis: University of Minnesota Press, 1986. Originally published as *La Jeune Nee*. Paris: Union Generale d'Editions, 1975.

Collins, Patricia Hill. *Black Feminist Thought: Knowledge, Consciousness, and the Politics of Empowerment.* New York: Routledge, 1990.

Crenshaw, Kimberlé Williams. "Demarginalizing the Intersection of Race and Sex." *University of Chicago Legal Forum* 139 (1989).

——. "Mapping the Margins: Intersectionality, Identity Politics, and Violence Against Women of Color." 43 *Stanford Law Review* 1241 (1991).

——. "Whose Story Is It, Anyway?: Feminist and Antiracist Appropriations of Anita Hill." In *Race-ing Justice, En-gendering Power: Essays on Anita Hill, Clarence Thomas, and the Construction of Social Reality*, ed. Toni Morrison. New York: Pantheon Books, 1992.

Davis, Angela. *Women, Race, and Class*. New York: Random House, 1981.

de Lauretis, Teresa. "Displacing Hegemonic Discourses: Reflections on Feminist Theory in the 1980s." *Inscriptions* ¾ (1988).

——. "Aesthetic and Feminist Theory: Rethinking Women's Cinema." In *Feminisms*, eds. Sandra Kemp and Judith Squires. Oxford: Oxford University Press, 1997.

——. "Popular Culture, Public and Private Fantasies: Femininity and Fetishism in David Cronenberg's *M. Butterfly.*" *Signs* 24:2 (Winter 1999).

Deleuze, Gilles. *Mille plateaux: Capitalisme et schizophrenie*. Paris: Minuit, 1980.

——. *The Logic of Sense*. Trans. Mark Lester. New York: Columbia University Press, 1990.

——, and Felix Guattari. *Kafka: Toward a Minor Literature.* Trans. Dana Polan. Minneapolis: University of Minnesota Press, 1986.

Derrida, Jacques. *Dissemination*. Chicago: University of Chicago Press, 1981.

——. "Des Tours de Babel." In *Difference in Translation.* Trans. and ed. J. F. Graham. Ithaca: Cornell University Press, 1985.

——. With Anne DuFourmantelle. *Of Hospitality*. Trans. Rachel Bowlby. Stanford: Stanford University Press, 2000.

Djebar, Assia. *Les alouettes naïves*. Paris: Julliard, 1967.

——. *Femmes d'Alger dans leur appartement*. Paris: des femmes, 1980. Translated as *Women of Algiers in Their Apartment*. Trans. Marjolijn de Jager. Charlottesville: University Press of Virginia, 1992.

——. *L'amour, la fantasia*. Paris: Edition Jean-Claude Lattes, 1985. Translated as *Fantasia: An Algerian Cavalcade*. Trans. Dorothy Blair. Portsmouth, NH: Heinemann, 1993.

Doane, Mary Ann. *Femmes Fatales: Feminism, Film Theory, Psychoanalysis*. New York: Routledge, 1991.

Donadey, Anne. *Recasting Postcolonialism*. Portsmouth, NH: Heinemann Press, 2001.

Dubey, Madhu. "The 'True Lie' of the Nation: Fanon and Feminism." *differences* 10:2 (Summer 1998).

Duras, Marguerite. *The Lover*. Trans. Barbara Bray. New York: Harper Collins, 1985. Originally published as *L'amant*. Paris: Les Editions de Minuit, 1984.

Enloe, Cynthia. *Bananas, Beaches, & Bases: Making Feminist Sense of International Politics*. Los Angeles: University of California Press, 1989.

Fanon, Frantz. *A Dying Colonialism.* Trans. Haakon Chevalier. New York: Grove Press, 1965.

——. *Black Skin, White Masks*. Trans. Charles Lam Markmann. New York: Grove Press, 1967.

Fausto-Sterling, Anne. *Sexing the Body: Gender Politics and the Construction of Sexuality*. New York: Basic Books, 2000.

Felman, Shoshana, and Dori Laub. *Testimony: Crises of Witnessing in Literature, Psychoanalysis and History*. New York: Routledge, 1992.

Foucault, Michel. *Discipline and Punish.* Trans. Alan Sheridan. New York: Vintage Books, 1977.

——. *The History of Sexuality vol. I.* Trans. Robert Hurley. New York: Random House, 1978.

——. "What Is An Author?" In *The Foucault Reader,* ed. Paul Rabinow. Trans. Donald Bouchard. New York: Pantheon Books, 1984.

Freud, Sigmund. *The Standard Edition of the Complete Psychological Works of Sigmund Freud*, vol. 22, ed. James Strachey. London: Hogarth and the Institute of Psychoanalysis, 1964.

Fuss, Diana. "Fashion and the Homospectatorial Look." *Critical Inquiry* 18:4 (Summer 1992).

——. *Identification Papers*. New York: Routledge, 1995.

Garanger, Marc. *Femmes Algériennes 1960*. Paris: Contrejour, 1982.

——. *La guerre d'Algérie vue par un appelé du contingent*. Paris: Seuil, 1984.

——. *Femmes des Hauts-Plateaux: Algérie 1960*. Paris: La Boite à Documents, 1990.

Garber, Marjorie. "The Occidental Tourist: *M. Butterfly* and the Scandal of Transvestism." In *Nationalisms and Sexualities*, eds. Andrew Parker, Mary Russo, Doris Sommer, and Patricia Yeager. New York: Routledge, 1992.

Garcia, Alma. "The Development of Chicana Feminist Discourse, 1970–1980." In *Unequal Sisters: A Multi-Cultural Reader in US Women's History*, eds. Vicki Ruiz and Ellen DuBois. New York: Routledge, 1989.

Gilman, Sander, ed. *Degeneration: The Dark Side of Progress*. New York: Columbia University Press, 1985.

Gilmore, Leigh. *The Limits of Autobiography: Trauma and Testimony*. Ithaca: Cornell University Press, 2001.

Grosz, Elizabeth. *Volatile Bodies*. Bloomington: Indiana University Press, 1994.

Haraway, Donna. *Simians, Cyborgs, and Women: The Reinvention of Nature*. New York: Routledge, 1991.

——. "Ecce Homo, Ain't (Ar'n't) I a Woman, and Inappropriate/d Others: The Human in a Post-Humanist Landscape." In *Feminists Theorize the Political*, eds. Judith Butler and Joan Scott. New York: Routledge, 1992.

——. "Universal Donors in a Vampire Culture: It's All in the Family: Biological Kinship Categories in the Twentieth-Century United States." In *Uncommon Ground: Toward Reinventing Nature,* ed. W. Cronon. New York: W. W. Norton & Company, 1995.

Harper, Mary. "The Poetics and Politics of Delacroix's Representation of the Harem in *Women of Algiers in Their Apartment.*" In *Picturing the Middle East: A Hundred Years of European Orientalism*. New York: Dahesh Museum, 1996.

Hayes, Jared. *Queer Nations: Marginal Sexualities in the Maghreb*. Chicago: University of Chicago Press, 2000.

Hélie-Lucas, Marie-Aimée. "Women, Nationalism, and Religion in the Algerian Liberation Struggle." In *Opening the Gates: A Century of Arab Feminist Writing*, eds. Margot Badran and Miriam Cooke. Bloomington: Indiana University Press, 1990.

Hirsch, Marianne. *Family Frames: Photography, Narrative, and Postmemory*. Cambridge: Harvard University Press, 1997.

Holloway, Karla. "The Body Politic." In *Subjects & Citizens: Nation, Race, and Gender from Oroonoko to Anita Hill*, eds. Michael Moon and Cathy Davidson. Durham: Duke University Press, 1995.

hooks, bell. *Ain't I a Woman: Black Women and Feminism*. Boston: South End Press, 1981.

——. *Black Looks: Race and Representation*. Boston: South End Press, 1992.

——. *Art on My Mind: Visual Politics*. New York: The New Press, 1995.

Huet, Marie-Hélène. *Monstrous Imagination*. Cambridge: Harvard University Press, 1993.

Hull, Gloria, Patricia Bell Scott, and Barbara Smith, eds. *All the Women Are White, All the Blacks Are Men, But Some of Us Are Brave: Black Women's Studies*. New York: Feminist Press, 1982.

Hwang, David Henry. *M. Butterfly*. New York: Penguin, 1989.

Irigaray, Luce. *This Sex Which Is Not One*. Trans. Catherine Porter. Ithaca: Cornell University Press, 1985.

——. *Speculum of the Other Woman*. Trans. Gillian Gill. Ithaca: Cornell University Press, 1985. Originally published as *Speculum de l'autre femme*. Paris: Les Editions de Minuit, 1974.

——. *I Love to You: Sketch of a Possible Felicity in History*. Trans. Alison Martin. New York: Routledge, 1996.

Jefferson, Margo. "The Tricks Mirrors Play." *The New York Times Magazin*e, October 17, 1999.

Jones, Amelia. "Tracing the Subject with Cindy Sherman." In *Cindy Sherman: Retrospective,* ed. The Museum of Contemporary Art. New York: Thames & Hudson, 1997.

Keller, Evelyn Fox, and Helen Longino, eds. *Feminism & Science*. Oxford: Oxford University Press, 1996.

Kessler, Suzanne. "The Medical Construction of Gender: Case Management of Intersexed Infants." *Signs* 16:1 (1990).

Khanna, Ranjana. *Dark Continents: Psychoanalysis and Colonialism*. Durham: Duke University Press, 2003.

Khatibi, Abdelkebir. *Love in Two Languages*. Trans. Richard Howard. Minneapolis: University of Minnesota Press, 1990. Originally published as *Amour bilingue*. Paris: Editions Fata Morgana, 1983.

——. *Maghreb pluriel*. Paris: Denoel, 1983.

Kim, Elaine, and Norma Alarcón, eds. *Writing Self, Writing Nation: Essays on Theresa Hak Kyung Cha's* Dictée. Berkeley: Third Woman Press, 1994.

King, Deborah. "Multiple Jeopardy, Multiple Consciousness: The Context of a Black Feminist Ideology." *Signs* 14:1 (Autumn 1988).

Kingston, Maxine Hong. *Tripmaster Monkey: His Fake Book*. New York: Vintage Books, 1987.

Kondo, Dorinne. "*M. Butterfly*: Orientalism, Gender, and a Critique of Essentialist Identity." *Cultural Critique* 16 (Fall 1990).

Kristeva, Julia. *Histoires d'amour*. Paris: Denoel, 1983. Translated as *Tales of Love*. Trans. Leon Roudiez. New York: Columbia University Press, 1987.

Kuhn, Annette. *The Power of the Image: Essays on Representation and Sexuality.* London: Routledge, 1985.

Kureishi, Hanif. *The Buddha of Suburbia*. New York: Penguin Books, 1990.

Lacan, Jacques. *Ecrits*. Trans. Alan Sheridan. New York: W. W. Norton & Company, 1977.

——. *The Four Fundamental Concepts of Psychoanalysis: The Seminar of Jacques Lacan Book XI*. Trans. Alan Sheridan. New York: W. W. Norton & Co., 1981.

——. *The Seminar of Jacques Lacan, Book I: Freud's Papers on Technique 1953–1954*. Trans. John Forrester. New York: W. W. Norton & Company, 1988.

Laqueur, Thomas. *Making Sex: Body and Gender from the Greeks to Freud*. Cambridge: Harvard University Press, 1990.

Lazreg, Marnia. *The Eloquence of Silence: Algerian Women in Question*. New York: Routledge, 1994.

Lejeune, Philippe. *On Autobiography*. Minneapolis: University of Minnesota Press, 1989.

Lemaires, Gérard-Georges. *The Orient in Western Art*. Trans. Harriet de Blanco. Cologne: Konemann, 2001. Originally published as *L'univers des Orientalistes*. Paris: Edition Menges, 2000.

Lewallen, Constance, ed. *The Dream of the Audience: Theresa Hak Kyung Cha (1951–1982)*. Berkeley: University of California Press, 2001.

Linker, Kate. "Representation and Sexuality." In *Art After Modernism: Rethinking Representation,* ed. Brian Wallis. New York: The New Museum of Contemporary Art, 1984.

Lionnet, Françoise. *Postcolonial Representations: Women, Literature, Identity*. Ithaca: Cornell University Press, 1995.

Lowe, Lisa. "Unfaithful to the Original: The Subject of *Dictée*." In *Writing Self, Writing Nation: Essays on Theresa Hak Kyung Cha's Dictée*, eds. Elaine Kim and Norma Alarcón. Berkeley: Third Woman Press, 1994.

Lutz, Catherine, and Jane Collins. *Reading National Geographic*. Chicago: University of Chicago Press, 1993.

Lye, Colleen. "M. Butterfly and the Rhetoric of Antiessentialism: Minority Discourse in an International Frame." In *Performing Asian-American Race and Ethnicity on the Contemporary Stage,* eds. Sucheng Chan, Josephine Lee, Michael Omi, and David Palumbo-Liu. Philadelphia: Temple University Press, 1988.

Marcus, Sharon. "Fighting Bodies, Fighting Words: A Theory and Politics of Rape Prevention." In *Feminists Theorize the Political*, eds. Judith Butler and Joan Scott. New York: Routledge, 1992.

Martin, Biddy, and Chandra Talpade Mohanty. "Feminist Politics: What's Home Got to Do With It?" In *Feminist Studies/Critical Studies*, ed. Teresa de Lauretis. Bloomington: Indiana University Press, 1986.

Martin, Emily. *The Woman in the Body: A Cultural Analysis of Reproduction*. Boston: Beacon Press, 1987.

Mathur, Saloni. "Wanted Native Views: Collecting Colonial Postcards of India." In *Gender, Sexuality, and Colonial Modernities*, ed. A. Burton. London: Routledge, 1999.

Matsuda, Mari. *Where Is Your Body? And Other Essays on Race, Gender, and the Law.* Boston: Beacon Press, 1996.

Maxwell, Anne. "'Native' Women and Tourism: A Contested Site of Orientalism." *Third Text*, vol. 25. London: Kala Press, 1993–1994.

McClintock, Anne. *Imperial Leather: Race, Gender, and Sexuality in the Colonial Contest*. New York: Routledge, 1995.

Menchú, Rigoberta. *I, Rigoberta Menchu: An Indian Woman in Guatemala*, ed. E. Burgos-Debray. Trans. A. Wright. London: Verso, 1984.

Mercer, Kobena. "Reading Racial Fetishism: The Photographs of Robert Mapplethorpe." In *Fetishism as Cultural Discourse*, ed. Emily Apter. Ithaca: Cornell University Press, 1993.

Merini, Rafika. *Two Major Francophone Women Writers, Assia Djebar and Leila Sebbar.* New York: Peter Lang, 1999.

Mernissi, Fatima. *Beyond the Veil: Male-Female Dynamics in Modern Muslim Society*. Bloomington: Indiana University Press, 1987.

——. *Dreams of Trespass*. Cambridge: Perseus Books, 1994.

Minh-ha, Trinh T. *Woman/Native/Other: Writing Postcolonial and Feminism*. Bloomington: Indiana University Press, 1989.

——. *When the Moon Waxes Red: Representation, Gender and Cultural Politics*. New York: Routledge, 1991.

——. "White Spring." In *The Dream of the Audience*, ed. Constance Lewallen. Berkeley: University of California Press, 2001.

Mitchell, W. J. T. *Picture Theory*. Chicago: The University of Chicago Press, 1994.

Mohanty, Chandra Talpade. "Under Western Eyes: Feminist Scholarship and Colonial Discourses." In *Third World Women and the Politics of Feminism*, eds. Mohanty, Russo, and Torres. Bloomington: Indiana University Press, 1991.

—— "Crafting Feminist Genealogies: On the Geography and Politics of Home, Nation, and Community." In *Talking Visions: Multicultural Feminism in a Transnational Age*, ed. Ella Shohat. Cambridge: The MIT Press, 1998.

Montrelay, Michele. "Récherches sur la féminité." *Critique* 278 (July 1970).

Mulvey, Laura. *Visual and Other Pleasures*. Bloomington: Indiana University Press, 1989.

Muñoz, Jose Esteban. *Disidentifications: Queers of Color and the Performance of Politics*. Minneapolis: University of Minnesota Press, 1999.

Nietzsche, Friedrich. *Thus Spoke Zarathustra*. Trans. R. J. Hollingdale. New York: Penguin Books,1961.

——. *Beyond Good and Evil*. Trans. Walter Kaufmann. New York: Random House, 1966.

——. *On the Genealogy of Morals*. Trans. Walter Kaufmann. New York: Vintage, 1967.

——. *The Gay Science*. Trans. Walter Kaufmann. New York: Vintage Books, 1974.

Nora, Pierre. "Between Memory and History: *Les Lieux de Mémoire*." *Representations* 26 (Spring 1989).

Olsen, Kare. *Krigensbarn: De norske krigsbarna og deres modre*. Oslo: Forlaget Forum, 1998.

Owens, Craig. *Beyond Recognition: Representation, Power, and Culture*. Berkeley: University of California Press, 1992.

Pêcheux, Michel. *Language, Semantics and Ideology*. New York: St. Martin's Press, 1982.

Pedersen, Susan. "National Bodies, Unspeakable Acts: The Sexual Politics of Colonial Policymaking." *Journal of Modern History* 63:4 (Dec. 1991).

Phelan, Peggy. "Broken Symmetries: Memory, Sight, Love." In *The Feminism and Visual Culture Reader*, ed. Amelia Jones. New York: Routledge, 2003.

Pon, Cynthia. "'Passages' in Mary Shelley's *Frankenstein*: Toward a Feminist Figure of Humanity?" *Modern Language Studies* 3:2 (Fall 2000).

Rapaport, Herman. "Representation, History, and Trauma: Abstract Art after 1945." In *Topologies of Trauma: Essays on the Limit of Knowledge and Memory*, eds. Belau and Ramadanovic. New York: Other Press, 2002.

Renan, Ernest. *Qu'est-ce qu'une nation?* Paris: Pocket, 1992.

Rimbaud, Arthur. *Poésies; Une saison en enfer; Illuminations*. Paris: Gallimard, 1965.

Rose, Jacqueline. *Sexuality in the Field of Vision*. London: Verso, 1986.

Rosello, Mireille. *Declining the Stereotype: Ethnicity and Representation in French Culture*. Hanover: Dartmouth College, 1998.

el Saadawi, Nawal. *The Hidden Face of Eve*. Trans. Sherif Hetata. London: Zed Press, 1980.

Said, Edward. *Orientalism*. New York: Vintage Books, 1978.

——. and Jean Mohr. *After the Last Sky*. London: Pantheon, 1986.

Sandoval, Chela. *Methodology of the Oppressed*. Minneapolis: University of Minnesota Press, 2000.

Sartre, Jean-Paul. *Nausea*. Trans. Lloyd Alexander. New York: New Directions, 1964.

Sebbar, Leila. *Sherazade (Missing: aged 17, dark curly hair, green eyes)*. Trans. Dorothy Blair. London: Quartet Books, 1982.

——, and Nancy Huston. *Lettres parisiennes: Histoires d'exil*. Paris: Barrault, 1986.

Sedgwick, Eve Kosofsky. *Epistemology of the Closet*. Berkeley: University of California Press, 1990.

Serres, Michel. *Le Parasite*. Paris: Grasset, 1980.

Shelley, Mary. *Frankenstein*. New York: W. W. Norton & Company, 1996. Norton critical edition of 1818 text.

Silverman, Kaja. *The Threshold of the Visible World*. New York: Routledge, 1996.

Sontag, Susan. *On Photography*. New York: Farrar, Straus, Giroux, 1977.

——, ed. *The Barthes Reader*. New York: Hill and Wang, 1982.

Spivak, Gayatri. "The Rani of Sirmur: An Essay in Reading the Archives." *History and Theory* 24 (1985).

——. *In Other Worlds: Essays in Cultural Politics*. New York: Routledge, 1988.

——. "Bonding in Difference." In *An Other Tongue: Nation and Ethnicity in the Linguistic Borderlands*, ed. Alfred Arteaga. Durham: Duke University Press, 1994.

——. *The Spivak Reader*, eds. Donna Landry and Gerald Maclean. New York: Routledge, 1996.

Sprinker, Michael. "The End of Autobiography." In *Autobiography: Essays Theoretical and Critical*, ed. James Olney. Princeton: Princeton University Press, 1980.

Stepan, Nancy. "Biological Degeneration: Races and Proper Places." In *Degeneration: The Dark Side of Progress*, eds. J. Chamberlin and S. Gilman. New York: Columbia University Press, 1985.

Stewart, Susan. *On Longing: Narratives of the Miniature, the Gigantic, the Souvenir, the Collection*. Baltimore: Johns Hopkins University Press, 1984.

Stoler, Ann Laura. *Race and the Education of Desire: Foucault's History of Sexuality and the Colonial Order of Things*. Durham: Duke University Press, 1995.

Tagg, John. *The Burden of Representation: Essays on Photographies and Histories*. Minneapolis: University of Minnesota Press, 1988.

Thomas, Rosemarie Garland. *Extraordinary Bodies*. New York: Routledge, 1996.

Wong, Shelly Sunn. "Unnaming the Same: Theresa Hak Kyung Cha's *Dictée*." In *Writing Self, Writing Nation: Essays on Theresa Hak Kyung Cha's* Dictée, eds. Elaine Kim and Norma Alarcón. Berkeley: Third Woman Press, 1994.

Woodhull, Winifred. *Transfigurations of the Maghreb: Feminism, Decolonization, and Literatures*. Minneapolis: University of Minnesota Press, 1993.

Woolf, Virginia. *Three Guineas*. New York: Harcourt Brace and Company, 1938.

Zimra, Clarisse. "Afterword." In Assia Djebar, *Women of Algiers in Their Apartment*. Trans. Marjolijn de Jager. Charlottesville: University Press of Virginia, 1992.

——. "Disorienting the Subject in Assia Djebar's *L'amour, la fantasia*." *Yale French Studies* 87 (1995).

Žižek, Slavoj. *The Sublime Object of Ideology*. London: Verso, 1989.

Index

About the Author

Karina Eileraas completed her B.A. at Wesleyan University in women's studies, international politics, and French. After completing Ph.D. coursework in French and gender studies at Northwestern University, she transferred to UCLA where she became the first graduate of the Ph.D. program in women's studies at UCLA in 2003. She recently completed a Mellon Postdoctoral Fellowship in Women's and Gender Studies at Carleton College, and is currently a visiting assistant professor in the women's studies program at UCLA.